Investing in India

Shanta Acharya

MACMILLAN
Business

First published 1998 by
MACMILLAN PRESS LTD
Houndmills, Basingstoke, Hampshire RG21 6XS
and London
Companies and representatives throughout the world

ISBN 0–333–68691–8

A catalogue record for this book is available from the British Library.

This book is printed on paper suitable for recycling and made from fully managed and sustained forest sources.

10 9 8 7 6 5 4 3 2 1
07 06 05 04 03 02 01 00 99 98

Printed in Great Britain by
Antony Rowe Ltd
Chippenham, Wiltshire

INVESTING IN INDIA

For my family and friends who invested in me

There is a tide in the affairs of men
Which taken at the flood, leads on to fortune;
Omitted, all the voyage of their life
Is bound in shallows and in miseries.
On such a full sea are we now afloat,
And we must take the current when it serves,
Or lose our ventures.
(William Shakespeare, *Julius Caesar*)

The working of great institutions is mainly the result of a vast mass of routine, petty malice, self interest, carelessness, and sheer mistake. Only a residual fraction is thought.
(George Santayana, *The Crime of Galileo*)

Man is condemned to be free.
(Jean-Paul Sartre, *Existentialism is a Humanism*)

Now, *here*, you see, it takes all the running *you* can do, to keep in the same place. If you want to get somewhere else, you must run at least twice as fast as that!
(Lewis Carroll, *Through the Looking Glass*)

Contents

List of Tables

Preface

This book came about as a result of my meeting Kalpana Shukla of Macmillan in Delhi. It was at her suggestion that I began writing about investing in the Indian stockmarket. As a portfolio manager in the City of London, my experience of investing in India epitomised the spectrum of problems that any investor could encounter. Inefficiency is not just the monopoly of India. By agreeing to share my ignorance in grappling with issues that confronted me as an investor, I hope the book will generate general interest; enough to have a benign impact on the investment environment in India. The book was written after the Election in July 1996 and economic data relating to India was updated after the Budget of 28 February 1997. Developments since April 1997 have been wholly ignored as the book went to press.

A word about data. India has now subscribed to the Special Data Dissemination Standards of the International Monetary Fund and has thus committed itself to bringing in a statistical system to produce most of the data with a shorter time lag, improved quality and coverage by 31 December 1998. If globalisation was being pursued in most sectors of the economy, there was no evidence of it in the data being issued by the government. Thus, timely and clean data will be most welcome as research on India tends to be corrupted without it. One hopes international accounting standards will also be introduced for the production of corporate data. The aim of the book is to identify broad trends and issues involved with investing rather than focus on accurate data. Thus, India is any quantitative investor's nightmare but a stock picker's paradise.

SHANTA ACHARYA

Abbreviations and Acronyms

ACC	Associated Cement Company
ADB	Asian Development Bank
ADR	American Depository Receipt
AI	Air India
APM	administered pricing mechanism
ATF	aviation turbine fuel
BIFR	Board for Industrial and Financial Reconstruction
BJP	Bharatiya Janata Party
BoP	balance of payments
BOT	build-operate-transfer
BE	budget estimates
BSE	Bombay Stock Exchange
CCI	Controller of Capital Issues
CGT	capital gains tax
CIP	central issue price
CMIE	Centre for Monitoring the Indian Economy
CMP	Common Minimum Programme
CPI	consumer price index
CPI(AL)	consumer price index for agricultural labour households
CPI(IW)	consumer price index for industrial workers
CPI(UNME)	consumer price index for urban, non-manual employees
CRR	cash reserve ratio
DoT	Department of Telecommunication
E	estimates
EAFE	Europe, Australia and the Far East
EM	emerging market
EMT	Efficient Market Theory
E&P	exploration and production
EPS	earnings per share
EU	European Union
EV	enterprise value
EVA	economic value added
FCI	Food Corporation of India
FCNR(A)	Foreign Currency Non-Resident Accounts
FCNR(B)	Foreign Currency Non-Resident (Banks)

FDI	foreign direct investment
FII	foreign institutional investor
FIPB	Foreign Investment Promotion Board
FX	foreign exchange
GATT	General Agreement on Tariffs and Trade
GDCF	gross domestic capital formation
GDP	gross domestic product
GDR	Global Depository Receipt
GDS	gross domestic savings
GFCF	gross fixed capital formation
GRT	gross registered tonnage
HLL	Hindustan Lever Limited
IA	Indian Airlines
ICICI	Industrial Credit and Investment Corporation of India
IDA	International Development Association
IDB	India Development Bonds
IDBI	Industrial Development Bank of India
IDF	Indian Development Forum
IFC	International Financial Corporation
IIR	The India Infrastructure Report
IMF	International Monetary Fund
IOC	Indian Oil Corporation
IPO	Initial public offering
IPP	independent power producer
Kwh	kilowatt hour
LDC	less-developed country
LIC	Life Insurance Corporation of India
LPG	liquefied petroleum gas
MAT	minimum alternate tax
MLR	minimum lending rate
MoF	Ministry of Finance
MNC	multinational corporation
MRTP	Monopolies and Restrictive Trade Practices Act
MSCI	Morgan Stanley Capital International
MSP	minimum support prices
Mtoe	million tonnes of oil equivalent
MTNL	Mahanagar Telephone Nigam Limited
MVA	market value added
Mw	megawatt
NCAER	National Council for Applied Economic Research
NEP	New Economic Policy

NH	National Highways
NIE	newly industrialising economies
NRI	non-resident Indian
NSE	National Stock Exchange
NTP	National Telecom Policy
OCC	Oil Coordination Committee
ODA	Official Development Assistance
OEA	Overall External Assistance
OECD	Organisation for Economic Cooperation and Development
OIL	Oil India Limited
ONGC	Oil and Natural Gas Commission
OPA	oil pool account
OPD	oil pool deficit
OPEC	Organisation of Petroleum Exporting Countries
P	provisional
PBVR	price-to-book-value ratio
PCFR	price-to-cash-flow ratio
PDS	public distribution system
PE	public enterprise
PEP	Personal Equity Plan
P/E	price-to-earnings
PLF	plant load factor
PLR	prime lending rate
POL	petroleum, oil and lubricant products
PPP	purchasing power parity
PSBR	public sector borrowing requirement
PSR	price-to-sales ratio
QR	quantiative restrictions
RBI	Reserve Bank of India
RE	revised estimates
RER	real exchange rate
RIL	Reliance Industries Limited
ROE	return on equity
ROCE	return on capital employed
SBI	State Bank of India
SCI	Shipping Corporation of India
SCST	Scheduled Caste and Scheduled Tribe
SDRs	Special Drawing Rights
SEB	State Electricity Board
SEBI	Securities and Exchange Board of India
SIL	Special Import Licence

SLR	statutory liquidity ratio
T&D	transmission and distribution
TELCO	Tata Engineering and Locomotive Company
TFC	Tenth Finance Commission
TFP	total factor productivity
TRC	Tax Reform Committee
TB	treasury bill
UF	United Front
UNDP	United Nations Development Programme
UT	Union Territories
UTI	Unit Trust of India
VAS	value added services
VSNL	Videsh Sanchar Nigam Limited
WMA	Ways and Means Advances
WPI	wholesale price index

Notes

- The Indian fiscal year runs from April through 31 March.
- Billion refers to a thousand million.
- $ or dollar refers to US dollars unless otherwise stated.
- Government or 'centre' refers to the central government of India and the Union Territories, which do not have a legislature. Delhi, which was earlier in the centre, has now been included in the states since 1993–94.

Acknowledgements

I am grateful to Kalpana Shukla for her original suggestion and to Stephen Rutt for commissioning me to write this book. I would like to thank Jane Powell for her suggestions in pruning the original text, Sam Whittaker and Keith Povey for their excellent editorial work and Julia Pike for her assistance in the proof-reading.

I owe thanks to Sanjay Acharya, Sushanta Acharya, Richard Chenevix-Trench, Peter Hodgman, Ashok Jambur, Vijay Joshi, Manmohan Singh, David Soden and Pavan Sukhdev for reading parts of this book.

I am grateful to Praween Napate and Pourus Panthake for their help in providing me with research and data. The support of brokerage houses like DSP-Merrill Lynch, ING Barings, James Capel-Batlivala Karani, First Global Finance, Peregrine, Socgen-Crosby, UBS and WI Carr Indosuez is gratefully acknowledged for sending me their Indian research.

I am indebted to Jay Birje-Patil, Keki Daruwalla and Sama Swaminathan for their help not just in locating various books and reports on India but also for their constant encouragement. My stay in India was transformed into a stimulating experience, thanks to the hospitality of friends like the Sukhdevs in Bombay and the Khoslas in Delhi. Robert Cassen, Homi Colah, Ajit Dayal, Sanjay Kathuria, Hemendra Kothari, D.R. Mehta, Nirmal Mohanty, Michael Patra, Ranjit Patnaik, Sadhana Shah, Lalatendu Swain, A. Vasudevan, Mahesh Vyas and Arvind Virmani were all generous with their time.

Other people who have helped me in this endeavour are too many to be named individually. I am grateful to all the officials of the Government of India, the Reserve Bank of India and the Securities and Exchange Board of India, members of the IMF and World Bank missions in Delhi, staff at the Confederation of Indian Industry at Delhi and CMIE in Bombay, academics, journalists, businessmen, stockbrokers, fund managers and analysts who have contributed in many different ways.

Last though not least, I cannot thank my parents, family and friends enough for keeping faith with me and investing in me without expecting anything in return.

SHANTA ACHARYA

Table of Events: Important Dates in the Development of the Indian Economy

1947–48   15 August 1947 India declares its Independence. Jawaharlal Nehru is sworn in as India's first Prime Minister. On 30 January 1948, Mahatma Gandhi is assassinated. The Reserve Bank of India is nationalised.

1948–49   India devalues its currency in line with Britain's. The UN proposes ceasefire in Kashmir and a plebiscite.

1949–50   On 26 January 1950 the Indian Constitution comes into force. Rajendra Prasad is elected India's first President.

1950–51   Near severe drought. The Planning Commission is established.

First Plan: 1951–56

1951–52   First Plan published on 9 July. Railways nationalised.

1952–53   First General Election, Congress wins 45 per cent and the Communist Party 3.3 per cent of the votes. Nehru continues as Prime Minister.

1954–55   The National Development Council is set up with members of the Planning Commission and Chief Ministers of all the states. The USA and Pakistan make an agreement whereby America offers military aid to Pakistan. India adopts the Pancha Shila with China.

1955–56   The Imperial Bank of India is nationalised and renamed as the State Bank of India. Bulganin and Khruschev make their first official visit to Delhi.

Second Plan: 1956–61

1956–57   Indian Companies Act comes into force. The life insurance industry is nationalised and the Life Insurance Corporation of India set up. Chou En-Lai makes his first visit to India. The Indian states are reorganised on a linguistic basis. Nehru launches the Non-Aligned movement with Nasser and Tito.

1957–58   Second General Election, Congress wins 48 per cent and Communists 10 per cent of the votes. Nehru continues as Prime Minister.

1959–60　President Eisenhower's first visit to India. The Fertiliser Corporation of India is set up.

Third Plan: 1961–66

1962–63　First Sino-Indian War. Third General Election, Congress wins majority of the votes. Nehru continues as Prime Minister. Dr. S. Radhakrishnan becomes the second President of India.

1963–64　The Unit Trust of India is launched in February.

1964–65　Nehru dies on 27 May 1964. Lal Bahadur Shastri becomes the second Prime Minister on 9 June. Severe drought. IDBI set up. FCI launched on 15 January.

1965–66　Near severe drought. First war with Pakistan. Shastri dies on 11 January 1966 at Tashkent during peace talks between India and Pakistan. Mrs Indira Gandhi becomes India's third Prime Minister on 23 January 1966.

Annual Plans: 1966–69

1966–67　The rupee is devalued by 36.5 per cent on 6 June 1967. Fourth General Election, Indira Gandhi continues as Prime Minister and Zakir Hussain becomes the third President of India.

1967–68　Gold Control Act comes into force.

Fourth Plan: 1969–74

1969–70　On 19 July, the 14 major commercial banks are nationalised. V.V. Giri becomes fourth President of India after the death of Zakir Hussain.

1970–71　MRTP Act comes into force on 1 June 1971.

1971–72　Severe drought in India. Poor harvests worldwide. A 20-year Treaty of Peace, Friendship and Cooperation is signed between India and USSR. Second War with Pakistan. India intervenes in East Pakistan leading to the creation of Bangladesh. Fifth General Election in India, Congress wins with Mrs Gandhi as its leader and the country's Prime Minister.

1972–73　Global business cycle reaches a peak.

1973–74　First Oil Crisis. The first 4 Plans delivered a Hindu rate of growth of 3.5 per cent.

Fifth Plan: 1974–79 (average growth rate 4.8 per cent)

1974–75　Near severe drought in India. First nuclear detonation by India on 18 May. Fakhruddin Ali Ahmed becomes the fifth President of India. The first Indian space satellite Aryabhatta launched with Soviet help.

1975–76   On 25 June 1975 Internal Emergency is declared by Mrs Gandhi in India. Offshore oilfield, Bombay High, goes into commercial production on 20 Feb 1975.

1976–77   The Janata Dal is formed on 23 Jan 1977. Internal Emergency is lifted on 21 March 1977. India's sixth General Election is held on 24 March and the country's first non-Congress government is elected. Janata Dal wins the election, Moraji Desai sworn in as the fourth Prime Minister.

1977–78   Neelam Sanjiva Reddy becomes the sixth President of India on 25 July.

Annual Plan: 1979–80

1979–80   On 7 June 1979, India's second satellite Bhaskara is launched. On 22 August, for the first time in India the Lok Sabha is dissolved. India's seventh General Election results in the overwhelming victory for the Congress and Mrs Gandhi becomes fifth Prime Minister.

Sixth Plan: 1980–85 (average growth rate 5.7%)

1980–81   Second Oil Crisis. World inflation peaks.

1981–82   On 14 Jan 1982, Indira Gandhi announces the 20-point economic programme.

1982–83   Near severe drought. On 25 July 1982, Zail Singh is sworn in as the seventh President of India.

1983–84   On 5 June 1984, the Indian Army enters the Golden Temple in Amritstar to evacuate it of Sikh militants.

1984–85   Mrs Gandhi is assassinated on 31 Oct 1984. India's eighth General Election is held in December, Congress wins more than 75 per cent of the votes and Rajiv Gandhi is reinstated as India's sixth Prime Minister. He had been appointed interim Prime Minister by the Congress Party after Mrs Gandhi's assassination.

Seventh Plan: 1985–90 (average growth rate 5.8%)

1985–86   Near severe drought in India.

1987–88   Severe drought in India. On 25 February 1988, India's first surface-to-surface tactical missile with a range of 250 km is successfully tested.

1989–90   India's ninth General Election is held in November. On 2 December 1989, Mr V.P. Singh, leader of the National Front, is sworn in as India's seventh Prime Minister.

Annual Plan: 1990–91

1991–91   On 7 November 1990, the National Front government gets voted out of power through a no-confidence motion in Parliament. Chandra Sekhar is sworn in on 10 November as India's eighth Prime Minister. On 6 March 1991, Chandra Sekhar resigns.

Annual Plan: 1991–92

India's tenth General Election is held on 20 May and 15 June. On 21 May 1991, Rajiv Gandhi is assassinated during his election campaign. Congress is elected in June 1991 with Narasimha Rao as the ninth Prime Minister. India begins structural adjustment programme in July with Manmohan Singh as Minister of Finance. The rupee is devalued and the liberalisation of the Indian economy is initiated.

Eight Plan: 1992–97 (aims at an average growth rate of 5.6%)

1992–93   Shankar Dayal Sharma becomes India's ninth President. In June 1992, the Bombay Stock Exchange Index hits an all-time high. In September 1992, Foreign Institutional Investors are allowed to invest in the Indian stockmarket. On 6 December, Hindu fundamentalists destroy the Babri Masjid in Ayodhya leading to the worst communal riots since 1947. On 12 March 1993, a series of bomb explosions in Bombay cause extensive damage to life and property.

1993–94   In July 1993, Foreign Institutional Investors start investing in India. On 30 September 1993, a massive earthquake hits Maharashtra.

1994–95   On 15 April 1994, India signs GATT. Congress loses Maharashtra to the BJP-Shiv Sena party.

1995–96   Eighth year of good monsoons. Depreciation of the rupee in the second half of the financial year.

1996–97   The eleventh General Election is held in May. Congress is defeated; the BJP form an interim government and resign due to lack of support. A coalition government of 13 parties, the United Front, is installed at the centre with the support of the Congress and the Left Front with H.D. Deve Gowda as India's eleventh Prime Minister. The UF government announce their CMP in July 1996. Charges of corruption are brought against Narasimha Rao and his telecommunications minister Sukh Ram. Ninth year of normal rains in India but drought conditions prevail in some states. The Finance Minister, P. Chidambaram, presents his second Budget on 28 February. On 30 March, the Congress withdraws its support for the UF government. The President is left with no choice but to ask the UF to demonstrate it has the confidence of the Lok Sabha by 11 April 1997.

1 The Long Path to Economic Liberalisation

INTRODUCTION

In July 1991, the government started to liberalise the Indian economy by addressing the structural inefficiencies inherent in the economic environment for investment by focusing on trade and industrial policies, the financial sector, taxation and the public enterprises. India began a structural adjustment programme to bring about supply-side reforms to help improve conditions for investment and employment. This also aimed to enable the capital market to assume an integral role in the allocation of resources in the nation's development. In less than six years, India has significantly altered its strategy for growth.

India's capital market is undergoing a fundamental change in its attitudes, goals and values as is government, industry and society. The changes are quite discernible but seem to have alienated many. Policy reforms remain incomplete but the free pricing of domestic share issues, the flotation of Euroissues, foreign portfolio investment in Indian companies, setting up of private mutual funds and the privatisation of public enterprises (PEs) have altered the scope of the market and its impact on investment. It is inevitable that in the process of adjustment, there will be winners and losers. The investment opportunity lies in the potential for higher growth as India continues to liberalise further.

Looking at the prospects for investing in the Indian stockmarket, one is confronted with an array of questions, many of which this book intends to address. Any investment decision, however, is ultimately linked to the risk – reward ratio that the individual investor seeks. All these factors are influenced by rational investor expectations within an economic framework that enables the investor to identify the opportunity early enough to be able to take advantage of it. The need to distinguish between the performance of the economy and that of the stockmarket involves a high level of *contrarian investing*. While a long-term investment strategy can be a lifebuoy, it is prudent when swimming in the rough seas of emerging markets that one takes into account the overall valuation of the market.

Hot markets are best avoided as the valuation of such markets tend to be easily distorted by short-term fund flows. With the increasingly international nature of capital, it is vital to understand the cycle of fund flows into the real economy as distinct from the stockmarket. Volatility is opportunity, but in illiquid markets active trading may not prove to be a winning strategy. For those interested in investing in India, the critical task is identifying the opportunity and timing one's entry into the market advantageously. The lack of depth and maturity in the market is manifested in its volatility, but trading the market volatility is a risky strategy due to the thinness of the market and the settlement problems inherent in trading domestic shares. The gap between a share being undervalued and fully valued can be elusive. Undervaluations can disappear within one settlement period. Thus, to compensate for the risk of entering a market with such 'trading' characteristics, one needs to adopt a contrarian investment strategy. With a limited number of investment opportunities, stock selection is the key to successful investing in India.

A country's performance is judged over decades rather than the latest business cycle, as its economic strength lies not only in the profitability of its corporations but in the prosperity of its people, more so in India where the private corporate sector accounts for less than 10 per cent of GDP but for most of its market capitalisation. The gap between the rich and the poor in India has widened over the past decades although the absolute level of poverty has improved significantly. As India operates within an unusual democratic set-up consisting of 26 governments, investing in India involves investing in 26 different economies – the Centre and the 25 States. When India embarked on its reforms in 1991, the Congress party at the centre did not have a majority in the Lok Sabha. Thus, the initial phase of reform was tackled mostly at the centre. Unless reforms are implemented at the state level, slippages and possible reversals could hold back economic growth.

India's stabilisation and initiation of reform has been a relative success. The United Front government's Common Minimum Programme as announced in July 1996 broadly reaffirmed the continuation of reform and identified the challenges ahead as reducing the fiscal deficit, liberalising the economy (particularly in the agricultural sector), rising to the infrastructural needs of the country and investing in the development of human resources. The coalition government's objectives embraced growth with the 'provision of basic minimum services, employment, macroeconomic stability, investment (particularly in infrastructure), human development and a viable balance of payments' as reiterated by the Finance Minister in his Budget statement on 28 February 1997. There has been no real progress in reducing the fiscal deficit and reforms in agriculture have not been attempted.

The progress in the implementation of reforms over the past two years has been slow. As India did not have the levels of inflation, debt or social disparities evident in Latin American or African countries, it was possible to stabilise the economy post-crisis without great social cost. India also had a relatively well-developed financial sector with an understanding of the basics of market economy and the existence of many institutions that supported private sector investment. The costly financial and industrial closures that accompanied the restructuring of several Eastern European countries have not happened in India but they may yet be necessary if the economy is to become fully competitive.

The resulting *gradual* approach to introducing reforms has been more the result of a lack of definition than a clear indication of ultimate aims. Hence, six years after the introduction of reforms, it is not fully clear if a market economy model with predominantly private ownership and public intervention to deal with market failure is accepted by the government, both at the centre and in the states, as the key to improving the standard of living for all Indians. India's planners need to pursue a clear strategy for development and not a patchwork of reforms as and when forced upon them as was the case in 1991. This crisis management approach has led to the dangerous conclusion that India needs another crisis to be able to take its reforms forward. The greatest asset any country's planners can have is to identify and respond to its needs without dogma. The Finance Minister, Mr P. Chidambaram, in his 1997 Budget clarified the direction of his government by continuing broadly with the spirit of reforms. But due to the nature of his government, doubts remain in the minds of investors as to the government's ability to tackle the more contentious aspects of reform. What has been lacking is a serious national debate about the nature of development as it takes decades for nations to radically alter their way of thinking.

Policymakers the world over have applauded the secret of the East Asian 'economic miracle' but the simple truth is that there is no substitute for pragmatic policymaking, a core of sound economic policies such as macro-economic discipline, an outward orientation as a means of achieving global competitiveness and high levels of investment in people. These values are instilled by governments in their people. No other group of developing countries succeeded in fostering growth, eradicating poverty, integrating with world markets and raising the living standards of its people as did the East Asians. Mismanagement and ineffective policymaking reversed the achievements of several Latin-American and African countries in the 1980s. The economic fortunes of Asian and Latin American countries in the 1990s equally goes to prove that there is no room for complacency in policymaking.

Starting from a very low base, the growth in per capita income in India has been low. While GDP grew at a rate of 4 per cent during 1950–92, per

Investing in India

capita income grew at a mere 1.8 per cent. Population growth at an annual rate of 2.2 per cent nullified the GDP growth rate of 4 per cent relegating India into the low-income category in world league tables. What is most worrying is that at current rates of growth, the population is expected to double by 2031. India is already lagging behind seriously in all aspects of human development. If the population continues to grow at current levels, the situation will become explosive and unmanageable by the middle of the next century. Economic trends compared to other countries are summarised in Table 1.1.

Table 1.1   Economic trends: a comparison

Country	GNP per capita (% growth per annum)		External debt (as % of GNP)		Debt service ratio*	
	1965–80	1980–93	1980	1994	1980	1994
India	1.5	3.0	11.9	34.2	10.0	26.9
Brazil	6.3	0.3	31.8	27.9	67.7	35.8
China	4.1	8.2	2.2	19.3	4.4	9.3
Indonesia	5.2	4.2	28.0	57.4	13.9	32.4
Korea	7.3	8.2	47.9	15.3	20.3	7.0
Malaysia	4.7	3.5	28.0	36.9	6.6	7.9
Mexico	3.6	−0.5	30.5	35.2	50.9	35.4
Russian Federation	NA	−1.0	NA	25.4	NA	6.3
South Africa	3.2	−0.2	NA	NA	NA	NA
Thailand	4.4	6.4	25.9	43.1	20.4	16.3

Note: * Debt service as a percentage of exports of goods and services.
Source: *World Development Reports*, 1995, 1996; *Human Development Report*, 1996.

It is true that calculations of per capita income can distort the picture somewhat as an annual per capita of $320 in 1994 could not have purchased a standard of living in the USA which could have been remotely comparable with what Rs 10 000 would have purchased in India. On a purchasing power party (PPP) basis, GDP per capita in 1994 for India was $1280. But, according to the *Human Development Report* of 1996, India's position in the Human Development Index was 135th out of 174 nations. While disparities in ranking between the PPP method and the conventional method are also enhanced at the per capita level, the fact remains that 20 per cent of India's population lives below the 'official' poverty level. In real terms the level of poverty is much worse. Even in the UK a similar percentage of the population lives under the poverty level. Thus, it is worth clarifying that the average Indian per capita income is 7 per cent of the average per capita income earned in the UK, and 5 per cent of that earned in the USA.

India is slowly establishing a political mandate for development and the freedom from ideology to be able to reassess its strategies. All the Asian success stories were achieved outside a democratic mandate. The high illiteracy rate means that the majority of Indians have no clue to the implications of the economic policies they vote for. They vote for decent, clean and well-managed governments that will provide them with the basic amenities of life like food, shelter, education and a means to earn a living. In India, the provision of the basic requirements for a living has been daunting. However, fifty years after Independence there is no excuse for the high level of poverty. What has undoubtedly been a failure is not just government policies but the democratic process itself which has been abused in electing government after government that implemented policies which the electorate did not understand and most likely would not have voted for had they done so. While reform aims to introduce market forces to India's economy with a view to injecting greater competition and providing the consumer with a better choice of product, in the political context such choices are limited.

Poverty alleviation is espoused as the main aim of every government in India but achievements belie the political rhetoric. The management of development is what successful governance is all about. India has just over three decades to prepare for the doubling of its population not to mention improving the living standards of the existing poor. The political developments today are a swift reminder of what democracy can deliver. A model for economic change has to deliver tangible improvement for the underprivileged, within a reasonable timeframe, to win the support of the people. Investing in people is increasingly becoming critical to the survival of governments around the world. As technology advances, the gap between skilled and unskilled workers has widened social disparities further. In an era of global competitiveness, there is no resting on one's laurels even for the leaders like the USA and Japan. It is not that India has performed badly but that others have done better. Thus, stagnation of reform is not a luxury that India's planners can afford, particularly in light of the fact that reform tends to be an ongoing process.

If India's success has been patchy, it is highlighted in the substantial variations that exist between the various states, between the urban and the rural populations as much as between the private sector and the public sector. Thus, there are many 'Indias' one can invest in or, more precisely, cannot invest in. There exists an India, in the private sector, where returns on investment are reasonably high at 18–20 per cent and so are savings. This India comprises of approximately 50 million people with per capita incomes and work skills comparable to those in the developed world. This is the India that the market represents. But this India does not have its own government and is not concentrated in any state; nor does it have the ability to formulate its own economic policies. While there is a growing middle class, at best it is not more than a tenth of the population. It was estimated that 12 million people paid personal income tax, or less than 5 per cent of the official labour force. There are other 'Indias' where agriculture is the major employer, yet the government is reluctant to tax agricultural income or liberalise the sector. Thus, higher agricultural production does not translate into higher revenues for the government or lower prices for the consumer. Returns on public sector investment vary from huge losses to as much as 20 per cent in the oil sector. Even within the public sector, returns vary from state to state and the centre. There is no method of evaluating returns or imposing minimum standards across the nation. There are many such anomalies in the Indian economy.

The defeat of the Congress Party in the General Election of May 1996 was no proof that the Indian electorate in voting the Congress party out of power also jettisoned reformist policies as the United Front (UF) government's policies are extremely supportive of reform. It is clear that the electorate voted against corruption and mismanagement as they have done tirelessly in every election over the last few decades. What did emerge from the 1996 election is that the historical standing of the Congress has been eroded and that the Bharatiya Janata Party (BJP) is a serious contender for power. It remains a party with a predominantly Hindu base although the BJP won 41 'Scheduled Caste and Scheduled Tribe' (SCST) seats in the 1996 election compared to 22 SCST seats in the 1991 election. The voting pattern of 1996 reflected the desire of the nation to remain secular while focusing its economic agenda on poverty alleviation.

As India has managed to muddle through for decades, it has been harder for the nation to reach a political consensus on the need for greater public efficiency and savings and the possibility of higher rates of growth in personal wealth. While it is clear that economic growth provides the revenues and the resources for development, it is important to recognise that investment in human capital development forms the basis for sustaining growth. Market oriented reforms, especially in developing countries, need to be accompanied with public spending on improving the prospects of the weaker sections of the community. The Indian government has a poor record for expenditure on education, health and infrastructure and for tackling the critical problems of population explosion, higher public spending and borrowing. Expenditure on education and health did not lead to a fall in birthrates; rapid population growth became both the cause and effect of the low levels of human resource development. It is worth noting that public expenditure has risen in these critical areas since reforms began but what has been neglected for decades cannot be reversed within a few years. What has not been introduced in the public sector is a system of evaluating returns on investment, particularly in the social sectors. Thus, for example, there are primary schools in villages without teachers or pupils turning up for classes. Both parties work elsewhere while accepting government handouts.

India needs a clear development policy framework that transcends party political concerns. In a democratic context, it is inevitably a slow process as reforms need to be discussed at various levels. But if economic policies can be implemented on an all-party basis, then it would help establish longer term investment in the country. In his Budget Speech in July 1996, the Finance Minister, Mr P. Chidambaram, declared the need to set up a commission on the reform of public expenditure. He had not been successful in establishing such a commission by March 1997. The lack of consensus in any party on expenditure reforms has made it difficult for any government to curtail its borrowing requirements. The ensuing uncertainty has stalled investment flows. India's consensus-building approach towards reform has helped to ensure that it is lasting but it tends to be a slow process which can be costly as investors tend to link future plans with the continuation of reform.

The example of Enron's investment plans in Maharashtra is a case in point. From Enron's standpoint, progress was frustrating even though lessons were learnt. It is unfortunate that the lack of transparency and a competitive bidding process by the previous state government was used by its successor as a political scoring point. As the country is crying out for investment, the policy framework for an investor friendly environment needs to be both transparent, competitive and above party politics. It is to any party's advantage that investment does not get diverted elsewhere due to bottlenecks in India. The economic liberalisation of India came about as a recognition of that reality. Unfortunately, it took a crisis to make that happen. In a democracy, with almost a billion people, where illiteracy and poverty are rampant, the price that the political system extracts can be high. India's consensus building approach to policymaking has been less successful where the entire structure needs to be changed as in the case of public expenditure reform.

It is possible to argue that India does not have the advantage of resources to plan its development in a more sensible way and that in the final analysis development management is crisis management. But India has its Five-Year Plans and decades of central planning created modern India. The idea that democracy was responsible for India's *Hindu rate of growth* is a feeble argument. Democracy was chosen by Indians to provide them with better government. Democracy and central planning made Indians poorer than they were 25 years ago in comparative terms because there was no forum to take stock of institutions, policies and values. Poverty is the worst form of discrimination and it appears to have been self-inflicted. The market orientation of today may not serve the needs of tomorrow just as India's 'mixed' economic policy failed in the past. But in the absence of a better economic approach to human development, greater market orientation with government intervention to compensate for market failure is the best available option.

THE FAILURE OF INDIA'S MIXED ECONOMIC POLICY

India's economic performance since 1950 shows that its protectionist policies failed to deliver rapid growth in real incomes. The large expenditures on subsidies to power, irrigation, fertilisers and food did not accrue to the poor but fostered high levels of inefficiency and corruption. The lack of an outward orientation contributed to low productivity and growth. India may have avoided the level of mismanagement encountered in some Latin American and African economies, but the spectacular growth rates of the East Asian economies is a measure of the opportunity cost of India's failed policy. Its past policies encouraged the growth of a flourishing black economy because enterprise and honesty became unrewarding. The clandestine flight of capital out of India was a major factor behind the lack of development along with the unwillingness of people to channel investments through proper, legal routes as government polices rewarded rent-seeking activities rather than an entrepreneurial culture.

Economic policy prior to 1991 created a diverse but inefficient industrial base. This was the result of a rigorous central licensing system which decided the choice of product, technology, scale of production, location, and the financing route. India's licensing regime, apart from erecting barriers to entry, created an oligopolistic system that became technologically backward and inefficient. It was the lack of an outward orientation that led India to ignore, at great peril to its own competitiveness, international prices as a guide to resource allocation. A high level of investment in education with the latest imported technology and the return of expatriates facilitated rapid productivity growth among the Asian Tigers. But India's distorted policies led to brain-drain, a decline in investment in both education and technology and a resultant decline in productivity.

Despite severe resource constraints, which resulted in massive under-investment in the country's infrastructure, the government did not attempt to rectify its policy by improving public savings while seeking private investment. For India's Planning Commission, even advocating private investment would have been perceived as a kind of failure. When Korea and Taiwan embarked on their first decade of development, both countries were heavily dependent on foreign aid which accounted for almost half of their fixed investment. For Korea, over three decades from 1946–76, the USA alone provided more than $500 per capita, in 1993 $ rates, in economic and military assistance. For Taiwan, the aid amount was $425 per capita. Once the growth engine had sparked off, high domestic savings took over and maintained the process of capital accumulation.

Considering the major role that the public sector played in the Indian economy, it is not surprising that it resulted in a low rate of industrial growth. Fall in investment was triggered by the insufficient growth in productivity due to poor project management, overmanning, under-investment in technology, inadequate attention to research and development along with poor human resource development. This was reflected in the low rates of return on investment made by the public sector. Excluding the oil and power sectors, the rate of return on capital investment was mostly negative during the 1970s. It improved during the 1980s but was still less than 5 per cent. The low rate of return on capital investment inhibited the ability of the public sector to regenerate itself by attracting new investment and technology. It was low productivity that triggered inadequate savings and investment resulting in the low rate of economic growth over the past few decades.

It is worth emphasizing that the results in the central PEs in the petroleum and power sectors reveal that acceptable rates of return were achievable within the limitations of Indian planning. If these had been replicated in the state sector, the improvements in public savings would have been considerable. The commercial losses of the State Electricity Boards (SEBs), excluding subsidies, were estimated at Rs 109.4 billion in 1996–97 and the rate of return was –17.7 per cent. If the effective subsidies for agriculture and the domestic sectors are included, savings to the tune of Rs 194.9 billion or 1.3 per cent of GDP could have been made. These hidden subsidies are projected to rise to Rs 218.5 billion in 1997–98. The irrational tariff structure has not been easy to dismantle and sales revenue recovered only 80 per cent of costs in 1995–96. There are large unrecovered revenue arrears which were estimated at Rs 75.7 billion in 1993–94 (four months of current revenue). This is an example of how inadequate assessment of investment impacted on potential savings and investment.

India's savings rate is substantially lower than in most Asian countries whose policies have been geared to providing incentives for it. There was a basic policy failure in India to provide incentives for higher private savings as well as a lack of fiscal prudence that would have generated greater public savings. The public and private sectors' share in India's gross domestic capital formation and savings is summarised in Table 1.2. Investment as a share of GDP in the East Asian economies rose sharply over the past quarter of a century and the share of private investment in GDP also rose to two-thirds higher in the more successful East Asian countries than in other developing economies. The core concept of development whereby a country with a savings rate of 5 per cent transforms itself into one with a savings rate of 30 per cent was most uniquely interpreted by the East Asians as most of these countries now make capital investment in excess of 30 per cent.

Table 1.2   Share of public and private sector in India's gross domestic capital formation and savings (as % of GDP at current prices)

| | Gross domestic capital formation | | | Gross domestic saving | | |
	Public	Private	Total	Public	Private	Total
1950–51	2.8	8.3	10.2	1.8	8.7	10.4
1960–61	7.0	8.9	15.7	2.6	10.1	12.7
1970–71	6.5	10.6	16.6	2.9	12.8	15.7
1980–81	8.7	12.3	22.7	3.4	17.8	21.2
1990–91	9.7	15.5	27.7	1.0	23.3	24.3
1995–96 E	8.2	18.1	27.4	1.9	23.7	25.6

Source: *Indian Economic Survey*, 1996–97.

At the current investment level, India lags behind all the other Asian economies except for the Philippines (see Table 1.3). The unacceptably low level of savings in the public sector is the prime reason behind India's low rate of investment. Expenditure reform remains the key to increasing public saving. There can be no real prospect of rises in public investment in the medium term. It is therefore crucial for the government to enable the private sector to step up its rate of investment while the public sector reduces its own expenditure.

Another development in the Indian economy was the shift in public investment from agriculture to industry as a means of creating jobs through rapid industrialisation. The outcome was a reduction in total demand for industrial products. With inadequate land reforms in the agricultural sector coupled with falling investments by the government, the individual farmer had very little collateral to borrow money from the banks to make any investments. The government became the ultimate source of the bulk of aggregate domestic demand as the private sector had been effectively castrated from playing a development role in the economy. Ironically, the steady rise in subsidies for fertilisers, irrigation and power to maintain status quo meant that the fiscal edifice of the country became increasingly unstable.

Table 1.3   Gross domestic investment as share of GDP
in select Asian countries

Country	1971–80	1981–90	1990	1991	1992	1993	1994
India	20.5	22.8	26.3	25.5	24.6	24.1	23
China	33.9	32.1	36.6	35.4	34.1	36.7	42
Indonesia	19.3	30.4	36.1	35.0	34.6	35.2	29
Malaysia	24.9	30.7	31.5	37.0	33.8	33.5	39
Korea	28.6	30.5	36.9	39.0	35.9	34.4	38
Philippines	27.8	21.9	22.5	20.4	22.2	24.3	24
Singapore	41.2	42.2	39.7	38.2	40.8	42.0	32
Taiwan	30.5	22.6	22.4	22.8	24.2	25.1	24
Thailand	25.3	30.6	41.1	42.0	40.1	43.5	40

Source: *Asian Development Outlook*, 1994; *World Development Report*, 1996.

The industrial regulatory environment promoted a costly, inefficient structure that fostered corruption and nepotism. This contributed to a gradual accumulation of excess capacity in industry from the mid-1960s onwards, the capital goods sector being the most affected. It has been argued that the decline in public investment led to a fall in demand for capital goods and with it the fall in capacity utilisation rates. It is true that the rate of fixed capital formation declined in the first half of the 1960s and the second half of the 1970s, but as a percentage of GDP total investment rose marginally from 14.7 per cent of GDP in the second half of the 1960s to 15.3 per cent of GDP in the early 1970s. The significant decline in capacity utilisation rates in basic and capital goods in the 1970s reflected policy problems, including a mismatch between supply and demand.

As the licensing system became rigid, industrialists had virtually no power to do anything without having to refer every decision to the bureaucrats in Delhi. It was prudent for companies to apply for industrial licences for the setting up of plants with much higher capacity utilisation rates than the market warranted, simply to minimize the cost of having to go back to the various Ministries to get the clearances. For others, it became an easy way of preventing competition as idle capacity was the key reason for denying licences. Established firms had the incentive to keep out potential entrants and possible competition. The policy of the government to prevent monopolies being built up via its Monopolies and Restrictive Trade Practices Act also prevented the same companies from exploiting economies of scale. India's industrial policies thus led to a proliferation of plants with uneconomic scales of production as the authorities felt obliged to avoid market concentration. Lack of specialisation was another result of this policy, it was easier to obtain a licence for a new product than for expansion within the same product line.

India's policy framework resulted in escalating capital to output ratios. Industrial policies in the 1960s led to the fragmentation of production, low capacity utilisation and declining growth in total factor productivity. A detailed study by Isher J. Ahluwalia of evidence over twenty-five years 1960–1986 indicated a strong rising trend in capital intensity (+ 4.9 per cent per annum), a weaker rising trend in labour productivity (+2.2 per cent per annum) and a decline in capital productivity (–2.5 per cent per annum) (Ahluwalia, 1991, p. 50). The high protection rate for the manufacturing sector increased its capital intensity over the decades. Capital intensity in the manufacturing sector accelerated significantly in the 1980s. By establishing an ethos of import substitution for industrial growth, the government introduced a system which did not have to take into account the comparative costs in the production of goods. By not linking investment to exports, industrial productivity suffered from a lack of international competitiveness.

A Crisis Waiting to Happen

The background to the 1991 crisis can be traced back to India's inadequate policy response to the previous crisis of 1979–81 when world oil prices doubled. India survived it mainly because of its economic prudence prior to that crisis. But the 1979–81 external shock led to India's current account position deteriorating from a balanced one in 1978 to a deficit of –2 per cent of GDP or 30 per cent of exports in 1981. The persistence of current account deficits from 1982 to 1985 was the result of a stagnation of exports. By the time Rajiv Gandhi's government came to power and initiated the new economic *glasnost*, India's fiscal situation had already deteriorated. Hence, the strong growth in exports between 1986 and 1990 was insufficient to cushion the effects of the rising interest payments on external debt caused by the growth in imports induced by higher exports.

India's ineffective exchange rate policy was partly responsible for the lack of current account adjustment and the subsequent accumulation of foreign debt, but the key issue was the reversal of its erstwhile fiscal prudence. The fiscal deficit of the government had averaged 4.5 per cent of GDP in the second half of the 1970s but it rose to 8.5 per cent of GDP by the mid-1980s and remained at that level. By the end of the decade the economy was suffering from high levels of inflation and current account deficits. The total debt of the government had remained at around 50 per cent of GDP during 1975–80. That ratio rose to 62 per cent of GDP between 1985–89. Interest payments by the central government as a percentage of its total expenditure virtually doubled from 11.8 per cent in 1980–81 to 20.7 per cent in 1989–90. By the end of the 1980s, interest payment amounted to 4 per cent of GDP and was responsible for half the increase in public expenditure.

Simultaneously, India's external position deteriorated sharply. In 1980–81, India's total external debt was $20 billion. That amount had escalated to $57.5 billion by 1988. This was accompanied by the deterioration in the country's debt service ratio – as measured by interest payments as a percentage of current receipts – which declined from 10 per cent in 1980 to 16 per cent in 1988. This is partly explained by changes in the composition of the external debt position. Prior to 1980, the government had shunned external commercial borrowing and stuck to long-term loans at low rates of interest from institutions like the World Bank and the International Development Agencies. Even in 1988, 90 per cent of the foreign debt was long term with an effective maturity of over 22 years and an interest rate of 2.5 per cent. The decline in this source of funding forced India to finance its current account deficit through direct and more expensive commercial borrowing. By 1990, commercial debt comprised 25 per cent of total debt. The days of cheap capital were over.

The government of Rajiv Gandhi pursued a policy of export-led growth through currency depreciation and the provision of large export subsidies. The value of the rupee declined from 7.89 against the dollar in April 1980 to 16.66 by March 1990. Export subsidies rose from Rs 4 billion in 1980–81 to over Rs 27 billion by the end of the decade. While these measures boosted exports, they put a tremendous strain on the fiscal position of the government. The current account deficit rose from –1.7 per cent of GDP in 1980 to –3 per cent of GDP by 1990. A country's current account deficit has to be balanced either by capital inflows or by running down the reserves of gold and foreign exchange (FX). As India was unable to finance its current account deficit through direct or indirect foreign investment, it was inevitable that its FX reserves declined to finance the rise in imports.

By 1987–88, India had a visible trade deficit of –$5.7 billion and an invisible deficit of –$2.4 billion. Private transfers, accounted for mostly by inward remittances from overseas Indian workers, amounted to $2.6 billion and official transfers just under $0.3 billion resulting in a current account deficit of –$5.2 billion or –1.9 per cent of GDP. India's current account deficit had averaged 25 per cent of exports from 1982 to 1984, but from 1985 to 1990 it averaged 40 per cent of exports. Compared to the current account deficits in other East Asian economies, India's deficit was by no means large. It became unsustainable due to the closed nature of the economy and the lack of export development.

India's external debt rose from $20 billion in 1980–81 to $65 billion by the end of the 1980s. The proportion of debt to GDP virtually tripled, debt service ratios and interest repayments went up dramatically. Currency devaluations aggravated the problem as the debt was incurred in dollars. Despite that, the total indebtedness of the country was no worse than other economies in transition. Foreign direct investment (FDI) had inspired the transfer of financing and technological know-how in the later generation of newly industrialising economies (NIEs). In 1991, Malaysia was the third largest recipient of FDI among developing countries after Mexico and China. In Malaysia, FDI accounts for over 20 per cent of gross domestic investment. Six years after reforms, FDI and foreign institutional investment together account for less than 10 per cent of domestic investment in India.

India's overseas commercial borrowing was mostly in the form of non-resident Indian (NRI) deposits. These short-term deposits provided India with its short-term foreign currency requirements. Although classifiable as hot money searching for arbitraging opportunities, it was precisely this *hot money* that comprised the bulk of the capital inflow during that critical period. What appears confusing, given the government's strategic dependence on inward private transfers of hard currency, is why the government made no concerted effort to pool the available NRI deposits into some form of long-term venture capital fund to bridge its financing needs as it did so effectively in issuing the India Development Bonds (IDBs) in the aftermath of liberalisation. The IDBs offered NRIs an excellent arbitraging opportunity. The immunity scheme attached to it encouraged Indians with funds illegally lodged abroad to repatriate it back home. These schemes were successful in raising $2.4 billion. Given India's credit rating, commercial borrowing would have been equally expensive.

A combination of factors – including higher debt service obligations, higher import bills due to the Gulf crisis, the collapse of the Soviet Union, domestic political instability brought about by successive changes in governments (Narasimha Rao came to head India's fourth government in two years), the flight of NRI deposits, the collapse of the Japanese stockmarket in January 1991 precipitating the withdrawal of Japanese assets abroad – meant that India's meagre reserves rapidly declined to a few weeks of essential imports. The macroeconomic imbalances of the past and the persistence of structural rigidities in the industrial and financial sector with the external shocks led the Indian government to the verge of defaulting on its external payments by March 1991.

India's crisis of 1991 was not brought about by the external shocks but they helped to undermine an economy which was in a highly vulnerable state due to unsuccessful macroeconomic policies over a prolonged period. The drying up of foreign credit was a reaction to India's macroeconomic instability. If its inherent economic position had been sound, India would have weathered the external shocks without precipitating a crisis. Most radical economic transformations are based on an unrepeatable set of disadvantages. This was the mother of all crises that India had to face and it was just bad enough to shake India's self-confidence in its long held policy of self-reliance and its determination to shun foreign participation in rebuilding its economy. The sense of external vulnerability vital to successful economic policymaking was finally introduced by this crisis even though the country's planners had been aware for quite some time of the need to jettison their failed policies. As the crisis made reform inevitable, India's policymakers cannot claim any accolades for managing the economy well. Prevention would have been better than a cure.

Faced with a major financial crisis, the government took measures both to address the issues in the short term as well as to prevent a recurrence of it in the future. In the short term, IMF borrowing enabled India to fulfill its overseas commitments. But, it was clear that the BoP crisis of 1991 was the result of structural weaknesses in the economy. While the objective was to restore macroeconomic stability, it was obvious that in the altered world order, India had to earn its FX by increasing exports. A stable macroeconomic and political environment with an outward orientation in policymaking to introduce competitiveness into all sectors was imperative for attracting inward investment. The government proceeded with its thrust towards unblocking the channels for directing private investment into the industrial and infrastructural sectors. But the changes have been slow and, more recently, stalled due to continuing political uncertainty. The 1997 Budget, though still failing to tackle critical expenditure issues, was a step in the right direction.

LAYING THE FOUNDATIONS: RECENT ECONOMIC DEVELOPMENTS

In July 1991, India's economic liberalisation was precipitated by the government's high fiscal deficit and external imbalances which had generated double digit inflation and, despite assistance from multilaterals and bilaterals, FX reserves had fallen to two weeks of imports by June 1991 pushing the country to the verge of defaulting on its external debt obligations. The reform programme initiated by this crisis focused on a plethora of issues ranging from trade policies, exchange rate management, financial sector reform, taxation, fiscal policy, privatisation of public enterprises and the overall investment environment for private sector participation. The capital intensity of India's policies needed to be addressed as investment had failed to deliver sustainable growth in either output or employment.

Stabilisation policies were intended to get the economy back on even keel in the short term so that structural reforms could address the problems inhibiting the economy from a higher growth trajectory. It was important to make the necessary policy shifts to allow the economy to enter a higher phase of growth while ensuring that the problems of the past did not recur. The major thrust of India's New Economic Policy (NEP) was to reduce the budget deficit from 8.4 per cent of GDP in 1991 to 5 per cent by 1993, to help contain inflationary pressures and to stimulate industrial growth by introducing competition. Encouraging an open trade regime by establishing rupee convertibility was necessary to attract foreign investment as much as liberalising private sector investment. These policy measures were meant to curtail the unsustainable rise in the internal and external debt of the government.

The sharply reduced availability of external finance during the crisis year forced India to cut its imports. Thus, expenditure switching played a major role in India's adjustment process. The devaluation of the rupee and the subsequent dismantling of the import tariff rates effectively spurred exports by March 1993 and inward investment significantly enhanced the country's FX reserves. India's liberalisation was implemented in the middle of a global crisis and the initial thrust at exports yielded a seemingly lacklustre response as the major economies of the world were still in the grip of a recession and India's traditional export markets like the USSR and Eastern Europe had collapsed in the wake of a new economic order.

It is worth noting that India's exports were far from slow in responding to changes in policy as the figures during 1991–93 may indicate for they mask an 18 per cent rise in exports to general currency areas with a 75 per cent decline to the rupee payment areas of Eastern Europe. Thus, the basic thrust towards exports had been clearly established even though a focussed policy within the export sector is yet to emerge. India's economic recovery since the crisis has been driven by exports and private investment. It has also been accompanied by a rise in domestic savings. The recovery has not put undue pressure on inflation or the external accounts. However, bottlenecks in infrastructure and the inability of the government to curb its fiscal deficit remain the most serious threats to India's long-term growth prospects.

Since the crisis of 1991 we have seen a commendable improvement in India's current and capital accounts accompanied by structural reforms but the same cannot be said of domestic public finances. To achieve greater fiscal prudence and improve public savings requires a concerted effort between the centre and the states to reduce public expenditure. The fiscal prudence exhibited at the centre needs to be complemented at the state level. Bureaucracies can either facilitate reform or hamper them. East Asia's technocrats have generally been recognised for being a vital element of the political mandate for reforms. India too boasts of an excellent civil service both at the centre and in the states. These institutions need to be motivated, particularly at the state level, to hasten development. Often policy changes made at the centre do not get acted upon at the state level as a result of various bureaucratic inefficiencies. The problem lies with the nature of India's political system whereby the balance of power prevents the 26 different governments from acting in concert. It is only in times of a crisis that the nation has been able to unite in its sense of vulnerability. It is time that the political parties unite in economic policymaking without having to precipitate the whole country into a crisis first.

The government aimed at reducing its overall public sector deficit from over 12 per cent of GDP in 1990–91 to a more manageable 7 per cent by the mid-1990s. The gross fiscal deficit was to be curbed to 5 per cent of GDP by end of fiscal 1992–93 which target was never reached. These involved significant cuts in government expenditure and budgetary support for the public sector. Subsidies and budgetary support to PEs comprised about 4 per cent of GDP in 1991. After cuts they went down to just over 3.1 per cent and most of the decline came from cuts in capital spending. Central PEs contributed to fiscal reduction both through lower capital spending and higher profits. At the state level, however, higher spending wiped out all the benefits made from higher revenue collection.

In the absence of a real fiscal adjustment, inflation has been contained by tight monetary policies which has led to high real interest rates making borrowing and investing unattractive. High real interest rates affected the

performance of the stockmarket in the wake of higher FII inflows in 1994
which led to a significant overvaluation of the market. High real interest
rates resulting in a volatile stockmarket depressed private sector borrowing
which affected investment, industrial production and economic growth
which in turn led to lower revenue collection and higher fiscal deficits.
Bank lending declined during 1996 as private sector borrowing fell due
to the high cost of capital; real interest rates were around 16 per cent in June
1996. A depressed stockmarket did not help corporates in their fund
raising activity, the total collapse of the Initial Public Offering (IPO)
market kept the retail investor away. High real interest rates usually hurt
the small and medium sized companies more than the large ones. Thus,
the more dynamic sector of the Indian economy pays the price for the
profligacy of the inefficient public sector. Such a policy is clearly
unsustainable.

It needs to be acknowledged that India's reforms have involved a relatively high fiscal cost. The lowering of import tariffs and excise with the
liberalisation of the financial sector impinged on revenues and increased
the cost of government borrowing while it has been politically difficult to
reduce subsidies. The fertiliser subsidy alone accounts for just under one
percent of GDP per year. The privatisation of PEs has not been successful.
Most of the fiscal adjustment has been achieved at the centre with little
contribution from the states. The government's desire to admit the private
sector into newer areas of the economy is commendable but the policy
framework was simply not ready for the private sector to fill the vacuum
created by the government's withdrawal.

The response of the economy to industrial deregulation, trade liberalisation
and currency devaluation along with the easing of constraints on external
financing was strongly positive. An analysis of potential GDP and output gaps
in the Indian economy by the IMF indicated that the 1991–93 recession was
considerably milder than previous recessions. India has had three severe recessions since the 1960s (in 1965–67, 1972–74 and 1979–82) with output gaps
of more than 4.5 per cent of potential GDP compared to the gap of less than
2 per cent in 1991–93. While India's industrial recovery took longer to establish itself, economic growth gathered momentum with both investment and
output registering higher growth by 1993–94. However, the political instability during 1995–97 led to a state of benign neglect in matters of fiscal
correction resulting in high real interest rates and lower rates of industrial
production and growth.

Adjustments in exchange rate, lowering of tariffs and easier credit
access has translated to higher productivity. GDP growth recovered from
0.8 per cent in 1991–92 to 5 per cent in 1992–93 rising further to the

6–7 per cent level between 1993–94 and 1996–97. The structural adjustment programme in India has been satisfactory by all accounts and to its credit the nation has managed to deliver higher levels of growth. The current account deficit position has improved substantially. Foreign investment has risen sharply resulting in the increase in FX reserves to $19.5 billion by 27 February 1997. While portfolio investment has declined since 1994, at $3–4 billion in 1996, it represented 8–10 per cent of global portfolio investment into emerging markets (EMs).

The monetisation of reserves that accompanied the initial inflows led to a rise in money supply. Coupled with increases in administered prices, inflation rose from 7 per cent in mid-1993 to 10 per cent in early-1995. The real exchange rate (RER) appreciated putting downward pressure on exporters. Fears that capacity constraints in the small and medium scale exporters and a stronger currency may slow down the rate of export growth posed a serious problem for India's policymakers. But the devaluation of the rupee was triggered by the slowdown of foreign currency inflows as imports continued to be firm. The rupee was stable at 31.37 to the dollar during 1994 and 1995, but fell to 35.8 to the dollar by March 1997.

As India does not allow the import of consumer goods, the strength of imports indicated a revival in demand and economic growth during 1994–95. Helped by rises in US interest rates and adverse developments in capital flows into EMs in the wake of the Mexican crisis, the Reserve Bank of India (RBI) tightened its monetary stance and inflation declined to below 5 per cent by mid-1996, coinciding with India's General Election. Rises in the administered prices of petroleum, oil and lubricating products (POL) and some food items after the election put upward pressure on inflation which edged up to the 8 per cent level by March 1997. The current account deficit at under 2 per cent of GDP does not pose a problem as FX reserves represent approximately 5.6 months of imports and the debt service ratio appears manageable at 26 per cent. As a percentage of GDP, external debt had declined from 37 per cent in 1992–93 to an estimated 28 per cent in 1995–96. But, fiscal pressures remain due to the government's inability to adhere to a stricter macroeconomic regime. Thus, the economy has responded well to reforms but macroeconomic stresses continue to remain the major challenge to policy.

With the abolition of industrial capacity licensing and the removal of import licencing for raw materials, intermediate goods and components, India's industrialists have greater discretion in responding to market forces and making their investment decisions. Industrial production after being stagnant in 1991–92 made a modest recovery in 1992–93 and rose 9.4 per cent during 1994–95. Industrial production growth was 12.7 per cent in

1995–96 and was estimated to be lower at 9 per cent for 1996–97. There was evidence of a broad-based recovery in the industrial sector during 1995–96 although the capital goods sector exhibited a particularly strong recovery suggesting a rise in investment in new machinery to expand capacity. The technological upgradation in the industrial sector should reflect in higher productivity growth in the future. The consumer goods sector recovered responding to the reductions in excise duties on automobiles and electronic goods. The impact of higher real interest rates and lower production in the infrastructural sectors resulted in lower industrial production for 1996–97. As the real cost of capital declined to the 8–10 per cent level by March 1997 from 16–18 per cent in June–July 1996, it is anticipated that industrial recovery will take place in 1997–98. Unless real interest rates decline to the 6–8 per cent level, there is little scope for any significant rise in investment or production. However, these investments need to be directed urgently to the infrastructural sector.

While output in the infrastructural sectors was little affected by short-term fluctuations, the lack of any significant rise in investment will impact on industrial investment in the future. During the years of transition, instead of upgrading infrastructure to prepare the path for higher foreign investment, the government was boxed in within the constraints imposed by its past policies. The production of basic goods has been steady. Among the non-industrial sectors, agricultural production has been helped by good monsoons but the sector has not been able to benefit from deregulation. If the government proceeds with the much awaited deregulation in the agricultural sector; the economy will respond much faster to reforms. India's service sector has benefited greatly from the recent policy of liberalisation with the financial services sector registering the strongest growth. The setback of 1992–93, due to the stockmarket scam, affected the entire sector.

There are fewer areas of the economy where private investors cannot invest. Despite this progress, the protection that still exists for some 822 products which are reserved for the small-scale sector has discouraged economies of scale and technological upgradation in those sectors. The constraints faced by the small-scale sector may impact on export growth in the future. The government has enhanced the investment ceiling for plant and machinery of small-scale industries and dereserved some 14 items with a view to reducing wastage in agricultural commodities. It will bring in new investment and improved technology. But, the constant need of the government to 'protect' various sectors of the economy only implies that these sectors will ultimately become too uncompetitive to survive without government subsidies. Annual growth rates for different sectors are shown in Table 1.4.

Table 1.4 Annual growth rates of real GDP (%, at factor cost by industry of origin)

	1981–90	1990–91	1991–92	1992–93	1993–94	1994–95*	1995–96**	1996–97***
Agriculture	3.4	3.8	–2.3	6.1	3.6	4.6	–0.1	3.7
Industry	6.9	7.2	–1.3	4.2	6.8	9.4	11.6	8.7
manufacturing	7.2	6.1	–3.7	4.2	8.5	10.2	13.6	10.6
electricity, gas, water	8.9	6.5	9.6	8.4	7.1	8.6	9.1	4.2
construction	4.4	11.6	2.2	3.4	1.3	6.9	5.3	4.6
mining & quarrying	7.4	10.7	3.7	1.1	2.0	8.1	7.0	1.7
Services	6.6	5.2	4.9	5.5	7.3	7.5	8.8	7.4
GDP	5.5	5.4	0.8	5.3	6.0	7.2	7.1	6.8

Notes: * provisional; ** quick estimates; *** advanced estimates.
Source: *National Accounts Statistics*, 1996; *Indian Economic Survey*, 1996–97.

In July 1991, the major objective of the government was to stabilise the economy and that was achieved primarily through expenditure cuts on subsidies, defence, capital expenditure and loans to the states and PEs. But the quality of fiscal adjustment was weak as it issued from a decline in public investment and not from higher public savings. Financial sector reforms and the intention of the government to reduce borrowing from the RBI increased the rates of interest paid on government debt aggravating the deficit situation as the burden of public borrowing was transferred. The marginal real interest rate that the government is paying for its domestic debt is nearer the growth rate of the economy itself. Unless, fiscal imbalances and real interest rates are reduced, India may be caught in a debt trap and will find it difficult to provide a lower inflationary path to growth.

The discretion of the government to curb expenditure is seriously hampered by the fact that about 70 per cent of its budgeted expenditure is accounted for by interest payments, defence, wages and grants and loans to the states mandated by the Constitution. The consolidated deficit of the government remains at 10 per cent of GDP, which is only less than 2 per cent below the level it was in 1991. While the central government has adjusted its finances, savings at the state level and those of the PEs has not improved. This is clearly unsustainable. It is essential that the centre–state fiscal relationship is restructured as the states need to address their inadequate tax collections, growing wage expenses, poor cost recovery and closure of uneconomic enterprises.

Since the restructuring programme began, of the 241 PEs operating centrally in 1994–95, there were 109 loss-making ones. The total profit of the 130 profit-making PEs amounted to Rs 121.24 billion, a 24 per cent increase over the previous year and the losses of the 109 loss-making PEs amounted to Rs 49.07 billion, a 6 per cent decline year on year. The overall performance of the central PEs has been encouraging: investment grew by 4.5 per cent in 1994–95 over 1993–94, sales grew by 18.4 per cent and net profit by 58.8 per cent. Gross internal resources rose by 20 per cent. The top ten loss-making PEs accounted for half of the losses of the PEs and the top ten profit-making enterprises accounted for 62.3 per cent of the total pre-tax profits of the profit making PEs. However, this level of improvement in efficiency and productivity needs to be replicated at the state level.

It is clear where efficiency gains can be achieved. The closure of chronically loss-making PEs will improve returns on capital employed. In March 1995, there were 271 206 sick industrial units locking up total bank credit worth Rs 137.4 billion amounting to 6.7 per cent of total bank credit and 13.3 per cent of bank credit to industry. The process of dismantling and restructuring sick companies has been hampered by highly 'politicised' labour and land laws. The will to face these challenges has been lacking as reforms in company, labour and land laws have not yet been seriously addressed. No political party in India has dared to challenge the main interest groups, even the public sector trade unionists who have little voting power have been left untouched, leave alone the powerful farmers' lobby. Since 1991, there have been improvements in industrial relations with decline in man-days lost through strikes and lock-outs and in the rate of disposal of cases registered with the Board for Industrial and Financial Reconstruction (BIFR).

 The whole question of labour reform which is vital to the privatisation programme can only be addressed when the government is in a position to generate greater investment and employment. The public sector divestment programme was a major initiative launched by the government. It marked the start of a process of improving the performance of public sector units and the state sector units to be able to divest them successfully. As the restructuring process entailed redundancies, a National Renewal Fund was set up to provide a means of assisting laid-off workers. But, privatisation was never part of the plan to reform PEs. The aim to inject greater efficiency into the PEs was through reducing their effective rate of protection, restructuring potentially viable PEs and liquidating others by providing greater autonomy and the mandate to be profit-oriented.

The strength of the labour unions has meant that retrenchments, corporate restructurings, closure or sale of loss-making units or joint ventures with the private sector cannot be implemented without referring the matter back to the government. The government has yet to accept the recommendations of the Rangarajan Committee to disinvest up to 49 per cent of equity for PEs in areas still reserved for public investment, and over 74 per cent in the others. Large scale disinvestment would be the surest and most effective way of transforming PEs into dynamic and profitable concerns. It would definitely have a positive impact on the government's fiscal deficit. Thus, the initiative for the restructuring and disinvestment of PEs needs to be accelerated as an increase in public savings will lead to a decline in the public sector deficit and enable the public sector to invest in vital areas of education, health and infrastructure. As the social and political costs of such massive restructuring of the economy can be high, the importance of a national debate to enhance a greater awareness of public expenditure cannot be over-emphasised.

India needs to increase its rate of public savings as that will help lower the burden of government borrowing from the banking sector and thus reduce the 'crowding-out' effect on private sector investment. The government has taken steps to address that issue by reducing commercial banks' forced holding of government debt, by rationalising subsidised credit to priority sectors and bringing it more in line with market rates and by relaxing controls over the financial sector's lending decisions. The main challenge for the government is maintaining fiscal prudence as chronic fiscal deficits hurt all productive sectors of the economy. Any improvement in public saving will not only help contain the fiscal imbalance but reverse the anti-investment bias of the fiscal adjustment programme which has led to a declining trend in public investment. This implies an improvement in the quality of public expenditure by the government. Due to poor resource allocation, generation of employment opportunities by the public sector has not been feasible.

Removal of barriers to private sector entry in areas previously reserved for the public sector indicates that the process of introducing private investment continues but an adequate policy framework is still not in place. The slow take-off in private investment was not so much the high cost of capital but high idle capacity in sectors where private investment could have gone into – for example, into manufacturing. But in areas relating to infrastructure, where there is mounting urgency to expand capacity, policy and institutional framework conducive to private investment is still not in existence. While the industrial sector has been greatly liberalised since 1991, radical changes in company law will be necessary to attract greater commitment from the foreign direct investor. The role of the private sector has been accepted in principle; in reality, many obstacles remain for the economy to benefit significantly from private enterprise.

The evolution of the industrial sector has been a slow one with the domination of the state-controlled leviathans inhibiting the rise of private enterprise. The good news is that private entrepreneurs are now able to fund their investments through the stockmarket patronised by institutional investors and individual shareholders supported by a developed banking sector capable of assessing industrial risk. Despite that, the government's hold on the banking sector is unhealthy for private enterprise. It is inevitable that the adjustment process will continue to be slow due to supply side constraints and structural rigidities reinforced by resource immobility giving industry a longer gestation period to equip itself for change. The reforms that have been put in place as a result of India's economic liberalisation are hardly revolutionary. Most areas of the economy have been opened to private investment; import licensing restrictions have been eliminated except for consumer goods; import tariffs have been reduced significantly albeit they remain at comparatively high levels; full convertibility has been established for current account transactions though capital account convertibility is not on the agenda. Financial markets have been greatly liberalised; banks have more discretion in their lending decisions and prudential regulations that meet international standards are in place. Yet in the Indian context, these seemingly business-school textbook measures have had a radical impact on industry.

CONCLUSION

India has fundamentally altered its development strategy over the last six years. The economic recovery has been unexpectedly robust, the external accounts both current and capital have improved but vital fiscal adjustments have not taken place except, to some extent, at the centre. Inflation has been controlled at high cost to private investment. There is growing evidence of a crisis of expenditure composition at the state level where resources for the operation and maintenance of key infrastructure like roads, irrigation, primary education and health facilities have been cut to sustain less-productive expenditure on subsidies. India's development strategy is unsustainable without the help of its states.

While liberalisation of the investment regime is virtually complete, FDI remains slow to pick up because of regulations and administrative constraints that are neither transparent nor uniform across the states. Trade and foreign exchange regimes have been liberalised considerably, yet protection levels remain among the highest in the world. The financial sector has been liberalised but it remains dominated by the public sector with limited discretion in their commercial lending policy. While the 1993–94 National Sample Survey released in 1996 indicates that the incidence of poverty has declined, direct evidence does not support that conclusion in terms of the quality of life or human development indicators. The failure to cushion the negative effects of structural reforms on the poor has had an adverse response to reforms. Urban degradation has risen over the period under discussion. Law and order problems have increased on a national level along with pollution and a marked decline in basic services.

However, reform and growth are ongoing processes. India's achievements over the past six years have been commendable but the momentum of reform needs to be maintained to sustain growth and spur private investment. The continuation of reforms stands to benefit the poor by eliminating the bias against investment and employment which was the trademark of India's past policies. The structural reform of public expenditure, including the question of subsidies, can only benefit the poor. The misutilisation of public funds is unacceptable in the context of India's poverty. Unfortunately, the partial implementation of reform has not benefited the poor; even the higher expenditure on the social sectors has been misdirected towards those who are better equipped to manipulate the system.

Long-term funds, be it FDI or FII, will not be able to find their way into India if the reform process is not revitalised by the government. The reform agenda stalled between 1995–97. But, for the portfolio investor, this lack of market distortion due to meagre fund inflows, offered valuations that were at their most attractive in December 1996. After a strong recovery in corporate profitability in 1993–94 of 40 per cent for the companies in the new Bombay Stock Exchange (BSE) Index and 63 per cent for 1994–95, earnings growth slowed down to 26 per cent in 1995–96 and is estimated to be between 0–10 per cent for 1996–97 due to a combination of the higher cost of capital, the introduction of a minimum tax, a general slowdown of domestic demand and increases in raw material prices in international markets. For the stock pickers of the investment world, the market had not offered such valuations since the initiation of reforms in 1991. As many of the factors hampering growth begin to unwind, a recovery in the industrial sector can be expected after 1997–98. But, the market tends to discount such growth within a short period. Thus, to sustain the momentum of growth for both the market and the economy will require more than short-term measures from the government. If political stability coincides with economic vision during the Ninth Plan period, India is poised to benefit hugely from its reforms. It is hoped that the country will not squander away such an opportunity.

This book aims to provide the reader with an understanding of India's achievements and failures, particularly since the reforms of 1991. Chapter 2 deals with the export effort, but the question of the liberalisation of trade has revenue consequences and impacts on fiscal policy. The partial liberalisation of trade reflects on fiscal policy which is analysed in Chapter 3. While progress has been made in macroeconomic management, it remains the major policy challenge for India. Chapter 4 deals with issues relating to savings and investment, both domestic and foreign. It examines the effect of past policy measures on incentives to save and invest. While the foundation for deeper reforms have been laid, much remains to be done. The 'politicisation' of reforms has stalled the entire agenda for liberalisation. Due to the limitations of space, discussion is confined to certain aspects of India's challenges ahead in Chapter 5. It has not been possible to discuss in any detail the desired investments needed in the social sectors or in the area of environmental preservation. Nor is there scope to assess the cultural and ethical aspects of liberalisation. Chapter 6 deals with industrial policy development and the problems involved in making long-term investment decisions with regard to portfolio investment in Indian companies.

It is the conclusion of the author that investment in quality management is ultimately the most successful strategy. But, investors can only ignore stock price movement or market valuations at great risk to their own long-term investment performance. There is no substitute for understanding the fundamentals of the individual company one invests in to remain a successful investor in the company. However, it is unrealistic to expect managements to work miracles or for the stock market to deliver returns that are equally fantastic. If such a phenomenon occurs, then surely it is an aberration. If a company's cost structure rises due to any combination of higher costs incurred on borrowings, wages, taxes or raw materials and the company is unable to pass it on to the consumer due to weaker demand or greater competition and fails to improve market share and reduce costs by not being able to lay off workers or decrease its cost of capital, then it is reasonable to conclude that profit margins will come under pressure. No amount of analysis or positive thinking can alter some basic facts.

As the Indian stockmarket reflects less than 10 per cent of the economy, it helps to have a working acquaintance with the remaining 90 per cent of the economy because the stockmarket is hostage to the policies that the government implements. Private investment is tuned in to the macroeconomic situation as business is sensitive to returns on capital employed. More importantly, foreign portfolio investment which accounts for a mere 10 per cent of market capitalisation but is responsible for much of the market's volatility, is highly sensitive to government policymaking. Thus, investing in India involves an inclusive strategy and the more one is able to combine the 'top-down' approach with the 'bottom-up' one, the more successful one can hope to be as an investor.

2 The External Sector

INTRODUCTION

India's historic policy of 'self reliance' discouraged the development of exports as a means of growth. The nation's resources were to be mobilised in building domestic industrial capability. The usual reason for protecting any industry is to improve the terms of trade. In India, it was the scarcity of foreign exchange that dictated a protectionist stance. It had an adverse effect on resource allocation resulting in a trade policy that was not developed in conjunction with the country's fiscal and industrial policy.

Given India's inward focus on self-sufficiency and import substitution, the need to import oil forced India to trade. Exports trailed imports, resulting in a conservatively managed current account deficit, until the trade balance rose from −2.9 per cent of GDP in 1960–61 to −3.1 per cent of GDP by 1966–67. This deterioration in the trade and current account balance was caused by a combination of factors including severe droughts and a war with Pakistan. A massive 36.5 per cent depreciation in the currency was made in 1966–67. But instead of liberalising trade, more stringent restrictions were introduced. This further restricted access to inputs for exports leading to a protected domestic market and created a high cost structure for industry which resulted in lower productivity.

India's anti-export bias led to a stagnation of exports through the 1950s. In the 1960s, despite the devaluation of the rupee to improve the current account balance and the need for greater export competitiveness, export growth remained muted at the 4 per cent level. In the 1970s, with a slow-down in the growth of the domestic market, some sectors of industry attempted to build an export market aided by government subsidies and import concessions. This coincided with the growth of the Middle-Eastern market. India saw a pleasant spurt in export growth of 17.8 per cent per annum during 1971–78. The share of oil-exporting countries rose from 6.5 per cent of India's exports in 1970 to 17.2 per cent by 1975. The composition of exports also reflected the need of these oil-rich economies; manufactured goods as a portion of exports rose to 58 per cent in the late 1970s. The trade balance even recorded a small surplus in 1972–73.

The slump in exports came with the first oil crisis in 1973–74. Following the second oil shock in 1980, petroleum products accounted for 42 per cent of India's import bill. The movement in oil prices thus have a major impact on India's trade. The compound annual rate of increase in the import of petroleum, oil and lubricant products (POL) between 1965–66 (India's first economic crisis-cum-recession since Independence) and 1991–92 (the lastest crisis) was 22.4 per cent while the same figure for the capital goods sector was 12.3 per cent. The restrictive import policy in the capital goods sector hampered productivity growth but did not contribute significantly to improvements in the current account balance. An open trade policy would have resulted in a swifter adjustment of the currency and a superior exchange rate policy would have boosted exports improving both trade and current account balance.

The growing deficits in the trade and current accounts during the 1980s was the direct result of a policy that failed to balance surging imports by encouraging inward foreign investment. The links between fiscal policy, trade reforms, investment and productivity growth are complex but they tend to influence each other. A stable fiscal environment and an open economic system attract higher private investment leading to technological upgradation which improves exports via increased international competitiveness. Foreign direct investment (FDI) tends to generate higher productivity gains in host countries whose economies are not subject to major domestic policy distortions. Investment by multinational corporations (MNCs) has indirect benefits like the rapid transfer of new technology, products, management techniques and the knowledge of export markets. Besides, competitive pressures from local firms tends to have a benign effect on FDI. But, six years after reforms foreign investment has not contributed more than 10 per cent of gross domestic capital formation (GDCF) in India.

This chapter aims to examine to what extent India has succeeded in incorporating trade into its overall policymaking as the taxation of trade impinges on fiscal issues and on the competitiveness of the economy. India's management of the external sector since the crisis of 1991 has been hailed as one of its major successes. It is true that exports have risen on average by 20 per cent each year between 1993–94 and 1995–96 from $22 billion in 1993–94 to $32 billion in 1995–96, while FX reserves rose from $1 billion in June 1991 to $19.5 billion by February 1997. India's current account balance is manageable at –1.4 per cent of GDP for 1996–97 having declined from the –3.2 per cent level in 1990–91. Improvements in the capital account have been significant with rises in FDI and foreign institutional investment. While FDI lags behind the levels seen in China, India now absorbs about 5–7 per cent of global portfolio investments into EMs. The fact that with the right policies, India could earn its rightful place in global international portfolios is another matter.

TRADE

India's trade policy needs clearer enunciation with the aim of creating and maximising competitive advantages while exploiting international market opportunities. India's lack of strategy in the export sector translated to its share of world exports declining from 1.8 per cent in 1950–51 to 0.5 per cent by 1990–91. As India's trade policy remains unfocused, the share of merchandise trade in its GDP compares poorly with other export driven economies. In 1995–96, exports accounted for 9.9 per cent and imports 12.6 per cent of GDP; together amounting to less than the share of merchandise trade in GDP achieved by China in 1985 which then represented 24 per cent of GDP.

India's first BoP crisis of 1965–66 was the result of two severe droughts leading to an increase in food imports. This crisis was precipitated in the aftermath of a weak BoP position induced by agricultural stagnation and low export growth. But the second and the third crises, in 1973–74 and 1979–81, were mainly due to sharp increases in the price of oil. The increasing industrialisation of countries like India and China will undoubtedly continue to support the global demand for raw materials. Economic reforms and improvements in technology is likely to have a significant impact on the consumption of energy. According to the International Energy Agency, the real price of oil in 2005 is likely to be higher by 50 per cent from levels in 1993–94. A gradual increase in the price will not pose a huge problem of adjustment, particularly in countries like India that are heavily dependent on oil imports. But a sudden external surge in oil prices could trigger another 'oil shock' that could greatly diminish the competitiveness of the products of many developing countries.

India's trade imbalance never recovered from the massive growth in imports between 1979 and 1981. The trade balance had been conservatively managed but the situation was aggravated in the 1980s by both external shocks and internal policy changes which encouraged a more liberal import policy. India had and still has one of the most protected economies in the world. Infact, import tariffs had been erected to contain the trade imbalance. Imports had been restricted via quantitative restrictions (QR) and high tariffs, enabling the government to control both the quantity and the type of goods imported through the allocation of foreign exchange. As the rupee was non-convertible, importers had to approach the central bank for FX clearance which involved a Kafkaesque experience of various government agencies.

It is worth bearing in mind that the trade gap in 1990–91, the year of India's economic crisis, was less than –2 per cent of GDP. The developments

Investing in India

in India's balance of trade with its major trading partners between 1989–96 reflects the changes achieved in its trade policy (see Table 2.1). The extent of value addition in exports is evident from the fact that India imported raw materials and project goods from countries like Australia, the OPEC, Latin America and Germany and exported manufactured goods to the USA and the NIEs of Asia. India's major trade imbalance currently remains with the OPEC countries and to that extent the economy remains vulnerable to sudden rises in oil prices.

Table 2.1   India's trade balance with its major trading partners*
(in Rs billion)

Country	1989–90	1990–91	1991–92	1992–93	1993–94	1994–95	1995–96E
OECD	−54.8	−58.8	−4.6	−30.7	−13.7	22.4	−50.3
EU	−48.3	−37.3	−20.7	−39.3	−37.8	−2.6	−45.3
North America	0.3	−7.3	20.6	33.4	39.4	66.5	53.0
Australia	−5.5	−11.4	−9.5	−17.8	−13.0	−17.9	−21.6
Japan	−0.9	−2.1	6.9	0.2	6.9	−0.4	−8.4
OPEC	−32.3	−52.1	−56.5	−85.1	−89.0	−113.7	−152.9
Eastern Europe	23.5	24.4	23.7	6.5	13.7	8.5	−1.3
Other LDCs**	−17.8	−25.0	−4.8	15.5	56.6	15.7	48.2
Asia	−8.2	−13.7	11.4	26.7	55.6	35.2	48.9
Others	4.8	5.1	4.2	−4.1	−1.0	−5.8	−7.0
Total	−76.7	−106.4	−38.1	−96.8	63.8	−73.0	−163.3

Notes: * The trade balance as derived above refers only to India's exports minus its imports from the countries mentioned; ** excluding members of OPEC.
Source: *Indian Economic Surveys*, 1994–95 and 1996–97.

The focus since 1985 has been to improve the competitiveness of exports. In response to policy measures involving easier access to imports, the performance of exports was encouraging. By 1989–90, the share of manufactured goods in exports rose beyond 75 per cent as impressive growth was seen in the export of engineering goods, chemicals, textiles and garments, leather goods, gems and jewellery. This growth was accompanied by the increasing cost of imports due to the rising import intensity of manufactured exports. The growth in import density enhanced the diversification of the export base as Indian manufacturers improved their competitive position in terms of pricing and technology. Export-linked imports rose from 13 per cent in 1980–81 to 20.8 per cent in 1991–92 reflecting the rise in the import content of India's manufactured exports. India's terms of trade, which measures the terms of exchange between a unit of exports with that of imports, has improved significantly since the introduction of liberalisation and reform.

The major thrust of the economic reform of 1991 was to enhance rapid and sustainable growth in exports while ensuring external sector viability by allowing inward foreign investment. The new export oriented industrial and trade policies included the removal of quantitative restrictions (QR) on imports and recognised that a progressive move towards full convertibility of the currency would facilitate foreign investment that was necessary to sustain the momentum of growth. In July 1991, the rupee was devalued by 19 per cent and export subsidies were abolished. By March 1992, India had adopted an explicit dual exchange rate whereby exporters were able to access the depreciated free market rate. In March 1993, the exchange rate was unified resulting in a net devaluation of 40 per cent in nominal terms and 25 per cent in real terms. Tariff reductions were also introduced in 1992–93 but it was less than the currency devaluation.

Exports were not slow to respond to these policy changes as the overall figures during 1991–93 masked an 18 per cent rise in exports to the general currency areas with a 75 per cent decline to the rupee payment areas of Eastern Europe. In August 1994, the rupee was made fully convertible for current account transactions. But the continuing restrictions on the imports of consumer goods and the trade of agricultural commodities stand in the path of India's integration with the world economy. The trade reforms undertaken since 1991 have dismantled many of the restrictions of the past and have reduced the anti-export bias of Indian industry. In July 1991, out of 5040 tariff lines 80 per cent were subjected to import licensing requirements which was based on 26 seperate lists. Several goods were exclusively reserved for imports by various state agencies. By December 1996, most tariff lines covering raw materials, intermediates and capital goods were freed of any import licensing requirement. While restrictions on the import of capital and intermediate goods has been eliminated, a single negative list is maintained because of 'strategic considerations, environmental and ecological grounds, essential domestic requirements, employment generation and on grounds of socio-cultural heritage.'

A significant number of items covering 1487 tariff lines, whose imports were restricted, were allowed to be imported under freely tradeable Special Import Licences (SILs) which are granted to export houses, trading houses, star trading houses and super-star trading houses. The list of freely importable consumer goods has been expanded. In addition, imports of various consumer items are permitted under the SIL schemes and these items vary from blank 8mm video tapes/cassettes to cable cars. These complex export promotion schemes express the desire to provide free trade conditions for exporters while protecting the home market. Substantial rationalisation in customs duties and export incentives have been made but the complexity gives rise to bureaucracy and with it the scope for corruption and mismanagement.

Trade reforms within India itself has a long way to go. India is not a free-trade zone. The states levy sales taxes on inter-state sales. Under the Central Sales Tax Act of 1956, the states are authorised to levy sales taxes on inter-state sales originating in their territories. The centre prescribes a ceiling of 4 per cent which applies only to sales to a registered dealer. But if the sale is to an unregistered dealer or a consumer, the local tax rate or 10 per cent applies or whichever is higher. While the centre is reluctant to tax exports as it recognises the harm that such a tax could do to the growth of trade, state politicians and officials seem oblivious to the harm that inter-state taxes impose on the internal distribution of goods and services.

The reduction of import tariffs was guided by the Tax Reform Committee (TRC) chaired by Raja J. Chelliah. The TRC recommended various rates to be implemented by 1997–98. In broad terms, the lowest rate of 5 per cent was recommended for fertiliser and newsprint inputs, 10–15 per cent for 'basic' inputs like metals, 20 per cent for capital goods, 25 per cent for chemical intermediates, 30 per cent for other final products and 50 per cent for inessential consumer goods. It is true that Indian industry, after 50 years of protection, does need time to get internationally competitive but the prospect of losing out in the competition is not fully recognised. The complex tariff structure is meant to promote domestic value added industries just as the protected public sector was meant to represent the 'commanding heights' of the economy. While maximum tariff rates have been reduced to 40 per cent, it is not clear that the concept of a global market pricing mechanism is fully recognised as the key to asset allocation policies in India. It has to be acknowledged that in many developing countries, the higher stages of production have higher protection when the truth is that protection is needed by uncompetitive industries or those with low value-added relative to value added at world prices.

The aim of policymaking should be to make industry competitive and to give consumers better choice. In the process, some sections of industry will disappear under pressure from cheaper imports. Industries need protection during the period of transition from a sudden collapse of output or employment as that can have social and political repercussions. But, a policy that compensates for present disadvantages ends up promoting industries with a comparative disadvantage. What India's planners are trying to achieve is a paradox; the survival of local industry without admitting that the key to survival is to be among the most competitive globally. The risk is there of market forces wiping out complete sectors of industry that lack competitive advantage which is something that can be created or destroyed by interventionist policies. Even in developed economies that have openly espoused market mechanisms, government intervention is required to compensate for the effects of such resource allocation. This dualism is at the heart of India's inability to proceed boldly with reforms. Hamlet-like, the country's planners are caught in limbo because much of Indian industry is highly uncompetitive.

After six years of reform, India's trade regime remains among the most protected in the world. The process of reducing tariffs has been a slow one due to concerns about loss of revenue as well as fears relating to the ability of industry to adjust to the rate of decline in protection. The continuation of high tariffs on consumer goods has to do with fears about an acceleration in the imports of consumer goods leading to a deterioration in the level of reserves. There is also limited imports of agricultural products. Apart from the imports of POL, most capital and intermediate goods' imports are for investment and value addition in the industrial sector. A phased introduction of the abolition and the lowering of tariffs on consumer goods and agricultural products is necessary to prevent a misallocation of resources and a continuing lack of competition in potentially dynamic markets for India. Replacing the ban on the imports of consumer and agricultural goods with tariffs could also aid revenue collection.

The relatively closed nature of India's import structure ensures that as long as the trade deficit is financed through greater export performance or inward investments, there is no great cause for worry on account of the external sector as most imports are for investment rather than for consumption. The resource gap is a measure of a country's dependence on the outside world, expressing the net difference between exports and imports of goods and services as a percentage of GDP. In the Indian context, as the import of consumer goods is severely restricted, the resource gap mainly expresses the country's dependence on imports to support its domestic investment and exports. The role of trade in India's economy has changed significantly since 1991, but the contributions that the development of trade can make to economic growth is not being fully exploited. The international environment is not devoid of risks but increased participation in the world economy comes with its rewards.

The benefits of increased participation in the world economy are not only improved resource allocation, heightened competition as a means to

achieving world standards of efficiency, wider options for consumers and
the ability to tap international capital markets, but also the exposure to new
ideas and developments in technology. But globalisation has a price too as
firms in developing countries face intense international competition needing the support of their governments in terms of a stable, political and economic environment, free access to imports, an efficient infrastructure,
freedom from red tape and clear policy guidelines for private investment.
Investment in the upgradation of skills becomes the key to addressing the
changes in the labour market. The nature of policies becomes critical to the
speed of integration and growth. Countries where policies stand still tend
to fall behind. While major changes have been made, the 'politicisation' of
economic policymaking in India led to the near stagnation of reforms over
the past two years. Even in his most recent Budget, the Finance Minister
admitted his failure to address the issue of government expenditure. One
has the illusion of progress in reforms when one looks at pre-1991 conditions but compared to the rest of East Asia or several Latin American countries, India continues to fall short of its enormous potential.

The extent to which countries have benefited from private capital flows
due to the increased integration of world trade and capital markets is well-
documented. The fastest growing regions over the past five years, including East Asia and Latin America, have shown major advances in integrating with the world economy as measured by capital inflows and the
growth of exports. Since 1991, India has joined in reversing restrictive
trade practices and participating in the growth of world trade. India is now
more open to trade with the ratio of total trade to GDP rising from an average of 12.7 per cent in the 1980s to 22 per cent by the mid-1990s. The strong
performance of the export sector since 1992 has been aided by currency de-
preciations and the removal of the anti-export stance of past policies. If
India is able to continue with its structural reforms, greater openness to
trade is expected to increase to 45 per cent of GDP by 2005 or the level
currently prevalent in China. This will usher in a higher level of FDI which
represented 1.5 per cent of GDP in 1996 in India compared to China's 3.5
per cent.

India's trade policy is slowly being integrated with its fiscal policy, but
it is difficult for reformists to take the concept of free trade to its logical
conclusion – namely, that it is better to import 'potato chips' as well as
'electronic chips' if one is not very good at making either. For 50 years, the
domestic market has been protected resulting in high cost but low quality
products for the consumers. Greater trade openness would ensure that
investment flows into sectors where India has an advantage. Import competition tends to encourage the absorption of the latest technology and

international standards of excellence. India's *swadeshi* mind-set can be well exploited through policies encouraging private investment that bring with it superior technology and higher productivity. The consumer can only benefit from greater competition. As is widely recognised, there is a valid macroeconomic argument for not banning the import of consumer goods. Reasonable tariffs on consumer imports not only boost consumption and increase government revenues but in times of crises, when it becomes necessary to restrict imports, a cushion of relatively inessential imports causes less damage to domestic production.

The Development of Exports

During 1955–92, world exports grew at 10.5 per cent annually while India's exports grew at 7.7 per cent. During 1993–94 and 1995–96, India's exports grew at 20 per cent in dollar terms. Government policy since July 1991 aimed to encourage exports to rise to the 9 per cent level of GDP during the Eighth Plan period, up from 5.2 per cent in 1985–90. Recognising the critical role of the external sector, a high-powered committee overseeing the BoP position recommended an export growth target of 15 per cent in dollar terms as both necessary and feasible in order to sustain the minimum level of FX reserves over the medium term and to maintain a current account deficit ratio of 1.6 per cent of GDP to contain the growth in the external indebtedness of the country. Manufactured goods were aimed to account for the bulk of exports, an estimated 76 per cent, while the share of primary commodities was to be 19 per cent. Most of these targets have been met. After a strong performance in exports, the growth in 1996–97 is anticipated to be modest. The situation is summarised in Table 2.2.

Table 2.2   Growth in exports in selected emerging countries
(percentage growth per annum)

Country	1990–91	1991–92	1992–93	1993–94	1994–95	1995–96	1996–97E
India	9.2	−2.7	2.8	20.0	18.4	21.0	6.0
Brazil	0.6	13.3	8.4	12.4	6.7	7.5	8.2
China	23.1	18.2	8.0	31.9	22.9	6.9	14.0
Malaysia	18.1	13.6	18.8	31.8	23.3	17.5	4.0
Thailand	23.2	13.1	13.0	21.3	24.3	13.2	3.5
Indonesia	13.2	16.5	8.4	8.9	13.4	11.4	12.4
Korea	10.6	6.6	7.3	16.8	30.3	10.8	14.0
Mexico	11.8	8.2	12.3	17.2	31.3	16.7	2.0
Taiwan	13.4	6.9	4.5	9.4	20.1	8.1	7.9
Turkey	4.6	8.1	4.7	17.5	19.3	15.7	12.0

Source: ING Baring Securities (India) Pvt Ltd.

The need to maintain competitiveness in the external sector could well imply a series of downward adjustments in the real exchange rate (RER) of the currency over the years unless the trade gap is bridged by net capital receipts through foreign asset inflows. The maintenance of adequate FX reserves so that a BoP crisis is not repeated is the paramount consideration. The new approach to the BoP management thus involves a strategic role for exports. But, tariff and tax exemptions, periodic devaluation of the currency and access to cheaper capital has provided a level of support to exporters that may have made them dependent on these aids for their future growth. The government's dependence on having to earn FX has created a new 'interest group' in addition to the existing ones. Each of these pressure groups extract a price in policymaking. At the end of the day, it is the Indian consumer who pays the price for the government's policies.

The composition of India's exports since the 1960s has undergone a shift reflecting the move towards greater value addition, and thus the share of manufactured goods in total exports has grown steadily while that of agricultural products has declined. But as a percentage of GDP, exports were marginally lower at 6.1 per cent in 1990–91 compared to 6.5 per cent in 1950–51. Agro-commodities dominated exports in the first four decades of India's reluctant trade effort consisting 30 per cent of exports in 1980–81. By 1990–91, it had fallen to 18 per cent of exports, impressive gains having been made in engineering goods, garments, gems and jewellery, leather goods and chemical products. Agricultural products accounted for 20 per cent of exports in 1995–96 but manufacturing products dominated exports at 75 per cent of the total.

While the import of consumer goods continues to be subject to restrictions, import of capital goods have been significantly liberalised and, when destined for exports, are subject to concessional tariff rates. The high cost of capital also has a negative effect on exports. The structural issues involved in lowering inflation and interest rates involve a long-term policy framework. But, in the interim, the government directed banks to ensure a minimum 10 per cent of net credit to the export sector. Export credit was as high as 20 per cent of gross bank credit in 1994–95 when exports were buoyant but fell to 7.5 per cent in 1995–96 when gross bank credit itself slumped to Rs 75.9 billion between April and September 1996. The high cost of capital during 1996–97 meant that both export credit and gross bank credit declined sharply.

Despite the domestic economic crisis and a global recession, India was able to maintain its level of exports in manufactured goods during the critical years of 1990–93 at \$13–14 billion. Manufactured exports continued to register strong growth in the following two years but failed to maintain the momentum of growth in 1996–97. There has not been any significant diversification in the constituents of exports as a result of reforms but the direction of trade has changed since 1991 with the rise in exports to East Asia which has more than compensated for the decline in exports to the Eastern European countries, mainly Russia (see Table 2.3).

The change in the composition of exports is reflected in the evolution of India's direction of exports. Until the 1960s, India was dependent on the UK for 27 per cent of its exports. By 1970, India had been successful in diversifying exports but the diversification strategy was skewed towards the former USSR which accounted for almost 20 per cent of India's exports in 1980–81 and was still high in 1990–91. Thus, when the Soviet Union collapsed, it had a catastrophic effect on India's foreign reserves as the trade with the ex-USSR was conducted on a bilateral rupee trade basis. Since 1993, the diversification of trade has been more stable. Exports to the barter trade region declined dramatically after the collapse of the Soviet-bloc. No soft-currency agreements in trade exist today. Exports to North America and the Asian NIEs comprised 49.6 per cent of India's exports in 1996–97 with the European Union accounting for 26.5 per cent. The changes are summarised in Table 2.4.

An analysis of India's exports of engineering goods reveals that growth in dollar terms doubled during the 1980s and that the major growth came from electronics and software products followed by transmission line towers, cables and wires, machine tools and auto-parts. In absolute terms, at just over $2 billion in 1990–91, it was miniscule in terms of global market share. If India is able to maintain its competitive edge in these sectors, its share in the world market for manufactured products is poised to grow. India's software exports for 1995–96, for example, were estimated at $1 billion but have potential for significant growth in increasing its share in the global market.

The government initiated a 'thrust sector' approach to spur exports by identifying products that are likely to achieve significant export growth by the removal of procedural delays. One such example was allowing foreign credit lines as a marketing aid. A major initiative by the Exim Bank involved a credit line to manufacturers to access the US market. The bank helped Indian manufacturers of chemicals and engineering goods to gain entry into the US market. With the right policies and the removal of infrastructural irritants, there is hope that India will become a global sourcing point for major MNCs. An analysis of the region-wise growth of exports in the engineering sector reveals that East Asia and Europe were the major importers of India's engineering products in 1990–91 compared to 1970–71 when Africa and North America were the major buyers.

Table 2.3   India's principal exports since 1991 (US$ billion)

Products	1990–91	1991–92	1992–93	1993–94	1994–95	1995–96E
Agricultural and allied products	3.52	3.34	3.26	4.15	4.37	6.32
Ores and minerals (excluding coal)	0.83	0.82	0.63	0.76	0.81	0.92
Manufactured goods	13.23	13.26	14.10	16.80	20.60	23.98
textile fabrics & manufactures (excluding carpets handmade)	3.81	4.02	4.32	4.74	6.35	7.22
cotton yarn, fabrics made-ups etc.	1.17	1.30	1.35	1.54	2.23	2.58
readymade garments	2.24	2.19	2.39	2.58	3.28	3.67
leather manufactures	1.45	1.27	1.28	1.30	1.61	1.73
gems and jewellery	2.92	2.74	3.07	3.99	4.50	5.27
handicrafts (including handmade carpets)	3.44	3.34	3.78	4.77	5.33	0.61
machinery, transport, metal manufactures	2.16	2.23	2.46	3.02	3.48	4.36
Total exports	18.14	17.86	18.54	22.24	26.33	31.79
Percentage of GDP	6.2	7.3	7.8	8.8	8.8	9.9

Source: Indian Economic Survey, 1994–95 and 1996–97.

Table 2.4 Direction of India's exports (percentage share)

Country	1960–61	1970–71	1980–81	1990–91	1991–92	1992–93	1993–94	1994–95	1995–96E
OECD	66.1	50.1	46.6	53.5	57.9	60.5	56.9	58.7	55.7
EU	36.2	18.4	21.6	27.5	27.0	28.3	26.1	26.7	26.5
Germany	3.1	2.1	5.7	7.8	7.1	7.7	6.9	6.6	6.2
UK	26.9	11.1	5.9	6.5	6.4	6.5	6.2	6.4	6.3
North America	18.7	15.3	12.0	15.6	17.4	20.0	19.0	20.1	18.3
USA	16.0	13.5	11.1	14.7	16.4	19.0	18.0	19.1	17.4
Other OECD	10.1	15.2	10.6	10.4	10.5	9.1	9.1	9.2	8.3
Japan	5.5	13.3	8.9	9.3	9.2	7.7	7.8	7.7	7.0
OPEC	4.1	6.4	11.1	5.6	8.7	9.6	10.7	9.2	9.7
Saudi Arabia	0.5	0.9	2.5	1.3	2.0	2.2	2.3	1.7	1.5
Eastern Europe	7.0	21.0	22.1	17.9	10.9	4.4	3.8	3.6	3.8
Russia*	4.5	13.7	18.3	16.1	9.2	3.3	2.9	3.1	3.3
Other LDCs**	14.8	19.8	19.2	16.8	17.5	20.8	24.2	23.9	25.7
Africa	6.3	8.4	5.2	2.1	2.2	2.7	2.6	2.5	3.4
Asia	6.9	10.8	13.4	14.3	14.8	17.4	20.7	20.1	21.3
Latin America & Carribean	1.6	0.7	0.5	0.4	0.6	0.7	0.9	1.3	1.1
Others	8.0	2.6	1.0	6.2	5.0	4.7	4.4	4.6	5.1
Total (Rs bn)	6.4	15.4	67.1	325.5	440.4	536.9	697.5	826.7	1063.5

Notes: * Refers to the former USSR before 1992–93; ** excluding members of OPEC.
Source: *Indian Economic Surveys*, 1994–95 and 1996–97.

India's share in world exports fell from 0.6 per cent in 1970 to 0.4 per cent in 1980 before rising to 0.6 per cent in 1995. By comparison, China's share rose from 0.9 per cent in the 1980s to 3 per cent by 1995 while Korea's rose from 1 per cent to 2.6 per cent over the same period. If India is able to deepen its reforms, the potential is there for achieving similar levels of success. As is evident from the growth in India's share of some principal commodities in world exports, there has been progress in value addition in areas of leather, textiles, precious and semi-precious stone exports. But, there is tremendous scope for improvement in the manufacturing sector.

The recovery in India's exports since liberalisation was the culmination of developments that came together in 1993–94. The slowdown in domestic demand, the lowering of import tariffs, improvements in the overall administration of exports along with the depreciation in the real exchange rate (RER) of the rupee and the waiver of income tax on export earnings motivated firms to reorient their production with a view to exports. However, export performance could come under pressure due to infrastructural constraints. According to World Bank projections on India's export performance, overall growth of exports in key sectors is expected to average 12.4 per cent between 1996–2005, compared to 12.7 per cent during 1985–94, due to the slow pace of reforms as political constraints imply that fiscal imbalances and structural weaknesses are going to be addressed rather gradually.

While world GDP growth is projected to average 3.5 per cent during the next decade, India's import penetration ratios in major industrial markets remains small. India's exports to Japan, for example, account for less than 8 per cent of total exports. Industrial nations' growth is projected at 2.8 per cent per annum over the coming decade. India will need to deepen its reform to take advantage of the growth in world trade because of its low penetration in the fast growing Japanese and Asian markets. Even in the clothing sector India is not a major supplier accounting for only 1 per cent of consumption in the European Community and North America. Compared to China, which is itself a relatively new player in world trade, India's share of the world market is much lower.

Estimates made by several institutions, including the Asian Development Bank (ADB) and the General Agreement on Tariffs and Trade (GATT) secretariat, show that the income effects of the implementation of the Uruguay Round package will be most noticeable in areas of clothing, agriculture, forestry and fishing products, processed food and beverages. Since India's existing and potential export competitiveness also lie in these areas, it is anticipated that India will be able to make progress in world export markets in these sectors. With imports into developed countries forecast to increase by 5.5 per cent, Asian manufactures stand to benefit the most. Key sectors poised to gain are machinery and transport equipment, office and telecommunications equipment and other consumer goods. According to various studies, Indian exports in textiles and garments along with gems and jewellery will benefit the most and rise to almost 60 per cent of India's exports by 2005. Indian exports of machinery are slowly gaining global market share. If India's share in world trade were to improve from the current 0.6 per cent to 1.5 per cent, the trade gains for India will provide significant cushion to its current account deficit.

India faces a favourable external environment over the next decade in terms of moderate world inflation, stable economic growth and increasing trade openness. World trade volume has recovered strongly since 1991–93 when it averaged a 4.1 per cent rate of growth. More importantly, intra-regional trade in Asia and in Latin America has been growing at a much faster pace. If India continues with its reforms and does not fall behind the trade policy standards set by other developing countries, India's export market growth is projected to grow at 6 per cent over the next decade.

The Evolution of Imports

During 1955–92, world imports grew at an annual rate of 10.4 per cent and, despite India's restrictive policy, imports grew at 8.1 per cent with POL crowding out imports necessary for industrial development. Capital goods imports and with it the induction of technology were the main casualty. The growing import of POL since the mid-1970s resulted in a decade of low capital imports which adversely affected industrial productiveness. The exclusion of the import of capital goods was the policy response to the non-availability of FX resources as it was necessary to be conserved for oil imports. POL soared from 9 per cent of imports in 1950–51 to 42 per cent by 1980–81 falling to 25 per cent by 1990–91. Capital goods imports fell from 35 per cent of imports in 1965–66 to 24 per cent by 1990–91. But export-linked imports grew steadily from 4 per cent of imports to 14 per cent of imports by 1990–91, putting pressure on the current account balance. With liberalisation, import and export intensity have increased in most sectors of the economy contributing to increased efficiency and improvements in quality.

The success of India's Green Revolution is clearly reflected in the decline of food and food-related items from around 20 per cent of imports in 1960–61 to zero by 1990–91. The rise in the imports of precious stones was for value added re-exports and thus contributed to FX earnings. The import of fertilisers and ammonia as feedstock reflects that there is scope for liberalisation in that sector to meet demand via domestic production. An analysis of imports since 1991 shows that non-POL imports peaked in 1990–91 at $18.04 billion. Imports of non-POL products declined by 22 per cent during 1991–92 due to the squeeze triggered by the FX crisis. Imports rose by 12 per cent in 1992–93 and by 11 per cent in 1993–94. In 1994–95, POL imports rose marginally while that of non-POL products rose strongly by 29 per cent. The composition of non-POL imports has also remained largely the same since 1992 with capital goods, pearls, precious and semi-precious stones, chemicals, fertilisers and iron and steel accounting for 45 per cent of imports. The major imports are summarised in Table 2.5.

The import of POL fell from 28 per cent in 1991–93 to 20.5 per cent in 1995–96 in value terms. In volume terms, POL amounted to 29 million tonnes in 1990–91, rising to 40.6 million tonnes in 1992–93, stabilising during 1993 to 1995 at 41–42 million tonnes of imports before rising again in 1995–96 to 48 million tonnes. The sourcing of India's imports also changed over the decades reflecting the shift in oil-imports. The share of the UK and the USA declined considerably and the collapse of the former USSR had a significant impact on India's direction of trade after 1991 (see Table 2.6).

India's record on imports since liberalisation is seen as a vindication of the new trade policy and exchange rate regime. While the evidence is not sacrosanct, it appears that imports have proven to be relatively price elastic; thus facilitating a smooth transition from import compression to market determined imports of necessary commodities. The process of dismantling the channelling of essential imports by the government via subsidised FX allocation implies that the international pricing mechanism is being introduced to all sectors. Defence-related imports have been removed from the subsidised FX allocation mechanism since 1992. This should help to establish a greater degree of long-term stability in the management of the external sector.

There are several areas in the Uruguay Round of GATT that refer to market access; the more relevant ones for India being tariffs, textiles and garments and agriculture. In most developed countries industrial tariffs are low – an average of 5 per cent – and do not constitute a barrier to trade. Most developing countries have been reducing their tariff rates but have been prevented from lowering them significantly as import tariffs constitute a significant portion of government revenue. In India, trade taxes amount to approximately 4 per cent of GDP and about 50 per cent of the c.i.f. value of imports with the latter figure being virtually a world record. The World Trade Agreement came into force on 1 January 1995 at which point about 68 per cent of India's tariff lines were bound, compared to other developing countries in both Asia and Latin America who have bound 90–100 per cent of their tariff lines at levels

Table 2.5 India's major imports since 1991 (US$ billion)

Products	1990–91	1991–92	1992–93	1993–94	1994–95	1995–96E
POL	6.03	5.36	6.10	5.75	5.93	7.53
Fertilisers & fertiliser material	0.98	0.95	0.98	0.83	1.05	1.68
Chemical elements & compounds	1.27	1.38	1.43	1.54	2.34	2.81
Pearls, precious & semi-precious stones	2.08	1.96	2.44	2.63	1.63	2.11
Iron and steel	1.18	0.79	0.78	0.79	1.16	1.45
Plastic materials	0.61	0.57	0.24	0.43	0.61	0.80
Capital Goods, of which:	5.83	4.23	3.74	5.31	6.37	8.46
non-electrical machinery	2.36	1.63	1.65	2.04	2.94	4.29
electrical machinery	0.95	0.63	0.20	0.20	0.25	0.38
transport equipment	0.93	0.37	0.46	1.27	1.11	1.11
Non-POL imports	18.04	14.05	15.78	17.56	22.72	29.15
Total imports	24.07	19.41	21.88	23.31	28.65	36.68
Percentage of GDP	9.4	8.3	9.8	9.7	10.5	12.6

Source: Indian Economic Survey, 1994–95 and 1996–97.

Table 2.6 Direction of India's imports (percentage share)

Country	1960–61	1970–71	1980–81	1990–91	1991–92	1992–93	1993–94	1994–95	1995–96E
OECD	78.0	63.8	45.7	54.0	54.2	56.1	56.1	51.4	52.4
EU	37.1	19.6	21.0	29.4	29.2	30.2	30.0	24.8	26.6
Germany	10.9	6.6	5.5	8.0	8.0	7.6	7.7	7.6	8.6
UK	19.4	7.8	5.8	6.7	6.2	6.5	6.6	5.4	5.2
North America	31.0	34.9	14.7	13.4	11.7	11.7	12.7	11.1	11.6
USA	29.2	27.7	12.9	12.1	10.3	9.8	11.7	10.1	10.5
Other OECD	7.1	7.4	7.4	11.2	10.4	10.6	9.7	10.6	9.7
Australia	1.6	2.2	1.4	3.4	3.0	3.8	2.8	3.2	2.8
Japan	5.4	5.1	6.0	7.5	7.1	6.5	6.5	7.1	6.7
OPEC	4.6	7.7	27.8	16.3	19.9	21.6	22.4	21.1	20.9
Kuwait	0.0	0.3	2.7	0.8	1.7	4.4	4.8	5.2	5.4
Saudi Arabia	1.3	1.5	4.3	6.7	7.4	6.8	6.6	5.5	5.5
Eastern Europe	3.4	13.5	10.3	7.8	5.1	2.5	1.8	2.4	3.4
Russia*	1.4	6.5	8.1	5.9	3.8	1.2	1.1	1.8	2.3
Other LDCs**	11.8	14.6	15.7	18.4	17.1	15.2	15.4	19.9	18.3
Africa	5.6	10.4	1.6	2.7	4.1	3.4	2.2	2.9	2.3
Asia	5.7	3.3	11.4	17.1	11.2	10.5	12.1	14.2	14.4
Others	2.2	0.5	0.5	3.5	3.7	4.6	4.3	5.3	5.0
Total (Rs billion)	11.2	16.3	125.5	431.9	478.5	633.7	731.0	899.7	1226.8

Notes: * Refers to the former USSR before 1992–93; ** excluding members of OPEC.
Source: *Indian Economic Surveys*, 1994–95 and 1996–97.

comparable to or lower than India's. The lowering of tariffs in India has been gradual as revenue collection from domestic sources was weak in the wake of a domestic recession induced by the restructuring programme. Significant improvements have been made in revenue collection since 1992–93 but trade reforms continue to be slow. Inadequate progress in the liberalisation of the agricultural sector and the completion of reforms in the trade sector continue to affect the overall fiscal adjustment.

The Import of Consumer Goods

Questions of greater market access and free trade inevitably lead to India's restrictions on consumer imports. It has been widely accepted that trade should no longer be regulated by QR but through taxes and subsidies, with a few prohibitions being kept on grounds of health, morality or defence. While major achievements have been made in dismantling import restrictions, the virtual ban on consumer goods remains a thorny issue for India's planners. A few concessions have been made in the import of consumer items since 1991, but the key decision to open up the economy to consumer imports has not been on the agenda. As a result of restrictive imports in the consumer goods sector, the domestic consumer has paid the price over the decades.

It is true that excessive imports of consumer goods in Mexico helped trigger an unsustainable current account balance which precipitated in a crisis. But it was more due to an insufficient and timely policy response to the escalating external account imbalance. The adjustment in the exchange rate which was made in response to the crisis should have been implemented early enough to compensate for the rising current account deficit. Other policy measures could also have been used. The Mexican crisis has provided ammunition to those in India unsure about managing the consequences of global markets pressures. While FX reserves look healthy at the moment, the liberalisation of the Indian economy has not been extended to lowering import tariffs on consumer goods to international levels. The Eighth Plan acknowledged the need to open imports of raw materials and components and thereafter of manufactured goods. It also recommended a reduction in a wide spectrum of tariff rates and to move towards a trade regime in which the average tariff level is brought down to 25 per cent within a period of three to four years. The objective of the import restructuring policy was aimed at boosting exports while restraining the current account imbalance.

The maximum tariff rate under the old policy was as high as 400 per cent, which was reduced to 150 per cent in 1991–92 and further to 110 per cent in 1992–93. It was then lowered to 85 per cent in 1993–94, 65 per cent in 1994–95, 50 per cent in 1995–96 and 40 per cent in 1996–97. These rates do not apply to the imports of consumer goods. On an import-weighted basis, average tariffs in India were estimated to be at 29 per cent in 1994–96. But the Chelliah Committee's suggested rates of tariffs to be achieved by 1997–98 remains higher than other developing countries and the report argues that lower rates would be inadvisable in the medium term.

The ratio of imports to exports in India is much higher compared to the other export-oriented East Asian economies, particularly when the level of FX reserves is taken into account (see Table 2.7). While India has staged a dramatic recovery in its FX position since 1991 and the ratio of imports to exports showed an improving trend between 1991 and 1993, trade liberalisation has spurred import intensity. It is clear that the removal of import controls is not on the government's agenda. Restrictions on the imports of consumer goods should be phased out rapidly while tariffs on consumer imports can be lowered more gradually as the economy is able to sustain a higher level of imports. It is expected that liberalisation on the capital account will also have to be deferred until after that adjustment is made. The two are not necessarily connected but given the government's priorities, changes on the capital account is likely to be introduced with improvements in the financial and banking sectors as well as the central bank's ability to manage capital flows better. It is also linked to the government's dependence on the central bank to finance its deficits. The slow disengagement in the latter process is an encouraging sign but unless the fiscal deficit is reduced substantially, the central bank remains the lender of last resort.

Table 2.7   Ratio of imports to exports – a comparison (in percentage terms)

Country	1990–91	1991–92	1992–93	1993–94	1994–95	1995–96E
India	151.1	115.3	123.1	105.2	118.6	127.6
China	85.9	88.9	94.9	113.4	95.5	88.8
Hong Kong	93.7	96.2	98.2	97.6	100.8	101.9
Indonesia	98.6	95.9	90.1	91.9	97.1	99.0
Malaysia	94.7	102.4	98.5	99.5	103.2	108.4
Philippines	123.5	112.6	119.8	125.7	120.2	125.3
Thailand	115.8	113.7	107.3	106.3	106.6	108.2

Source: Socgen-Crosby Research; *Indian Economic Survey*, 1996–97.

Economists have long argued the advantages of an open trade policy. The question of trade boils down to how trade should be taxed or subsidised. Trade taxes and subsidies, along with the issue of protection, should be considered within the context of public expenditure and social utility. The debate regarding the desirability of an active governmental industrial policy and whether protection of the domestic market is necessary to support such a policy continues in the light of the economic success of countries like Korea and Taiwan. While policy errors were made in both countries, both governments achieved significant growth through exports; as their economies developed they 'traded up.' But, there appears to be no sustainable argument for permanent trade restrictions. Some may argue that there is a fiscal constraint to implementing an optimal system of subsidies and taxes, but the fact remains that the sooner the fiscal adjustment is made, the better it may be for the revival of productivity in the development of the economy.

THE CURRENT ACCOUNT BALANCE

India's economic planners believed in the 1950s that the country could emerge stronger as an exporter of manufactured products after its industrial base had been established with the help of foreign technological resources but without foreign financial aid. To achieve that level of industrial sophistication, import substitution was emphasised to conserve the nation's reserves. The BoP situation was managed conservatively. It was not until 1980–81 that the trade balance deteriorated to −4.4 per cent of GDP, but the current account deficit at −1.2 per cent of GDP was being financed by strong inflows. By 1989–90, the balance on the 'invisibles account' was down to $616 million from $5.45 billion in 1980–81. While private transfers on the capital account had risen to over $3 billion in 1989–90, the outflow of funds on the invisibles balance had built up a total deficit of $3.7 billion. As FX reserves had never been high, India's ability to service its external liabilities was considerably reduced with the decline in the availability of external commercial borrowing by May 1991.

The improvement in India's external accounts has been one of the achievements of the stabilisation and reform programme. After two years of export adjustment, the recovery in exports began firmly in 1993–94. India's current account deficit improved from −$9.68 billion in 1990–91 or −3.2 per cent of GDP, to −$1.16 billion or −0.5 per cent of GDP in 1993–94 and was estimated at −$5.48 billion or −1.7 per cent of GDP in 1995–96. The current account deficit for 1996–97 was estimated to be at 1.4 per cent of GDP. The decline in the rate of growth of imports in 1996–97 may impact on export growth for 1997–98. But export growth has been broadly based both in terms of markets and commodities since the recovery began. There is scope for necessary adjustments in the exchange rate to sustain the export effort. What might hinder exports is the country's infrastructural constraints.

Investing in India

The depreciation of the real exchange rate (RER) with cuts in import tariffs helped export competitiveness. Improvements in the administration of export promotion schemes have provided exporters with better access to raw materials and financing facilities at international prices. The capital account has been strengthened by increased foreign investment resulting in higher foreign currency assets. Private transfer of funds has been buoyant and the share of concessional and commercial debt-creating flows in total capital inflows has declined. This has had a positive effect on the debt service ratio which declined from 35 per cent of current receipts in 1990–91 to an estimated 25 per cent in 1996–97. FDI is higher at around $2 billion and portfolio investment has stabilised at $2–3 billion. These developments have translated into a comfortable level of reserves which has recovered from less than a month's of import cover in 1990–91 to over 5 months' cover in 1996–97. A breakdown of India's BoP is shown in Table 2.8.

Table 2.8   Select items in India's balance of payments (US$ billion)

Key indicators*	1990–91	1991–92	1992–93	1993–94	1994–95	1995–96E
Exports	18.48	18.26	18.87	22.68	26.86	32.47
Imports	27.92	21.06	23.24	25.07	31.84	41.41
Total trade as % of GDP	15.6	15.6	17.6	18.5	19.3	22.5
Trade balance	−9.44	−2.80	−4.37	−2.39	−4.98	−8.95
as a % of GDP	−3.2	−1.1	−2.0	−0.9	−1.6	−2.7
Net invisibles	−0.24	1.62	0.84	1.23	2.35	3.51
Current account balance	−9.68	−1.18	−3.53	−1.16	−2.63	−5.43
as % of GDP	−3.2	−0.4	−1.8	−0.5	−0.9	−1.7
External assistance	2.21	3.04	1.86	1.90	1.43	0.78
Commercial borrowing**	2.25	1.46	− 0.36	0.61	1.03	0.53
IMF	1.21	0.78	1.29	0.18	−1.15	−1.71
NRI deposits	1.53	0.29	2.00	1.21	0.81	0.94
Foreign investment	0.10	0.14	0.55	4.23	4.89	4.14
Capital account	8.40	4.75	4.25	10.02	7.59	2.51
Reserves (-increase)	1.28	−3.57	−0.73	−8.86	−4.96	2.91

Notes: * Data for the years 1990–91, 1991–92, 1992–93 and 1993–94 are 'preliminary actuals' and those for 1994–95 and 1995–96 are 'quick estimates'; ** figures include receipt on account of India Development Bonds in 1991–92 and related repayments, if any, in the subsequent years.
Source: *Indian Economic Survey*, 1996–97.

The continued accumulation of reserves reflects the onset of an improvement in the external sector. To sustain this achievement will require the continuation of reforms in trade, macroeconomic policies and the easing of infrastructural constraints. A significant feature of the structural change in the BoP situation is the increase in the coverage of imports by export earnings. The ratio of exports to imports deteriorated sharply from 1980–81 onwards, and without matching foreign investment to bridge the resource gap a FX crisis in India was waiting to happen as policy adjustments were not made over a long period of time. The ratio was the lowest in 1980–81 at 53.5 per cent. Although, it had recovered to the 75 per cent level by 1990–91, the decline in inflows and the government's inability to borrow funds abroad was the reason behind the crisis of 1991. Since then the ratio of exports to imports has been healthy and with it the FX reserves.

External Account Vulnerabilities

India's dependence on capital inflow rose to 2.9 per cent of GDP in 1988–89. This was matched by the rise in trade deficit to 3.4 per cent of GDP. By 1990–91, the situation had not improved; imports were strong at 8.1 per cent of GDP and the current account deficit had deteriorated to –3.2 per cent of GDP. The fall in invisible earnings translated to the FX crunch of 1991. Despite the improvements in India's BoP position since then, the situation remains prone to stresses from increased oil imports as India's domestic oil production is expected to level off in the medium term. Government subsidies on POL is stimulating the demand for oil at a rate higher than the rate of GDP growth. Demand for POL is growing at over 8 per cent per annum compared to real GDP growth at 6–7 per cent. The expansion in the power sector is becoming more dependent on oil rather than on domestic coal-based thermal plants. Thus, any rise in the price of oil will not bode well for India's BoP position.

Debt repayments over the next few years, along with volatile NRI deposits which account for 18 per cent of total external debt, may cause concern if policy response is not adequate. According to the World Bank, India will need to mobilise about $46 billion of external finance, excluding the rollover of short-term debt and NRI accounts, in addition to the financing requirements of the current account deficit. Neither FDI nor portfolio investment will be available unless the macroeconomic position is perceived to be secure and the necessary infrastrucutre is available. As is evident, the growth enhancing effects and the output impact of FDI is substantially higher in more competitive, export-oriented economies. Fiscal adjustments in the OECD countries has necessitated a reduction in multilateral and bilateral concessional development aid. Thus, developing countries' borrowing costs will increase making them more exposed to foreign interest-rate shocks and resulting currency adjustments. Increased recourse to non-debt capital flows has already become important in the development agenda of most developing countries including that of India.

The healthy performance of exports since 1992–93 has been encouraging, but maintaining export competitiveness will remain the critical task of both policymakers and industrialists. The higher export to import ratio coupled with an improvement in the invisibles account has led to the recovery in the current account position. The surplus in the invisibles account of $1.6 billion in 1991–92 and the subsequent years is mainly the result of strong private transfers. With the liberalisation in the current account, the black market in currency trading disappeared making the legal transfer of money through banking channels attractive. Growth in tourist income also recovered after the Ayodhya crisis in 1992–93. The higher deposit interest rates during 1994–96 increased the inflow of NRI transfers. The improvement in the flow of invisible receipts along with higher export earnings helped in reducing the current account deficit. The decline in imports during 1996–97 continued to keep the deficit at around the 1.5 per cent level of GDP.

India's dependence on external assistance and commercial borrowing has declined since liberalisation. This was reflected in the advance repayments made in April 1994 of $1.15 billion to the IMF. It is expected that the role of external assistance in financing the external deficit is going to decline further. The share of external assistance as a percentage of capital inflows has been declining since the 1980s. In 1980–81, a crisis year for India, it represented 61 per cent of capital flows, but by 1990–91 it was lower at 26 per cent and declined further as private inflows began to recover. In 1991–92, the year of the most recent FX crisis, external assistance was 64 per cent of total capital inflow. During the late 1980s, without recourse to either cheap long-term credit or access to foreign investment, the government had depended heavily on external commercial borrowing to finance its widening current account deficit. External commercial borrowing declined from over 30 per cent of capital flows in 1991–92 to 21 per cent in 1995–96. The economy has moved to a more stable and sustainable BoP position with a structural change in the capital account with a shift from debt-creating inflows to non-debt creating foreign investment flows.

India's large NRI population has had little confidence in their home country's business milieu or the stability of the rupee. But, during the time of Rajiv Gandhi's prime-ministership (1985–91), enterprising NRIs started looking for opportunities to invest in India. With the change in attitudes and policies in India, there was a strong increase in NRI flows into India and NRI deposits became a major source of external financing in the middle to late 1980s rising from $2 billion in 1983–84 to $14 billion by 1990–91. The major attraction for NRIs was the higher interest rate compared to global market rates offered on foreign currency deposits as the exchange risk was also covered. But the decline in that source of funding due to the Gulf crisis and the deterioration in India's macroeconomic stability pushed the nation to the verge of defaulting on its external debt repayments (see Table 2.9).

Table 2.9 Non-resident Indian deposits (US$ billion)

Name of account or deposit*	1991	1992	1993	1994	1995	1996
Foreign currency non-resident	10.10	9.79	10.62	9.30	7.05	4.25
Non–resident external rupee	3.59	2.53	2.86	3.59	4.56	3.92
Foreign currency non-resident (banks)	0	0	0	1.07	3.05	5.72
Non-resident (non-repatriable) rupee	0	0	0.61	1.79	2.48	3.54
Foreign currency (banks & others)	0.26	0.61	1.04	0.53	0	0
Total	13.95	12.93	15.13	16.29	17.14	17.44
As % of external debt	17.0	15.4	16.8	17.6	17.3	18.9

Notes: * As at the end of March.
Indian nationals and persons of Indian origin resident abroad are able to open bank accounts in India out of funds remitted from abroad. Authorised dealers offer six different types of accounts to NRIs with varying rates of interest on their deposits. Outstanding stock under all these schemes except the Non-resident (Non-repatriable) rupee deposit constitute part of India's debt.
Source: *Indian Economic Surveys*, 1994–95 and 1996–97.

While in absolute terms NRI deposits only declined 7.4 per cent from $13.9 billion in March 1991 to $12.9 billion in March 1992, its share in total capital flow fell sharply as external assistance rose strongly. The following year, NRI deposits rose 17 per cent to $15 billion by March 1993 and comprised of the entire bulk of capital inflows as all other sources, ranging from commercial borrowing to private transfers, declined dramatically reflecting the country's critical funding situation. External assistance was curtailed once the worst of the funding crisis was over in 1991. The slowdown in NRI deposits as a source of external finance since 1993–94 reflected the decline in India's dependence on external borrowing. As FX reserves improved, the government needed to reduce the cost of bearing the exchange risk on NRI accounts as these deposits were brought under cash reserve ratio (CRR) requirements. Inflows under the Foreign Currency Non-Resident Accounts (FCNR(A)) schemes were discontinued from 15 August 1994. Interest rates on the FCNR(A) deposits were also adjusted downwards to moderate the cost to the banks. But commercial banks were permitted under the Foreign Currency Non-Resident (Banks) FCNR(B) scheme to continue to bear the exchange risk as the statutory cash and liquidity ratios did not apply to these accounts.

India's capital account has benefited by the decline in debt service payments to Russia since 1991–92. This arose due to the inability of Russia to absorb a higher level of imports from India. Foreign investment was the major contributing factor to the surge in capital flow. Total capital inflow has been rising steadily since 1993–94 and the share of portfolio investment has grown significantly. While approvals for FDI has been strong, actual investment has been slow to materialise due to various infrastructural constraints. The ratio of actual inflows to approvals needs to improve radically if FDI is to be actively encouraged. MNCs encounter the same level of frustration as direct portfolio investors. As the former is a more secure and longer term source of funding, it is paramount that the government improves the infrastructure needed to attract such investments. FDI represents a greater commitment and such investment tends to wait and see that reforms are fully entrenched before making any significant investments which will become difficult to reverse. The time lag for the build-up of FDI is longer than portfolio investment which tends to be more mobile and less secure.

In 1993, India benefited along with other EMs, from the opportunities opened up by liberalisation. The high interest rates due to the combination of fiscal and monetary policies prompted Indian companies to raise equity capital from overseas investors. The issuance of Global Depository Receipts (GDRs) by Indian companies can be viewed as a form of FDI as the funds raised went to the firms concerned directly. While portfolio investment into India has been encouraging since 1993–94, these flows slackened during 1995–97 as overall investment in EMs declined and the political uncertainty in India did not help (see Table 2.10). The Mexican crisis and the macroeconomic adjustments in various emerging countries coupled with the superior growth performance of the OECD economies led to a lower asset allocation towards EMs in global funds.

India's FX reserves had never been healthy because of the closed nature of the economy. In 1950–51, FX reserves at $1.9 billion were high, representing 16.8 months of import cover. By 1960–61, they had dwindled to $0.39 billion accounting for 2 months of imports. In 1970–71, at $0.58 billion, FX reserves were adequate for about 3 months of imports and a decade later, in 1980–81, reserves had risen to $5.85 billion or 4.5 months of imports. By 1990–91, once again FX reserves had declined significantly to $2.2 billion or less than a month in terms of current payments due. It was the lack of access to FX that forced India to borrow from the IMF and thus comply with its directives on structural adjustment. So when India pre-paid $1.1 billion of its loan to the IMF in April 1994, it was interpreted by many as the first step towards financial irresponsibility – namely, that India was paying up to free itself of the constraints and obligations of IMF-induced policymaking. It was the unexpectedly higher level of capital flow during a recession in the domestic economy that prompted the prepayment to the IMF.

Table 2.10   Foreign investment flows (US$ million)

	1991–92	1992–93	1993–94	1994–95	1995–96	1996–97#
FDI	150	341	586	1314	2133	1700
Portfolio investment	8	92	3649	3581	2214	2343
FII	0	1	1665	1503	2009	1002
Euro-equity	0	86	1602	1839	149	812
Offshore funds	8	5	382	239	56	20
Total	158	433	4235	4895	4347	4053

Notes: # From April till December. Figures in this table are based on actual inflows and may differ from foreign investment flows in the Balance of Payments Table 2.8 which are on accrual basis.
Source: *Indian Economic Survey*, 1996–97.

The future momentum in investment flows and the absorptive capacity of the economy will determine the level of India's FX reserves. An import cover of three months is considered adequate by countries more open to trade and investment and better experienced in the management of FX. Until the pattern of trade and foreign investment is more clearly established, it is unlikely that the Indian authorities will open up the economy to consumer imports for fear of a repetition of the 1991 crisis, particularly in light of the Mexican crisis of 1994 and its devastating impact on the local economy, the stockmarket and investor confidence. In August 1994, the final step towards current account convertibility was taken whereby India became committed to forsake the use of exchange restrictions on current international transactions as an instrument in managing the BoP. The rupee is not yet convertible on the capital account and needs to be liberalised in concert with fiscal stabilisation, reform of the financial sector and greater openness in trade.

India's policymakers have been concerned to limit the current account deficit to safe levels even when the infrastructural requirements would demand a higher recourse to foreign savings. While some of the East Asian countries have run current account deficits in the region of 6–8 per cent of GDP, they have also had much higher levels of exports and FX reserves. Unsound private borrowing and lending can lead to crises, and experience shows that the pool of international long-term funds is limited and does not flow to countries vulnerable to structural weaknesses. Such capital inflows tend to have higher risk-sharing characteristics but they also require higher returns on their investments and a stable macroeconomic and political environment is required to ensure that.

In India, during 1993–94 as the country was recovering from a domestic recession, the delay in imports resulted in the escalation of FX reserves. This appears to have been a one-off response as international fund managers did not have an exposure to India prior to the liberalisation of the capital market in September 1992 and thus invested heavily in Indian GDRs and Offshore Country Funds as settlement constraints prevented them from entering the market directly. The companies that issued GDRs were more opportunistic in their fund raising when there was no immediate need to raise funds for investment due to the low capacity utilisation ratios. Some firms reduced their debt but the bulk of the capital raised did not translate into imports but contributed to a rise in FX reserves.

China's had eight months of import cover in 1991 which declined to less than three months' cover by 1993, necessitating a firm policy response before reserves recovered to five months' of import cover in 1994. While a country's dependency on foreign investments can impede growth when that source of funding is not available, it also enforces a certain discipline on the authorities concerned to ensure that the funding remains unhampered. If the return on capital is competitive enough on a global basis and there are no obvious impediments to capital flows, investments tend to find their way into such markets. The rise in actual FDI into India will be the real driving engine for future economic growth. Unfortunately, the cost structure in India remains high for an adequate return on capital to spur FDI. When FDI accelerates, it will be a signal to investors that the cost structure for Indian companies is beginning to offer an adequate return on investment.

It has been argued by the Indian authorities that as payments on current and capital accounts become more open, the need for holding higher FX reserves must increase. India's reserves have not been considered adequate enough compared to the size of the economy. One of the major concerns for the Indian authorities in the management of the external account is the price of oil which is a significant and an irreversible import item. The price of oil is not expected to fall as it did in the 1980s and early 1990s contributing 1.5 per cent every year to India's terms of trade during 1985–90 and an estimated 5–6 per cent gain over 1991–93. In the absence of these windfall gains, India's terms of trade are expected to be flat over the next decade or so. The external environment will be both more supportive of reforms but will pose greater competitive challenges. Whether India can exploit it to its advantage will depend on domestic policy developments.

The prospect for higher economic growth in India hinges on the growth in investments, savings and exports as experienced in other East Asian countries. The ability to attract FDI into labour intensive, export oriented industries has been the established path to greater economic prosperity. Thus, the sustainability of a prudent current account position depends on exports and foreign investment. Greater openness to trade and with it improvements in infrastructure is expected to accelerate the flow of FDI. According to World Bank projections, India's real current account revenue is expected to grow at 8.3 per cent per annum between 1996–2005 compared to its pre-reform growth rate of 5.5 per cent. The current account deficit is expected to remain around 2 per cent of GDP, a level considered to be prudent.

EXTERNAL DEBT

India's external debt had risen from $20.5 billion in 1980 to $92.2 billion by March 1996 which, in present value terms, is almost twice the value of the country's exports. The level of debt remains a matter of concern. While the total debt figure is high, 45.5 per cent of it was on a long-term, concessional basis as of March 1996 and 5.5 per cent was short-term. This ratio has been fairly stable over 1990–96. Total interest paid was $4.3 billion and principal repayment was $8.1 billion adding up to a total debt service payment of $12.38 billion. India's debt service ratio at 25.7 per cent is an improvement on its level in 1990–91, but when compared to that of China's at 9 per cent, India's is rather high. With a current account deficit of −1.4 per cent of GDP, India would require about $12 billion in gross financing each year over the next few years.

Bilateral and multilateral participants in the Indian Development Forum (IDF) pledged $6.7 billion in official assistance in 1996–97, an amount similar to last year's, as a recognition of India's commitment to reform and poverty reduction. The government has taken measures to improve its utilisation rate of overall external assistance (OEA) which has gone up from 53.6 per cent in 1989–90 to 90.6 per cent in 1995–96. Overall external assistance in 1995–96 stood at Rs 110 billion. The Finance Minister has outlined his commitment to raise FDI to $10 billion annually, but total foreign investment flow during 1995–96 was $4 billion. Besides, such inflows cannot materialise unless the policy framework for private investment is clearly established and the infrastructure is available to support the investment. The international financial community has been supportive of India's economic performance but concerns remain on various critical areas ranging from the high fiscal deficit, restrictions on trade relating to consumer goods and agriculture, higher overall tariffs, lack of capital account convertibility and the general slowing down of structural reforms over the past few years. Even after an encouraging second budget by the Finance Minister in February 1997, it is not clear to the investing community whether the present coalition government is an interim one or is here to fulfil its electoral mandate and means business. As a result, long-term investment decisions have been delayed, if not cancelled.

The improved BoP situation has helped in reducing the rate of growth of external debt. As a percentage of GDP, external debt rose from 12 per cent in 1979–80 to over 28 per cent in 1989–90, peaking at 41 per cent in 1991–92 and declining to 29 per cent in 1995–96. The profile of external debt has undergone a fundamental change since the 1960s and 1970s with a shift from long-term, low interest bearing development assistance loans to medium and short-term, high interest bearing commercial loans in order to meet the increasing FX-needs of the economy. Many investors are cautious of an escalation of external debt as the rate of interest payable on the outstanding amount rises over the years. The rate of growth of exports is thus the key to the stability of India's external sector.

The share of short-term debt as a component of aggregate debt declined from 10 per cent in March 1990 to 5.5 per cent in March 1996. While this level of short-term indebtedness compares favourably with other emerging economies globally, the share of concessional debt to total debt is exceptionally high. As a result, the present value of India's external debt is much lower than that of other developing countries. The ratio of short-term debt to total debt is bound to rise in the future and along with it India's debt service payments. The question of debt has to be assesed by the level of cash flow available from the exports of goods and services to finance the debt and by analysing the utilisation of the external debt.

The bulk of India's imports are capital goods and raw materials needed for investment which tend to stimulate growth through improved exports and productivity. Thus, as long as exports continue to grow consistently at the 15–18 per cent level, the servicing of the rise in external debt will be manageable. Debt sustainability requires that the rate of interest of foreign borrowing should be less than the rate of growth of export earnings. Hence, the focus has to be on debt service as a percentage of current receipts rather than as a percentage of GDP. India's ability to service its external debt compares favourably with several developing countries but lags behind that of China.

Table 2.11   India's debt service payments – select ratios

Key indicators	1990–91	1991–92	1992–93	1993–94	1994–95	1995–96E
Debt service ratio*	35.3	30.2	28.6	26.9	27.5	25.7
External debt/ GDP	30.4	41.0	39.8	35.9	32.7	28.7
ECB/net capital flows	26.8	30.6	–8.4	6.1	13.6	21.0
External assistance/net capital flows	26.3	63.9	43.7	19.0	18.9	31.0
Import cover**	0.6	2.1	2.8	5.2	8.7	6.1
Current payments cover**	0.8	2.3	2.5	5.4	5.8	3.8
Rate of growth in debt service	21.1	–8.1	–7.2	12.3	27.0	13.3
Rate of growth in exports	9.2	–1.1	3.3	20.2	18.4	20.8
Debt service/ exports	49.5	46.2	41.3	37.9	40.7	38.1
Exports/imports	66.2	86.7	81.2	90.5	84.3	78.4

Notes: * total debt service repayments as a percentage of current receipts; ** in number of months.
Source: *Indian Economic Surveys*, 1995–96 and 1996–97.

India's debt service payments have been at the $8–9 billion level since 1990–91 but rose to $10.9 billion in 1994–95 due to higher repayments to the IMF and a rise in repayments on external commercial borrowing and further to $12.4 billion in 1995–96. The debt service ratio, expressed as a percentage of current receipts, declined from 35.3 per cent in 1990–91 to 25.7 per cent in 1995–96 (see Table 2.11). Success in sustaining exports is crucial to India's ability to reduce its external debt. The need to maintain export competitiveness will result in a gradual devaluation of the currency putting an increased burden on servicing the debt with the bunching of re-payments coming together periodically. External debt, denominated in dollars, can rise or decline reflecting the weakness or strength of the dollar

Investing in India

versus other major currencies in which the debt has been incurred. For example, the rise in India's external debt in March 1995 was attributed mostly to the changing value of the dollar rather than a significant increase in India's borrowing.

Economic reform has led to an improvement in the FX constraints on growth which had been a major drawback previously. However, there is tremendous scope for further relaxation in the area of debt. India's future ability to attract a larger share of global investment will also bear on the success of future reform. External debt management will remain an area of policy priority. Optimisation of currency, interest and maturity mix of debt to minimise costs and exposure risks all constitute part of the government's debt management strategy. But, greater liberalisation in the area of debt management, both internally and externally, could ease the debt constraints of the government.

FOREIGN EXCHANGE RESERVES

It was the scarcity of FX reserves prior to Independence that initially steered India towards a protectionist regime. Partial import controls were introduced in 1940 to save FX during the Second World War. By 1942, all imports were under direct quantitative control and the fluctuations in the BoP position meant that the ideology of protection was favoured as a practical measure by India's policymakers. India's FX reserves, including gold and Special Drawing Rights (SDRs), reached the $1 billion level only in March 1970 or two decades after the country had launched its development programme in 1950. It was also the same year that India's import cover rose above the three month's level; it represented 5.5 months of imports. Thus, it took India two decades to build up its FX reserves for their accumulation was not considered vital to macroeconomic stability.

The severe drought in India in 1971–72 and the global oil crisis in 1973–74 meant that import cover plummetted to critical levels between 1973–75. The second oil crisis also had a severe impact on India's import cover in 1981–82. Thus since 1969–70, India's FX reserves fell below the critical level on three occasions but only once did that breach persist for two consecutive years and that was between 1973–75. In 1973–74, an official grant from the USA helped India tide over the FX crunch. After the second oil crisis in 1981–82, India's planners became keenly aware of the need to increase the level of FX reserves for greater macroeconomic stability.

One of the more easily accessible sources of FX for India has been the savings of NRIs. This aspect of India's FX earnings goes back to the mid-

1960s when the exodus of Indians led to the inflow of foreign savings back into the homeland. The dependence on NRI savings has not been without some cost to the country. To attract these inflows in the 1980s, the interest rates offered were higher than the global market interest rates and the exchange risk also had to be covered. Such expensive deposits were finally wound up in August 1994. Since then the rate of influx of funds has slowed down. NRI deposits as a percentage of capital flows rose from 9.7 per cent in 1980–81 to 33.6 per cent in 1985–86 and represented 28.4 per cent of capital inflow in 1989–90. It was the decline in private transfers due to the collapse of NRI earnings from the Gulf region that partly contributed to India's FX crunch in 1991.

India's policymakers did attempt to address the country's precarious FX reserves position. By 1984–85, with the arrival of Rajiv Gandhi as Prime Minister, exports were already recognised as the key to improving India's external resources. But the inadequate sequencing of the spectrum of reforms necessary to sustain the export effort meant that by 1988–89, FX reserves represented less than 22 per cent of India's imports and import cover had fallen under the critical level. Drastic remedial action was required but none was taken. Imports kept rising along with exports and the inflow of NRI funds. The government was lulled into a false sense of security. Lack of adequate policy response meant that by 1989–90, the central bank had less than two months of import cover. This was directly the result of economic mismanagement over a period of time that left the country vulnerable to external shocks. By May 1991 India came close to defaulting on its external debt obligations.

The importance of building up and being able to sustain a higher level of import cover had been recognised by India's policymakers prior to the crisis of 1991, but sustainable policy changes were only implemented after the crisis. India's FX reserves went up from $2.2 billion in 1990–91 to $20.8 billion in 1994–95. Such a strong build-up in reserves was possible due to a combination of buoyant exports, subdued imports and a surge in non-debt creating foreign investment. The cover of foreign currency assets to total payments in the current account balance also improved from less than a month in 1990–91 to about 8 months during 1992–93 and 1993–94 before declining to 5.5 months in 1995–96. The need for a higher level of import cover coupled with foreign investment in 1993–94, which did not translate immediately into higher imports, led to the accumulation of FX reserves.

During 1993–94 and 1994–95, India had a high level of import cover. If import cover rises as a result of a strong growth in exports compared to imports, it can help the economy to withstand sudden upsets in the BoP position. In India, the recycling of foreign capital into reserves only put upward pressure on money supply and inflation leading to higher interest rates which had a punitive effect on industry, particularly the small scale manufacturing sector. It deterred foreign investment as accumulation of reserves through such a method reflects the inability of the economy to absorb a higher level of foreign savings. What can be disconcerting is that a rapid deterioration in reserves can also transpire when the cycle reverses and imports rise leading to current account deficits, currency depreciation and loss of confidence by investors which leads to a further cycle of capital outflows.

As the investment cycle picked up in India, it was not possible to continue to maintain higher levels of import cover in the wake of lower capital inflows. By 1995–96, imports had risen to the extent that the foreign currency assets of the RBI had fallen to $17 billion by the end of March 1996, equivalent to slightly over five months of imports and about four months of current payments. This goes to illustrate how rapidly reserves can rise or fall. The current level of import cover for India is by no means high considering the import needs of the economy. Thus, the build-up in reserves between 1993–96 was not a trend that is sustainable unless the rate of foreign investment is stepped up through unblocking channels for private investment in infrastructure with the formulation of an export policy.

The breakdown of foreign investment in India illustrates the nature of the problem that the country's planners had to face. There was no significant rise in FDI into the country. The major inflow was portfolio investments made by FIIs. The funds thus raised went to the private corporate sector that did not have the means to invest in the infrastructural sector due to various restrictions in government policies relating to that area of investment and the unutilised capacity in the industrial sector delayed investments in that sector. The major portion of this capital raised did not translate into investments or imports. However, the need to boost exports dictated India's exchange rate policy during these critical years of transition from an artificially managed currency to a market determined one.

There is a certain absorptive capacity for any economy to be able to utilise capital investments without spurring inflation. In a relatively open economy, controlling capital flows becomes the major policy challenge. Sterilising the inflows can be costly for governments but more importantly can attract even greater inflows of speculative capital. As a stable currency is also perceived as the cornerstone of economic policy, the only options left are usually administrative ones like increasing reserve requirements on non-resident accounts or taxing currency swaps as was the case in Thailand in 1996. Malaysia faced similar unmanageable capital flows between 1992 and 1994 which culminated in the imposition of capital controls. While in theory large capital inflows should enable a country to increase its investment rate, expand its production base and boost its growth rate; in reality, large inflows are not an unmitigated blessing. They involve complex choices for policymakers as they threaten the competitiveness of the real exchange rate (RER) which is crucial to expanding the export base from which the capital inflows can be serviced.

MANAGEMENT OF THE EXCHANGE RATE

The rupee after Independence had been pegged to the pound sterling, but domestic prices rose faster than foreign prices during the 1960s leading to the appreciation in the RER and export stagnation. The combination of wars and droughts precipitated an economic crisis in 1965 whereby a 36.5 per cent devaluation in the rupee was made in June 1966 to adjust the RER. Between 1947–70, India was virtually on an adjustable peg. The severe drought of 1972 and the first oil crisis of 1973, resulting in high inflation, led to the depreciation of the RER and with it a recovery in export competitiveness. In September 1975, the rupee's peg was altered from the pound sterling to a basket of currencies, with undisclosed weights, though sterling continued to be the currency of intervention. This was done to protect the rupee from the generalised floating of major currencies.

Inflation in India had been reduced to zero and a link with a weak currency (the pound sterling) was not thought to be beneficial to the rupee. The improvements in the FX position in 1975 was accompanied by import liberalisation. Thus, from 1975–79 there was an export boom which generated the hope that India was finally adjusting its trade policy to the global environment. After the second oil price rise in 1980–82, the exchange rate was not adjusted in response to India's rising trade and current account imbalances which were financed by a combination of external borrowing and the drawing down of reserves. The subsequent deterioration in the RER led to export stagnation in the mid-1980s. Once again between 1986–90, when the exchange rate policy became more active, the rupee was depreciated by 35 per cent. Thus, between 1972–90, India had succeeded in 'depoliticising' its exchange rate policy.

While in the past or until 1981, the devaluations were caused due to external shocks like wars, the oil crisis, droughts and famines; the devaluations during the 1980s were directly the result of government policy to boost exports. Finally, the rupee was devalued by 40 per cent in 1991 to correct the BoP crisis. Initially, India had a dual exchange rate policy or an official rate for certain government-related activities determined by the RBI and a market rate for commercial activity determined in the inter-bank market versus the dollar. In March 1993, India merged its dual exchange rate system to a single, market rate.

As there was to be no centrally determined fixed rate for the rupee, the rise in portfolio investments in 1993–94, without a matching rise in imports, meant that there was a greater demand for rupees than for dollars. To have allowed the currency to appreciate would have implied the acceptance of market forces as the determinant of the price of capital transference. That was perceived by the authorities to have been detrimental to exports while making imports more attractive. As a stable exchange rate was perceived to be critical to a successful export policy, it was decided that the RBI should intervene to maintain the level of the rupee by buying dollars in the market. Between March 1993 and December 1994, $13 billion was added to India's foreign currency reserves as a result of this intervention. This led to deficit financing and the monetisation of reserves. But, inadequate sterilisation led to higher than planned rises in money supply and higher rates of inflation and interest rates. Reduction in foreign portfolio investment in 1995–96 eased the pressure on the RBI for such intervention. Once again, such pressures emerged in 1996–97 as imports declined and foreign inflows remained stable.

The RBI is not an independent entity. Thus, its actions reflect government policy which opted for unsterilised or partially sterilised intervention to build up reserves even though it was at the cost of higher money supply and inflation. As inflation is also determined by the government's administered pricing policy, the transition to a market-determined rate of currency exchange was made relatively smoothly without inducing a crisis. In real terms, the currency appreciated against a basket of currencies. The prolonged period of enforced stability of the rupee/dollar rate from March 1993 to July 1995 (at Rs 31.37 to the $) meant that India's competitiveness in international markets was not eroded by the higher inflow of foreign currency. But, the partial sterilisation of the RBI intervention contributed to higher inflation which put downward pressure on the currency when imports started to rise.

With a recovery in imports and a slowdown in foreign investment, the process of downward adjustment of the value of the currency from August 1995 onwards resulted in fluctuations in the exchange rate until it settled at Rs 37 to the dollar on 9 February 1996, having fallen to Rs 38 to the dollar on 6 February 1996. The RBI intervened in the market from October 1995 onwards to curb excessive speculative activity in the rupee. To redress the

whole situation, the RBI announced several measures to end market speculation. RBI intervention led the RER of the rupee back to the level it was in
March 1993. While the official management of the RER will be crucial in
maintaining competitiveness of exports, prolonged fluctuations in currency levels as experienced in the second half of 1995–96 can deter investment and encourage speculative trading. Investment decisions are
postponed in a climate of uncertainty; more so if a currency risk is perceived to be imminent.

The management of the exchange rate as a basis of trade policy or an
instrument in controlling inflation was not on the agenda prior to 1991.
Therefore, there is little historic evidence to prove the ability of India's
policymakers to manage an efficient exchange rate policy. Nor does India
have a track record in the management of capital flows. Thus, periodic
devaluations of the currency will remain a cause for concern. India's
protectionst policies have discouraged the import of consumer goods.
While that has had serious and negative implications for the Indian consumer, the closed nature of the economy has helped to limit the magnitude
of the current account deficit. Even if Indian industry were to rise swiftly to
the challenge of international competition by the next millenium, the fact
remains that greater consumer spending along with the need to export more
will translate to a higher level of imports which will exert downward pressure on the currency.

Official policy on the rupee has demonstrated India's determination to
keep exports competitive. A policy of gradual depreciation is best suited
for such an option as opposed to sudden and rapid changes in the exchange
rate. As investment activity rises, it is inevitable that imports will rise.
India is starting out from a very low base in both exports and imports.
With increasing liberalisation in trade, both export and import density of
India has risen. India's GDCF at 23–25 per cent of GDP is closer to the
rate of investment in Indonesia rather than in Korea or Malaysia. Exports
and imports as a percentage of GDP are also significantly lower for India at
under 25 per cent of GDP. However, as the economic infrastructure gears
up to be able to absorb a higher level of investment, imports are bound
to continue to outstrip exports in the next decade. The management of
the exchange rate along with the foreign currency assets will remain
critical to India's ability to attract major foreign investment. India needs
a significant boost in investments to be able to accelerate growth and alleviate poverty. However, until the convertibility of the currency on the capital account is in place and the investment parameters are fully evolved,
foreign investors will find it difficult to allocate substantial capital into
India.

Extensive capital inflows, accompanied by a real appreciation of the exchange rate, can hurt exports. And when the cycle of inflows is reversed, the detrimental effects on exports may not be reversed equally effectively. The rise in portfolio flows into EMs, as was the case with India in 1994, indicated the rise of external financing of development coming from private sources and going into private destinations. The benefit to any developing economy of this type of capital is that a large part of the risk is transferred to the investor. A sudden reversal of equity investment in the open market can prove costly to the investor but it also has a negative impact on the market. In India's case, the GDR route of financing corporate development has proven to be highly lucrative to the private sector as any reversals in investment would not have seriously affected the individual firm. However, the speed with which large amounts of money can move in and out of developing countries can have a detrimental effect on their economies requiring sudden changes and reversals in policy. Thus, the role of financial institutions becomes crucial in helping to channel capital flows effectively.

In the face of large and persistent capital inflows, a tightening of fiscal policy can help to cut inflation, lower interest rates and reduce the incentive for such inflows. However, in the case of India, these were foreign portfolio investments and not bank deposits. Besides, fiscal adjustment was difficult as it coincided with a significant loss of revenue for the government coupled with higher expenditure. A reduction in government consumption had enabled Malaysia to move from a fiscal deficit of 5 per cent of GDP in 1986 to a small surplus by 1992. In Thailand, the fiscal deficit was wiped out even faster, from 5 per cent of GDP in 1984–85 to a surplus of 5 per cent of GDP in 1989–90. In India, investment surged when the fiscal deficit was relatively high and domestic investment activity was low, thus putting pressure on the exchange rate to appreciate. The RBI sought to maintain a competitive RER by targeting the nominal exchange rate and that was an elusive goal. Accumulation of FX reserves via such a method proved to be costly. When the inflows are large compared to the monetary base, unless sterilisation follows monetisation, it leads to an expansion of the monetary base resulting in higher inflation and higher interest rates.

Sterilised intervention also involves higher domestic interest rates and can be expensive for the central bank resulting in additional capital inflows into the banking system, increasing the level of liquidity in the banking sector. In India, foreign capital flows remain severely restricted despite the liberalisation of the economy. Thus, a high level of sterilisation could not have attracted additional foreign inflows but only added to the government's domestic debt which was already rising due to higher market rates of public borrowing. The whole purpose of sterilisation is that the central bank buys foreign reserves by issuing debt. The central bank debt pays for the higher domestic interest rate while the international reserves pay the foreign interest rate. These reserves stand to be revalued in domestic currency as the exchange rate depreciates. When these foreign assets go out on the back of higher imports, the central bank will be able to sell some of the reserves and realise the capital gains. In the end, the policy of sterilisation pays off. In the interim, it tends to be costly.

Since the second half of the 1980s, large capital flows into Latin America and East Asia had led to widening current account deficits of these countries. While in Latin America this increase in the current account deficit was the result of an increase in consumption, in the case of East Asia it was accompanied by an increase in investment. Essentially, there are two avenues open to any country in responding to capital inflows – widening the current account deficit or accumulating FX reserves. However, whether the current account deficit is increased on the back of investments or consumption is critical to the long-term growth prospect for a country. The Asian investment-driven rise in the current account deficit was helped by the fact that these countries were better able to utilise the capital inflow cycle as it coincided with full capacity utilisation rates and higher domestic investment cycles. In India, capacity utilisation rates were not high and the investment cycle was in temporary decline. That led to a forced accumulation of reserves in order to preserve a competitive exchange rate. India's policy response to larger than expected capital inflows implied that a real appreciation of the currency even temporarily was perceived to have disruptive effects on resource allocation. As India was developing its export base, the policy was to maintain a stable and competitive currency.

India's experience in processing capital inflows has been a recent one even though foreign private capital accounted for 1 per cent of GDP per year during 1988–92 in Korea, 5 per cent in Mexico, 10 per cent in Malaysia and 12 per cent in Thailand. All these countries faced the effects of such inflows on their RER, exports and domestic inflation rates while planning to cope with the effects such reversals would cause. Countries like Malaysia and Chile received the largest capital inflows as a share of their GDP during 1989–92. However, they also managed to avoid any significant appreciation in their RER by stepping up investment and export growth. While sterilised intervention has provided short term relief to some countries in preserving the RER, the most effective policy response in the long term has been through higher public savings.

CONCLUSION

Improvements in the external account has been India's key achievement since the introduction of reforms. Changes in trade policy have had a positive impact on the industrial sector and boosted exports. However, infrastructural constraints and inadequate fiscal adjustments since liberalisation remain the major problem areas for the economy. It is difficult to deal with trade-related issues without examining macroeconomic ones. The fiscal consequences of introducing a freer trade environment, including free trade within the country, with reforms in taxation that are equitable and efficient and, as such desirable, need to be dealt with as part of an integral economic policy. Lack of adequate fiscal adjustment has resulted from inadequate reforms leading to high real interest rates which in turn has impacted on the private sectors' ability to finance its borrowing and investment. The impact of infrastructural constraints on growth tends to be long term and has only been evident in comparative terms when expressed as lower rates of FDI as a percentage of domestic investment. Inadequate infrastructure could also hamper India's export potential. Thus, India's trade policy needs to be developed in conjunction with its plans for infrastructural investment.

Investors will need to factor in these issues in the periodic downward adjustments in the RER of the rupee. These can be periods of great volatility and can hurt the unwary investor or could potentially benefit the informed one. In the long term, markets tend to adjust for most things including currency devaluations. However, it is prudent to avoid overvalued markets both in terms of currency or stock valuations. Sometimes, the two are inextricably linked. As currency hedging is still a difficult task in the Indian context, if not an impossible one; switching investments into companies that stand to benefit from currency depreciation like hotels or exporters (remember in the Indian context, most exporters are also high importers) or into companies whose sales are unlikely to be affected by currency movements like the utilities or companies in the consumer sector could act as surrogate hedges against devaluations. It is worth noting, for example, that among the top 100 companies monitored by the Confederation of Indian Industry, there were only five companies whose net exports (exports minus imports) accounted for over 10 per cent of sales in 1994–95. In short, an effort has to be made in understanding the sources of the companies' profitability and how it might be affected by developments at home and abroad.

As India's external account is vulnerable to oil price adjustments, keeping an eye on the price of oil in the international market is vital. In 1995–96, the POL import bill rose by 27 per cent to $7.5 billion. The domestic price of oil will also need to be raised periodically to reduce the deficit in the oil pool account (OPA) which had escalated to approximately Rs 180 billion by 1996–97 or 1.45 per cent of GDP. The oil price hikes will translate to higher inflation and increased energy and transport costs to industry. The shortage in India's power supply is an additional constraint on industrial production. Thus, the external sector is not as secure as it appears to be because the macroeconomic situation is still fragile and the issue of India's indebtedness cannot be treated in isolation. Trade policy has an impact on macroeconomic policy and vice versa. The fiscal cost of reforms has been high; revenues from trade declined while public expenditure did not. To sustain the export effort, the process of trade liberalisation needs to be deepened to embrace the agricultural sector. But, the effort needs to be supported by reforms in the financial sector and improvements in the infrastructural sector.

Indian companies have to operate within the policy parameters defined by the government. Six years after liberalisation, industry's cost structure remains high and is more sensitive to domestic factors rather than international market forces. India's private sector does not benefit from the advantages arising from such factors but pays the price of inadequate policymaking. More importantly, the private sector still represents less than a tenth of the economy. But, it is linked to the rest of the economy and has to compete within the constraints of that environment. While the resiliency of the manufacturing sector in light of the high real interest rate environment needs to be applauded, the opportunity cost for the companies and the economy as a whole cannot be ignored.

The bulk of the Indian economy is not driven by market forces. One of the major considerations in favour of introducing market forces to India is the injection of efficiency into the system with a view to increasing the rate of return on investment. Even the administration of a simple cure can be mismanaged in the hands of inept practitioners. The political uncertainty over the past couple of years has prevented any real progress of reforms. While short periods of stabilisation are necessary for the consolidation of reforms, lack of direction and the inability of investors to make strategic plans can be a significant deterent to higher investment and growth. If these periods of stabilisation can be used in thrashing out policy issues domestically, that would be an achievement. Unfortunately, that has not been the case.

What has emerged are areas of weaknesses in policymaking reflected in the deceleration of export growth, a drop in domestic crude oil production, the sluggish performance of the power sector and other infrastructure, a rise in the rate of inflation and the declared inability of the government to cut its expenditure. In an environment of strong capital flows, a high fiscal deficit can prove to be inflationary leading to a reversal of such flows. The success of the external sector is linked to a stable macroeconomic situation. Indian corporates cannot compete globally without the support of the government in pursuing economic policies that encourage enterprise and competition. In assessing the prospects for investing in India, one is expected to take into account the ability of management to rise to the challenge of global competition via superior strategies but not in their ability to deliver miracles. Thus, the importance of understanding the role of governments and the effect of their policymaking on the future profitability and success of Indian companies.

3 Macroeconomic Developments

INTRODUCTION

The major challenge for India's planners remains the management of the fiscal deficit as it is crucial to sustaining higher growth. The structural adjustment programme initiated in 1991 was to address that issue. Unfortunately, the rise in the fiscal deficit in 1993–94 did not inspire confidence in the ability or the willingness of the government to manage the fiscal situation efficiently. While there is no risk of reforms being reversed, the rule of populism and the decline in the quality of expenditure management mean that reforms continue at a pace slower than warranted. However, the downward trend in the fiscal deficit since 1993–94 has been encouraging. If the deficit is maintained below the 5 per cent level of GDP with higher public spending on infrastructure and the social sectors, India could sustain higher growth and investor confidence.

Unless the momentum of reform is maintained, the beneficial effects of India's economic liberalisation will be 'crowded out' by the prolonged pain of adjustment. Reform aims to empower the economy to grow at rates experienced by its more successful peers whose policies allowed private investment in wider areas of the economy along with public sector investment. Making that a reality remains a challenge for the Indian government so that it contributes to a higher rate of return on capital employed while increasing social sector expenditure. Improving the overall policy structure for private investment in key areas of the economy like infrastructure is necessary for sustaining growth. Electricity generation was estimated at 3.5 per cent between April–December 1996. Clearly, power shortages will not deliver growth. Infrastructure needs to grow at 1.5 times that of GDP.

The consolidated non-financial gross deficit of India's public sector was 12.3 per cent of GDP in 1990–91. It has declined to about 10 per cent in 1995–96 raising serious doubts about the government's ability to tackle the fiscal situation. Successive governments, while recognising the need for continuing reforms, have been deadlocked over critical issues impacting on fiscal management. Thus, much needed reforms in agriculture, raising user-charges in various sectors of the economy or the implementation of the exit policy to increase public savings have not been introduced. There

71

has been no policy move towards full privatisation or reform of the 'sick' public sector units. The issue of increasing public savings has not been addressed seriously. It is thus fair to assume that the fiscal deficit cannot be reduced significantly below 5 per cent of GDP in the near future. What can be done though is better assessment of government spending and better targeting of subsidies and other public expenditure.

The government has declared its aim to boost long-term growth rate and reduce the fiscal deficit to less than 5 per cent of GDP which is clearly laudable. But, it is not clear from recent policy statements if that will definitely be achievable. By reducing taxes, the Finance Minister, Mr Chidambaram, has gambled on consumption growth fuelling higher revenue receipts leading to a lower deficit for the government. Unable to reduce expenditure, the Finance Minister replaced the issuance of *ad hoc* TBs to finance the budget deficit with a 'Ways and Means Advances' (WMA) scheme to accommodate temporary mismatches in the government's receipts and payments. The WMA is seen as a short-term bridging scheme and not a permanent means of financing the deficit. Unfortunately, the WMA will not by itself reduce government spending or redirect it to those most deserving. Besides, the interest rates payable on WMA are still not at market rates. Only a limit has been placed on the amount but it remains to be seen if it is adhered to.

It has been incumbent upon various governments to implement reforms and pave the path for higher growth but the search for consensus has slowed down the process. When the Congress-led government came to power in 1991, it did not have majority support in the Lok Sabha and the reforms were ushered in under IMF conditionality. Even after the Congress had mustered greater support for its policies, the Finance Minister, Manmohan Singh, found it difficult to move ahead with the necessary changes in policy to curb the fiscal deficit. It indicated that India's reforms had not succeeded in dissociating politics from economic policymaking. The present UF government is a thirteen-party coalition of disparate political ideologies. Their Common Minimum Programme (CMP) interprets their mandate to promote growth with social justice. In light of these constraints, it was to everyone's surprise that the budget estimate of the fiscal deficit for 1996–97 was at 5 per cent of GDP, thanks to higher revenue intake and delay in certain government expenditures.

The only tax-raising measure introduced under such a mandate has been the imposition of a minimum alternative tax on companies that paid zero tax. The effective tax rate works out to be 10 per cent of book profit. The imposition of a 2 per cent special customs duty levy was targeted for investment in infrastructure. The Finance Minister expected to raise Rs 16 billion via this levy, which was aimed at infrastructural spending. But the decline in imports for 1996–97 translated to a lower than planned revenue intake, including the levy for infrastructure. On the contrary, the Finance Minister raised subsidies and committed himself to other welfare measures which increased public expenditure. The Finance Minister also announced in July 1996 the setting up of an Expenditure Management and Reforms Commission to generate 'an informed public debate on an issue that has a vital bearing' on India's economic future. However laudable his intentions, no such commission was in existence by March 1997. His bold gamble with higher growth fulfilling his lower deficit projections may pay off in 1997–98 but the quality of public expenditure needs to be examined as there is scope for higher savings and investment. Both are essential to sustain the growth momentum.

The legacy of India's high government indebtedness has been a 'crowding out' of private investment. The Ministry of Finance's discussion paper of June 1993, regarding the overall objectives of the stabilisation and reform plan, noted in no uncertain terms the key impact of high fiscal deficits on various aspects of the economy:

> Rising fiscal deficits (in the 1980s) had created many problems. They had led to high levels of borrowing by the Government from the Reserve Bank, with an expansionary impact on money supply leading directly to high rates of inflation. High fiscal deficits contributed directly to the large current account deficits in the balance of payments and thus aggravated the problem of external indebtedness. Large fiscal deficits also, pre-empted a significant proportion of the savings of society to support the Budget, with a consequent scarcity of funds for productive investment. This was reflected in very high interest rates facing the commercial sector, which discouraged new investment and also reduced our international competitiveness.
>
> (*Economic Survey*, 1993–94)

The Ministry of Finance recognises the pitfalls of running an economic policy based on high fiscal deficits as it poses a real threat to the financial stability and the prospect for accelerated development of the country over the medium term. But no government over the past decade has been better equipped to usher in reforms at the state level as well as at the centre than the UF government. As improvements in fiscal adjustment remain the key to India's long-term success, this chapter aims to analyse the fiscal cost of India's reforms since 1991 and its impact on the economy in its effect on money supply, inflation, interest rates, internal indebtedness, private investment and public saving.

AN ANALYSIS OF THE GOVERNMENT'S FISCAL POSITION

Historically, the gap between government revenue and expenditure was managed conservatively until 1979–80. During the 1970s, the government ran a revenue surplus in eight out of the ten years. The fiscal deficit was 3 per cent of GDP in 1970–71 but doubled to 6 per cent of GDP by 1980–81 deteriorating further to 9 per cent of GDP by 1986–87. It was during the 1980s that fiscal conservatism gave way to higher spending which was not matched by domestic revenue receipts or FDI. The increased spending, not being directed at productive investments, made it unsustainable in the long term. Development or plan expenditure was 6.6 per cent of GDP in 1980–81 compared to 5.3 per cent in 1990–91 while expenditures on interest payments and subsidies were 1.9 per cent and 1.4 per cent of GDP respectively in 1980–81 compared to 4.0 per cent and 2.3 per cent of GDP respectively in 1990–91. By 1990–91, the gross fiscal deficit had escalated to 8.3 per cent of GDP and the revenue deficit was 3.5 per cent of GDP (see Table 3.1).

The budgetary deficit is the difference between total receipts and total expenditure, on both revenue and capital accounts. The revenue deficit denotes the gap between revenue receipts and revenue expenditure. The gross fiscal deficit is the difference between revenue receipts plus certain non-debt capital receipts like the recovery of loans and divestment proceeds from the sale of the government's PEs and total expenditure. The net primary deficit refers to the fiscal deficit less interest payments and the monetised deficit indicates the portion of the fiscal deficit that is monetised.

The revenue deficit was at 2.6 per cent of GDP during 1991–93 but rose to 4.1 per cent of GDP in 1993–94. Most of the factors contributing to the high deficit – namely, the cutback in government spending that triggered off a domestic recession resulting in low revenue collection or the deregulation of the financial sector that entrusted the central bank with the formulation of monetary policy to control money supply and inflation which led to high rates of interest – were precipitated by the structural adjustment programme. The failure of the government to raise any funds through the divestment of its PEs did not help. The initial decline in the growth of expenditure was encouraging, particularly in areas of subsidies and defence. The lack of consensus on a wide range of issues like subsidies and wages point to the failure of expenditure reform but the gradual decline in the revenue deficit since 1993–94 is encouraging.

Table 3.1   The irresistible rise of government deficits (as percentage of GDP)

Year	Budgetary deficit	Revenue deficit	Gross fiscal deficit	Primary deficit	Monetised deficit
1980–81	1.9	0.6	5.7	5.5	2.6
1985–86	1.9	2.1	8.3	5.5	2.4
1986–87	2.8	2.7	9.0	5.8	2.4
1987–88	1.8	2.7	8.1	4.7	2.0
1988–89	1.4	2.7	7.8	4.2	1.6
1989–90	2.3	2.6	7.8	3.9	3.0
1990–91	2.1	3.5	8.3	4.3	2.8
1991–92	1.1	2.6	5.9	1.6	0.9
1992–93	1.8	2.6	5.7	1.3	0.6
1993–94	1.4	4.1	7.4	2.9	0.0
1994–95	0.6	3.3	6.1	1.4	0.1
1995–96	0.5	2.7	5.8	0.9	0.7**
1996–97 RE	0.5	2.3	5.0	0.4	0.5**
1997–98 BE	NA*	2.1	4.5	−0.2	0.1

Notes: * With the discontinuance of *ad hoc* treasury bills (TBs) from 1 April 1997, the concept of the budgetary deficit will lose its significance and is no longer to be reported by the government; ** no estimates were provided by the government, estimates given here are based on those made by ING Baring Securities (India) Pvt. Ltd.
Source: Indian Public Finance Statistics, 1995; Budget 1997–98; ING Baring Securities (India) Pvt Ltd.

For many years prior to 1991, the growth in non-plan expenditure had been faster than the growth in plan-expenditure. Non-plan expenditure is the term used by the Ministry of Finance in India to refer to expenditure on items like subsidies, wages, interest or defence and is often referred to as non-productive or non-developmental spending when, in reality, all expenditure benefits some sector of the economy. Even the expenditure on subsidies cannot be classified unequivocally as unproductive for it depends on who it aims to benefit and how it is assessed. It is the gross misutilisation of subsidies or interest expenditure rather than the expenditure *per se* that makes it unproductive. The lack of adequate mechanisms for monitoring and assessing the return on public expenditure needs to be addressed. It is the major problem with all government expenditure, including plan-expenditure which is often categorised as productive. In India, return on public investment is unacceptably low, irrespective of whether it is in the non-plan or plan category. Thus, the focus should be on increasing productivity rather than simply cutting down on 'unproductive' spending as that might involve shutting down the government *en masse.*

The introduction of reforms was to reverse the rise in non-plan expenditure which was contained in 1991–92 and 1992–93, thus registering a decline in real terms compared to the growth in plan expenditure. But this new regime was unsustainable due to the increase in interest costs. The budget for 1996–97 aimed at curbing non-plan expenditure, thereby boosting plan expenditure. It remains to be seen if the government will be successful in meeting its deficit targets while increasing its plan spending as no real progress has been made in expenditure reduction. What needs to be emphasized is the absence of quality control mechanisms in assessing returns on government spending. Even in countries where such mechanisms are in place, there is no guarantee that spending is being assessed and directed efficiently. In India, no serious effort has been made to address the meagre return on public spending. Unqualified reduction in spending to contain deficits may help in the short term but will prove to be quite the opposite in the long term.

The government is caught on a slippery slope where it has to borrow at increasingly higher rates to sustain declining returns on investment. Interest expenditure rose from 1.9 per cent of GDP in 1980–81 to 4.8 per cent of GDP in 1996–97. As interest expense has been escalating, by netting out interest payments which are caused by prior borrowing, the primary deficit reflects the fiscal improvements at the centre. The primary deficit has declined from 4.3 per cent of GDP in 1990–91 to an estimated 0.4 per cent by 1996–97. But, the budget target for 1997–98 at −0.2 per cent of GDP appears to be unrealistic. Increased borrowing as well as increases in the cost of borrowing could potentially lead to an internal debt trap for the government as the primary deficit is unsustainable if the rate of growth in interest payments continues to be higher than the rate of growth of GDP. Interest payments have been growing at the rate of 16 per cent or more and constitute some 45 per cent of revenue receipts. Government receipts and expenditures are summarised in Table 3.2.

The lack of fiscal prudence will make it difficult for any government to finance its fiscal deficit by borrowing abroad. Even if it were to do so, a high primary current account ratio would imply a high external debt to exports ratio which would be equally unsustainable if the rate of growth of exports did not continue to outpace the rate of growth in external interest repayments. While excessive internal borrowing tends to crowd out the domestic private sector, high external borrowing has an equally negative effect on exports and on potential FDI. The current level of domestic borrowing is unsustainable as it will become increasingly expensive to attract

Table 3.2 Receipts and expenditure of the government (in Rs billion)

	1990–91	1991–92	1992–93	1993–94	1994–95	1995–96	1996–97 (budget estimates)	1997–98 (budget estimates)
Revenue receipts	549.5	660.3	741.3	754.5	910.8	1101.3	1307.8	1531.4
of which tax revenue (net to centre)	429.8	500.7	540.4	534.5	674.5	819.4	972.1	1133.9
Revenue expenditure	735.2	822.9	927.0	1081.7	1221.1	1398.6	1589.9	1834.1
of which interest payments	214.9	265.9	310.7	367.4	440.6	500.3	585.0	680.1
subsidies	121.6	122.5	119.9	128.6	129.8	137.3	166.9	182.5
Revenue deficit	−185.6	−162.6	−185.7	−327.2	−310.3	−297.3	−282.1	−302.7
Capital receipts	389.9	385.3	361.8	554.4	686.9	583.4	646.2	790.3
Capital expenditure	317.8	291.2	299.2	336.8	386.3	384.2	433.1	487.7
Total receipts	939.5	1045.6	1103.1	1308.9	1597.8	1684.7	1953.9	2321.7
Total expenditure	1052.9	1114.1	1226.2	1418.5	1607.4	1782.7	2022.9	2321.7
of which plan expenditure	283.6	309.6	366.6	428.5	473.8	463.7	548.9	628.5
non-plan expenditure	769.3	804.5	859.6	989.9	1133.6	1319.0	1474.0	1693.2
Fiscal deficit	−446.3	−363.2	−401.7	−602.5	−577.0	−602.4	−631.3	−654.5
Primary deficit	−231.3	−97.3	−90.9	−235.2	−136.5	−102.1	−46.3	−25.5

Source: Indian Economic Surveys, 1995–96, 1996–97; Budget, 1997–98.

the savings of the private sector into government bonds. The higher rates of interest offered by government bonds has made the holding of government paper more attractive to banks than corporate lending; thus 'crowding out' the private sector.

An analysis of the government's budgetary transactions reveals that an attempt has been made to reduce the gap between government outlay and current revenue as well as to reduce dependency on both external assistance and deficit financing to meet budgetary requirements. The burden of financing the gap between outlay and current revenue of the government has been transferred to domestic capital receipts. The share of domestic capital receipts in meeting this gap rose from 67 per cent in 1990–91 to 92 per cent in 1994–95 and fell to about 86 per cent between 1995–97, while the share of deficit financing declined from 25 per cent in 1990–91 to 1.4 per cent in 1994–95 rising to 10 per cent in the next two years. This has been achieved at the expense of capital formation out of budgetary resources which declined from 40 per cent of total expenditure in 1980–81 to less than 30 per cent in 1996–97. Thus, the fiscal adjustment has been far from adequate.

The government recognises the need to establish control over its fiscal imbalances to be able to curb the growth in money supply, inflation and interest rates; thus releasing resources for productive investment. However, it is seriously constrained in controlling expenditure as 72 per cent of it is targeted towards interest payments, defence, wages, grants and loans to the states which are mandated by the Constitution. On the revenue side, tax reforms with the lowering of import tariffs has meant that it has been difficult to contain the shortfall between expenditure and revenue below 6–8 per cent of GDP as the direct tax revenue base is too small. The efforts required to improve public finances will involve broadening the entire reform process to state governments, PEs and sectoral ministries other than Finance, Industry or Commerce at the centre. In short, a mandate for reform from the states rather than only at the centre. This can be obtained if social safety nets are made available by the government but more importantly opportunities for job creation are generated through greater private investment.

The Impact of Reforms on Investment

When the structural adjustment programme was introduced, it was inevitable that growth would suffer due to a decline in government spending on development programmes as the non-plan component of public expenditure was more inelastic. The main objective of stabilisation was to slow down the economy by switching expenditure and inducing a contraction of aggregate demand. The strategy of increasing revenue and decreasing expenditure was commendable except that cutbacks in expenditure were achieved at the cost of growth and not through public savings in non-plan spending. Simultaneously, the momentum of private investment was held back due to various structural impediments to its participation in vital areas of the economy, like infrastructure.

The key indicators of reforms since 1991 have not only been the question of fiscal discipline but whether reforms have succeeded in stimulating private investment. While the user cost of capital has been lowered for industry, significant barriers to entry remain deterring private investment. Due to the stabilisation programme, the government was not able to resuscitate demand in the economy by initiating large public spending programmes. The increased interest burden also hampered public investments. The privatisation programme was not successful. Fiscal improvement was achieved at the expense of public investment while reforms, aimed at increasing the role of private investment in the economy, did not succeed in compensating for the withdrawal of public spending due to policy bottlenecks to private investment. Thus, greater fiscal adjustment has to come from the government. Public investment in infrastructure needs to be stepped up along with that of the private sector to spur employment creation. At the same time, social expenditures need to be protected and targeted more effectively.

Gross capital formation out of budgetary resources declined from 6.5 per cent of GDP in 1990–91 to 5.7 per cent in 1994–95 and was estimated at 4.9 per cent in 1996–97. Most of this decline was reflected in the decline in financial assistance for capital formation in the economy. The improvements in public sector finances were achieved through savings in domestic capital formation. With the recovery in domestic demand and a rise in investment in 1994–95, average public investment between 1992–96 was 8.6 per cent of GDP and grew at 4.2 per cent over the same period. The major boost came through in the private sector where investment rose to an average 15.4 per cent of GDP between 1992–96 and grew at an average rate of 17.6 per cent with the strongest growth of 30 per cent coming through in 1994–96. Private fixed capital formation remained at around 13 per cent of GDP between 1992 and 1995, rising to 16.3 per cent in 1995–96 indicating that the shift in investment from public towards the private sector was slowly working its way through. Trends in investment are summarised in Table 3.3.

International experience indicates that real investment often declines in the initial phases of structural reform and it was no different in India. The pattern of private investment also confirms that the private sector's response has been fairly positive to reforms and that the prospects for private investment remains good. The rate of growth in capital formation in the private sector has been restrained mainly due to the continuing constraints in policy framework for investment in various areas of the economy hitherto not open to the private sector. As these obstacles are slowly removed, it is expected that private investment will accelerate. India's fiscal imbalances have not been reflected in the external accounts due to the higher growth in exports and the rise in foreign investment. The recent deceleration in the economy may have helped in containing the fiscal situation. However, a strong economic recovery could increase domestic investment levels to higher than the pre-crisis years. Unless public savings increase or foreign investment flows accelerate, a strong investment recovery could have a destabilising effect on the BoP.

Table 3.3   Trends in investment since 1991 (as a percentage of GDP at 1980–81 prices)

Year	GDCF** total	Public	Private	GFCF** total	Public	Private
1990–91	25.9	9.0	14.7	21.3	8.6	12.7
Growth rate*	18.1	4.6	17.5	9.9	4.8	13.6
1991–92	21.6	8.3	12.7	20.3	8.7	11.6
Growth rate*	−16.3	−7.2	−13.3	−4.0	2.0	−8.1
1992–93	22.4	8.1	14.3	20.6	7.7	13.0
Growth rate*	9.2	2.7	18.7	7.0	−7.2	17.5
1993–94	22.7	8.1	12.7	20.8	7.8	12.9
Growth rate*	6.3	4.4	−6.7	5.6	6.9	4.8
1994–95P	25.6	8.4	15.3	21.9	8.5	13.4
Growth rate*	21.5	12.1	29.3	13.3	17.2	11.0
1995–96Q	27.1	7.6	18.4	24.1	7.8	16.3
Growth rate*	13.7	−2.5	29.1	18.3	−1.5	30.9
1992–96	24.4	8.0	15.2	21.8	8.0	13.9
Growth rate*	12.7	4.2	17.6	11.0	3.9	16.1

Notes: * Growth rate (in percentage terms) in capital formation at 1980–81 prices; ** GDFC – gross domestic capital formation, GFCF – gross fixed capital formation; P – provisional estimates; Q – quick estimates.
Source: *Indian Economic Survey*, 1996–97.

The economic crisis of 1991 emphasised that fiscal excess, political instability and governmental inaction can combine to have devastating consequences on investment. The meagre rate of growth of public investment between 1992–96 emphasises the point. If the basic goal of sustainable, employment-generating growth is to be achieved, the path of fiscal prudence has to be followed. As the momentum of growth accelerates, the competition for investible resources will increase. If the fiscal deficit is high, growth in private investment tends to be 'crowded out' by high interest costs. The problem with large fiscal deficits is that sooner or later a portion of it gets financed by governments with money creation which spurs inflationary growth as was the case in the 1980s.

Since 1993–94, the government has been successful in raising finance by placing government securities in the capital markets. It has led to little asset creation and the amount of money raised has not been large enough to impinge excessively upon funds available to the private sector. But, the market rate of interest that the government has had to pay for its securities has risen steadily. Government borrowing escalated to levels that ultimately forced the government to renege on its agreement with the RBI made in September 1994 that if the net issue of *ad hoc* TBs exceeded Rs 90 billion for more than 10 continuous working days, the RBI would automatically sell these bills in the market to reduce it to the agreed level. The RBI automatically steps in to purchase any government paper when the response at an auction is insufficient. Such purchases are directly linked to money creation and tend to be inflationary. However, this rarely happened in 1993–94.

Between 1995–97, the government followed a looser fiscal policy saddling the RBI to respond to inflationary pressures with a tighter monetary policy. Real interest rates rose from the 6 per cent level to 16–18 per cent for blue-chip companies in India. While foreign inflows augment domestic savings and compensate for the crowding out of private investment, such inflows are usually linked to improvements in fiscal trends, ongoing reforms and political stability. The crowding out of domestic private investment tends to keep foreign investors out as well. The globalisation of capital has created opportunities for increased flows of private capital but the price is fiscal prudence and political stability. India's inability to implement a more prudent fiscal policy recently has stemmed from political instability and resulted in tighter monetary policies. It is often the case that small industrial enterprises suffer the most under high real interest rates which defeats the governmental effort to shift the burden of investment to private enterprise.

Currently, 31 per cent of central revenue is transferred to the states and Union Territories (UTs). If they are left to borrow or raise resources directly, the liquidity crunch brought about by a tight monetary policy would help in streamlining such entities by injecting a higher level of efficiency. Considering that the central government has no control over the finances of the states, one of the ways of introducing greater efficiency is by endowing these units with greater autonomy to make their own management and financial decisions. The process has already been initiated with some of the PEs under central control with remarkable results. Whether the same level of success can be replicated at the state level remains to be seen, for greater autonomy by itself does not automatically usher in superior management. The more-successful central PEs have had competent management in place who have been the real architects of this success.

PUBLIC FINANCE: EXPENDITURE

The government's total outlay in its budgetary transactions rose from 19.7 per cent of GDP in 1970–71 to 27.1 per cent in 1980–81 and further to 34.6 per cent by 1989–90. The concern in this rising trend in public expenditure was the declining share of development expenditure. Non-plan expenditure had accounted for a third of government spending in 1960–61. By 1970–71, it had risen to 40 per cent of total expenditure. It declined to 33.7 per cent of total outlay in 1980–81 but rose to 40 per cent by 1990–91, deteriorating further to 44 per cent by 1995–96. As a percentage of GDP, non-plan spending went up from 9.1 per cent in 1980–81 to 13.2 per cent and was estimated at 13.6 per cent in 1995–96.

Reforms aimed at reversing the rising trend in non-developmental spending of the 1980s, but, liberalisation of the financial sector meant that the cost of government borrowing had to rise. Had the fiscal deficit been the result of productive investments, the future benefits to the economy may have compensated over the medium term. When the fiscal deficit is directly the result of non-development expenditure, it places serious constraints on the flexibility of the economy to cope with any internal shocks. It places a greater burden on the government to protect itself from sliding into the internal debt trap which deficit financing leads to, severely restricting the development potential of the economy.

The compound annual growth rates of various items of government expenditure when compared to inflation reveals the misutilisation of precious resources over decades, with the gap between the rate of inflation and the rate of investment in development projects widening over the decades. By 1990–91, development expenditure had fallen to 60 per cent of government expenditure from 66 per cent in 1980–81. The inability to curb non-plan expenditure since the introduction of reforms in 1991 has meant that development expenditure has been affected; down to an estimated 56 per cent of total expenditure in 1995–96 while non-development spending had risen to 44 per cent with interest expenses alone consuming 18 per cent of the total outlay. Interest payments also accounted for 44.7 per cent of revenue receipts in 1996–97. While the overall figure is high, the trend has been improving. Interest payments were an estimated 47.2 per cent of revenue in 1995–96.

The inability of the government to control its non-plan expenditure was one of the main causes of the economic crisis in 1991 and remains the major fiscal challenge for the country. The introduction of reforms itself involved a high fiscal cost. The centre has met only partially the challenge posed by the fiscal deficit in reducing 'non-interest' spending and privatising PEs. Interest payments claimed an increasingly larger share of government revenue, leaving little scope for accelerating its developmental agenda. In 1996–97, total debt servicing which includes repayment of debt with interest payments amounted to an estimated 95.6 per cent of revenue receipts down from 113 per cent of receipts in 1995–96. The budget estimate for 1997–98 projects total debt service to be 93 per cent of revenue receipts indicating that revenue is rising faster than total debt repayments. The overall figure is still high but the declining trend is encouraging for lower public deficits.

The rise in the proportion of interest payments in expenditure is a result of both an increase in government borrowing as well as the rise in the cost of borrowing on the back of the government's plans to de-monetise its deficit. The monetised deficit of the government had reached 3 per cent of GDP by 1989–90, but was reduced to 0.1 per cent of GDP by 1994–95. With the emphasis on lowering the fiscal deficit, development expenditure is unlikely to go up in the medium term. Until interest payments decline, there is no hope of a real take-off in public investment. While development expenditure was ahead of inflation in 1980–81, its pace of growth declined substantially with the introduction of reforms. The economic crisis cut into development spending which grew at 9.2 per cent while inflation was over 10 per cent in 1991–92. The rate of growth in plan expenditure at 17–18 per cent was higher than inflation during 1992–94 but declined in 1994–95 to 10.6 per cent. Plan expenditure was hit sharply in 1995–96 as it fell by 2 per cent but recovered in 1995–96 to grow at over 18 per cent and is estimated in the 1997–98 budget to rise to 14.5 per cent. Thus, the cost of financing the government borrowing has been high in developmental terms.

Subsidies accounted for 14 per cent of non-plan expenditure in 1980–81 and rose to 15.8 per cent in 1990–91. With the initiation of reforms, subsidies declined to 10.2 per cent of non-plan expenditure by 1995–96 but rose to 11.3 per cent in 1996–97. As a percentage of GDP, however, subsidies have remained unchanged at 1.4 per cent of GDP in 1980–81 and 1.3 per cent in 1996–97, having been at 2.3 per cent in 1990–91. In nominal terms, subsidies rose from Rs 18.5 billion in 1980–81 to Rs 167 billion in 1996–97. As a percentage of revenue receipts, subsidies fell from 22 per cent in 1990–91 to an estimated 12.7 per cent in 1996–97 and were expected to decline further to 12 per cent of revenue in 1997–98.

Defence expenditure has also declined from 27.6 per cent of non-plan expenditure in 1980–81 to 14 per cent in 1990–91 and has stabilised at that level. Defence spending was 2.6 per cent of GDP in 1980–81 but had fallen to 1.7 per cent by 1995–96. Improvements have been made in curbing real expenditure on defence. But the government's inability to generate savings by pruning subsidies further or redistributing it more equitably and reining in administrative expenses have added to the soaring expenses on interest charges which have been buoyed by the higher cost of borrowing.

The Failure of India's Expenditure Reform

The critical issue in India's reform is the question of improving public savings. Public savings, compared to private savings, have never been high. In the 1980s, it was about 3 per cent of GDP but was virtually negative by 1990. Thus, improvements in public savings are vital in reducing the public sector borrowing requirement (PSBR) and in easing the pressure on monetary tightening as a means of containing inflation. High real interest rates impact negatively on investment and subject the economy to the effects of a higher financial burden, thus placing it on a lower growth path. An analysis of the gross savings of the government showed an improvement during the initial years of reform, but the gains made were not consolidated as reflected in the rise in consumption expenditure to 4 per cent of GDP in 1993–94. It was estimated to be marginally lower at 3.8 per cent of GDP in 1996–97.

The increase in current payments on the interest account has been the major source of rises in expenditure. It has hampered the government's ability to increase its investments in capital formation out of budgetary resources. The decline in government savings has meant that capital formation out of budgetary resources fell from 6.5 per cent of GDP in 1990–91 to an estimated 5.3 per cent in 1995–96 and declined to below 5 per cent the following year. Consumption expenditure accounted for 21.3 per cent of government expenditure in 1990–91 and investment on its own capital formation in physical assets accounted for a further 9.2 per cent. The remaining 69.5 per cent was for current and capital transfers to other sectors of the economy for financing their current and capital operations. The ballooning interest expense meant that the government's commitment to reduce dependance on the *ad hoc* issuance of TBs could not be honoured. Loose public spending with tight monetary policies has undermined investor confidence in the government's preparedness to address the issue of reducing public expenditure. This has been reflected in high interest rates and volatility in the currency and equity markets.

While such reflections capture the financial consequences of an increasingly indebted government, the consequences for human development are far more serious. As the cost of domestic borrowing has gone up and the term of the new-securities issues has gone down, the average rate of interest paid on the government's internal liabilities increased from 4.9 per cent in 1980–81 to an estimated 9.9 per cent in 1996–97. The rate of interest paid on internal debt will continue to rise unless the government improves its savings and reduces its expenditure. The staggering accumulation of debt through the second half of the 1980s, the currency devaluations, the payment of market rates of interest are all responsible for the spurt in interest expense payments in the 1990s (see Table 3.4). But increases in public savings is essential before the government can get to grips with its developmental agenda. Total internal debt had risen an estimated 117 per cent in nominal terms between 1990–91 and 1996–97 while interest payments on that debt have risen by 178 per cent over the same period. The role of domestic small savings and provident funds in financing government debt rose significantly between 1980–81 and 1990–91. But it is inconceivable to expect private savings to sustain the growing indebtedness of the government. To be able to generate a virtuous savings cycle, the government will need to exhibit greater fiscal discipline and increase public savings.

A study of the government's historical debt management record reveals that in 1950–51 it started from a position where its total assets represented 70 per cent of total liabilities and interest received was just under 50 per cent of interest paid out. Over the next 25 years the government was successful in building up its asset base. In the early 1970s assets had overtaken liabilities. By 1977–78, almost 95 per cent of interest paid out by the central government was covered by interest received. But the government's interest cover declined very rapidly thereafter. By 1979–80 interest received had fallen to 61.5 per cent of interest paid even though the asset-liability match was over 100 per cent. By 1990–91, the central governments' assets represented 75 per cent of its total liabilities and 40 per cent of interest paid out was covered by interest received. Between 1980–81 and 1990–91, total liabilities of the government went up by 428 per cent while assets rose up by 301 per cent in local currency terms. Both the assets to

Table 3.4 Liabilities of the central government (in Rs billion)

	1980–81	1990–91	1991–92	1992–93	1993–94	1994–95	1995–96RE	1996–97BE
Internal liabilities	485	2830	3177	3597	4306	4877	5533	6133
average rate of interest paid*	4.9	8.2	8.5	8.7	9.2	9.3	9.7	9.9
as % of GDP	35.6	52.9	51.5	50.9	53.2	51.1	50.4	49.1
External liabilities**	113	315	370	423	473	509	527	549
average rate of interest paid*	2.0	6.5	7.3	9.6	8.8	8.5	9.6	10.0
as % of GDP	8.3	5.4	6.0	6.0	5.8	5.3	4.8	4.4
Total outstanding liabilities	596	3146	3547	4019	4779	5386	6059	6681
average rate of interest paid*	4.4	8.0	8.5	8.8	9.1	9.2	9.7	9.9
as % of GDP	43.9	58.7	57.5	56.9	59.0	56.5	55.2	53.4

Notes: * Average rates of interest are calculated by taking the amount of interest paid as a percentage of the net liability;
** external debt figures represent borrowings by the central government from external resources and are based on year-end rates of exchange – for example, for 1980–81 the rates prevailing are at the end of March 1981 and so on.
Source: Indian Economic Survey, 1996–97.

liabilities ratio and interest received as a measure of interest paid declined substantially between 1991–92 and 1996–97 reflecting a build-up of liabilities due to the higher PSBR since the economic crisis of 1991 and the inability of the government to boost its programme of rebuilding assets.

While the excess of liabilities over assets rose from a low of 0.3 per cent of GDP in 1980–81 to an estimated 19 per cent of GDP by 1995–96, this may be misleading as assets continue to be valued at book. The current value of assets created over the decades should be many times higher as a substantial part of these assets are in physical form. But it has to be noted that although assets may be valued many times higher than stated, realising their value in the market is not the same thing. However, liabilities have to be met on debt incurred in the past. As the rupee continues to devalue, the current value of debt has increased substantially. The external liabilities shown in the accounts are at historical rates of exchange. Currency devaluations have led to an escalation in the current value of the debt.

It is useful to examine the distribution of assets across major economic classes and the liabilities incurred by the central government on behalf of the states, UTs and the PEs, bearing in mind the fact that the centre has no control over certain policy decisions made by these entities. In 1996–97, for example, capital outlay by the centre accounted for an estimated 53.5 per cent of total assets. The remaining assets were in the form of loans advanced by the centre to the states and UTs, PEs and others. Also, some 66 per cent of the centre's capital outlay was in economic services, 31 per cent in general services and 2.8 per cent in social services. The low proportion of asset creation in social services by the centre reflects the policy that social sectors come under the states. The centre's borrowing was mainly for the acquisition of capital for the provision of economic services. About 74 per cent of the loans advanced by the centre went to the states and UTs, and some 25 per cent to the public enterprises.

Economic assets were estimated to be 26 per cent of outstanding liabilities (non-RBI) of the central government at the end of 1995–96, loans made to the states and UTs comprised about 30 per cent and loans to PEs another 8 per cent. Non-RBI outstanding liabilities are defined as those excluding the non-marketable securities held by the RBI as these represent the amount of monetisation whose cost has already been paid for by the public through higher inflation. The sale of the centre's economic assets could in principle help repay some 26 per cent of the total liabilities of the central government. Depending on the timing and structure of the sale, these assets could reduce the government's liabilities and ease the fiscal burden of paying for uneconomic enterprises. The same is true for the state enterprises where returns on investment are deplorable.

To put it differently, about 38 per cent of the centre's non-RBI liabilities in 1995–96 would have been lower if these entities had been in a position to borrow directly. Loans advanced by the centre had been higher at about 62 per cent in 1980–81 and 42 per cent in 1990–91. The declining trend of central government loans to entities over which it has little control in terms of determining policymaking is encouraging. A decline from 42 per cent in 1990–91 to 30 per cent in 1995–96 is not an insignificant improvement. Unfortunately, the central government had not considered it appropriate to stipulate a minimum rate of return on its loans as any sensible banker would. These loans are treated as expenditures of the central government and are reflected in the central fiscal deficit. As they are also mandated by the Constitution, the centre has very little choice in terminating this arrangement without making amendments to the Constitution which process requires greater political will.

The privatisation option has not been given due emphasis by the government. While privatisations can be unpopular, it is up to governments to make the process democratic by introducing greater transparency in negotiations as well as by developing independent regulatory systems for the effective monitoring of privatised services. Malaysia has led the field in the privatisation of infrastructural facilities like telecommunications, roads and power. It was estimated that the private sector would provide approximately 78 per cent of Malaysia's total infrastructural spending under the current five-year plan to the year 2000. In India, a concerted attempt at privatisation will help in reducing government borrowing for non-development expenditure thereby releasing vital resources for developmental spending. Equally, reducing the loans made to states and UTs and the PEs should help in easing the centre's debt liabilities.

Increases in government borrowing due to the poor financial performance of the states and their PEs continues to be a matter of grave concern. As a percentage of the centre's loans, those made to the states and UTs went up from 64.6 per cent in 1990–91 to 74.2 per cent in 1996–97, while those made to PEs declined from 33 per cent to 25 per cent over the same period. The internal resources of the state PEs pose a problem as they continue to be negative, having doubled from −0.1 per cent of GDP in 1993–94 to −0.2 per cent in 1994–95. Sale of loss-making enterprises will reduce the overall borrowing of the states and make resources available for investment in social and physical infrastructure. But, the entire question of privatisation is linked to progress in other sectors of reform, namely changes in company and labour laws. The central PEs have been encouraged to become less dependent on the centre for their financing requirements but the same cannot be said of the state PEs.

The inability of the centre to bring about changes in the performance of the states and their PEs has put tremendous pressure on the fiscal position of the centre. As the resources of the centre have tightened, a continuation of the high level of transfer of funds to the states may not be feasible unless the states improve their savings. But, if the states default in their payments to the centre; that can be equally traumatic for the centre. The centre's periodic unconditional loan waivers and refinancing pledges to the states also undermined financial discipline and encouraged expectations of debt relief in return for political favours.

Expenditure on Subsidies

Reform in the area of subsidies is critical to lower government borrowing as much as to improve the return on such spending. Subsidies accounted for 4 per cent of expenditure in the early 1970–71 period, but more than doubled to 8 per cent of government spending by the early 1980s and peaked at 12 per cent in 1989–90. In 1990–91, central subsidies at Rs 121.6 billion accounted for 11.5 per cent of expenditure by the centre and represented 2.3 per cent of GDP. Total central subsidies were slashed to 8.3 per cent of government expenditure by 1996–97 and represented 1.3 per cent of GDP. The budget estimates for total central subsidies in 1997–98 at Rs 182.5 billion represented 7.8 per cent of total expenditure. A recent report on subsidies calculated the cost of implicit and explicit subsidies by the states and central government at 14.4 per cent of GDP in 1994–95.

Apart from export and interest subsidies, no real progress has been made in the reform of fertiliser subsidies. Overall subsidies to agriculture like fertiliser, power supply and irrigation have imposed severe burdens on the budgets of both the centre and the states. The State Electricity Boards' (SEBs) internal resource generation and surpluses that could have been invested for growth have given way to substantial losses. Subsidies have become too political for the various governments to confront the issue of escalating non-plan expenditure. The governments have only themselves to blame as the farmers' lobby point out that subsidies have become necessary due to inaccurate pricing of inputs as they are not aligned with international prices. A serious attempt at reforming the uneconomical subsidy for fertilisers was made in July 1991 when fertiliser prices were hiked by 40 per cent but a month later the rise was scaled back to 30 per cent and small farmers were exempted. A year later, the controlled price of urea, which accounts for half of fertiliser sales, was further reduced by 10 per cent. In the final analysis, the fertiliser subsidy is a subsidy to the fertiliser industry rather than to the poor farmer. Better utilisation of this subsidy would yield higher returns but it would be politically inexpedient to do so. A greater awareness, through a higher level of national debate on public spending, would usher in the necessary change in political sentiment to enable the government to target subsidies to those more deserving.

An analysis of the central government's subsidies reveals that almost 98 per cent of it is for food and fertilisers. The interest subsidy has declined substantially and so has the subsidy for export promotion. While at the current level of GDP, central subsidies do not compare unfavourably with other developing economies, it is the misutilisation of resources that has prevented subsidies from playing their developmental role in the economy. Thus, subsidies to farmers for fertilisers on top of power subsidies and tax concessions on agricultural income coupled with government pricing of outputs, has done little to boost recent productivity growth in agriculture while subsidies and the Minimum Support Pricing mechanism had initially helped in delivering the Green Revolution. The public sector units' losses in fertilisers during 1996–97 was estimated at Rs 6.8 billion.

Under the present policy framework there is little scope for higher investment in the sector. The losses on irrigation projects are high due to low user charges; utilisation rates are also low. Further gains in productivity can only be made by providing the incentives for investment in the sector by reducing subsidies and distributing it in such a way that it encourages private investment. The bulk of India's population is employed in agriculture. So, encouraging greater productivity growth through technological upgrading, better marketing and distribution facilities, market pricing of products and the removal of existing barriers to trade could lead to a transformation of agriculture as delicensing altered the productivity profile of industry. The current subsidy on fertiliser could be better spent on the development of agricultural infrastructure rather than on the fertiliser industry which could do with greater competition.

The decline in the rate of growth of total subsidies by the centre is encouraging. This needs to be matched by the states as they account for over half of total subsidies. Agriculture is the prerogative of the states; electricity and irrigation subsidies are determined by the states while fertiliser and credit subsidies are decided by the centre which are then topped up by the states (see Table 3.5). Initial government protection was responsible for the success of the Green Revolution but years of protection subsequently led to a fall in efficiency. It has thus become necessary to inject higher productivity by lowering protection. The initial impact of aligning domestic prices, of both inputs and outputs, with global ones will be positive for producers. The rise in productivity will attract investment and consumers will benefit in the long term. However, any rise in the price of agricultural products will be hugely inflationary in the short term and will necessitate government expenditure on food subsidies for the poor. The extent of the reduction in government spending as a result of agricultural liberalisation will not be large; it will entail a redistribution of government subsidy to revitalise the agricultural sector.

Table 3.5   Estimates of total subsidies (in Rs billion)

Year	Central govt.	% of total	Total	% of GDP
1960–61	0.31	33.3	0.93	0.6
1970–71	0.94	27.9	3.37	0.8
1980–81	20.28	64.2	31.60	2.3
1985–86	47.96	56.1	85.43	3.3
1986–87	54.51	55.7	97.95	3.3
1987–88	59.80	52.0	114.97	3.5
1988–89	77.32	53.9	143.54	3.6
1989–90	104.75	56.3	185.90	4.1
1990–91	121.58	65.3	186.09	3.5
1991–92	122.53	54.1	226.30	3.7
1992–93	119.95	58.7	204.50	3.1
1993–94	128.64	55.2	232.91	2.9
1994–95	129.82	49.4	263.06	2.8
1995–96 RE	166.94	NA	NA	NA
1996–97 BE	182.51	NA	NA	NA

Source: Reserve Bank of India; Centre for Monitoring the Indian Economy; Expenditure Budget, 1997–98.

As the current system of subsidies is not adequately targeted towards poverty relief, the liberalisation of the agricultural sector will need to be preceded by a genuine strengthening of anti-poverty programmes. There is economic and social justification for food subsidies aimed at poverty relief. However, the way the food subsidy is currently structured and implemented, it fails to achieve its true purpose. The food subsidy represents the difference between the economic cost of procuring foodgrains by the Food Corporation of India (FCI) and the issue price of the public distribution system (PDS) which is determined by the government from time to time. The food subsidy is thus paid to the FCI. In 1990–91, this cost Rs 24.5 billion or 0.45 per cent of GDP, and in 1997–98 it was budgeted at Rs 75 billion or approximately 0.5 per cent of GDP. A redirection of total subsidies of both the centre and the states, towards genuine poverty relief programmes will more than compensate for the liberalisation of agriculture. The resulting efficiency in the system could lead to higher public savings and encourage higher public investment in agricultural infrastructure.

Expenditure on Defence

The reduction in government spending on defence, like subsidies to a lesser extent, is a more strategic issue. History has a way of making people pay for their mistakes. India's defence spending is largely a mirror of Pakistan's high defence expenditure. It can equally be stated that Pakistan's high defence expenditure is linked to India's. The high defence spending in the Indian subcontinent is hardly justifiable taking into account the level of poverty in the region. Both countries are accountable for this state of affairs and need to display a higher level of pragmatism and maturity in resolving their problems over Kashmir. From Ireland to Israel, peace is being talked about if not fully established; the opportunity should be seized in the Indian subcontinent as well.

The threat from China has been reduced dramatically and India needs to defuse the defence issue politically with Pakistan. The lack of better diplomatic relations between the neighbours has not helped at all. Having fought three expensive wars, the two countries should have learnt that the exercise is both futile and costly. Improved relations in areas of trade and tourism should help to enhance the relationship between its peoples.

The lack of any exchange in ideas and the general atmosphere of distrust between the two nations, often whipped up to unrealistic levels by the media, resulted in a woeful lack of cooperation between the two countries that lived as one nation for centuries before Partition. Despite the relative freedom of the press in India, the media has only recently recognised its role in influencing public opinion which is vital to the working of any democracy. Whether it is a question of spending on subsidies or on defence, it is the role of the media to generate greater public awareness. It is difficult to say to what extent such debates are becoming entrenched in the public domain. Developing trade between the two countries should help ease the tension in the region. The subcontinent forms a natural trading block and a higher level of exchange of goods and services will help both countries in dealing with various problems from high defence spending to terrorism and drugs.

Defence accounts for a quarter of Pakistan's expenditure and 15 per cent of India's total expenditure estimated for 1997–98. India's defence expenditure has declined from 3.6 per cent of GDP in 1987–88 to an estimated 1.5 per cent by 1996–97. It would be difficult for the country to scale down its defence expenditure from these levels. Defence had taken up 19 per cent of government expenditure in 1963–64 when India's relation with Pakistan was fragile. India has managed to bring its defence spending down in the 1990s; the rate of growth of defence expenditure has been less than inflation, thus registering a real decline in spending. Taking into account the tension in the area, it is highly unlikely that this component of non-plan expenditure can be reduced dramatically from current levels. An examination of defence spending by various developing countries in the world reveals that India's record is relatively conservative. Given the political constraints of the South Asian defence strategy, it will be difficult for India to reduce its defence expenditure unilaterally.

There is little flexibility for the government to reduce its non-development expenditures significantly from these levels without upsetting the status quo. The next stage of reforms will necessarily involve greater involvement of the states and better negotiations with vested interest groups. Government borrowing needs to be reduced for interest payments to decline. The path to lower real rates of interest is through expenditure reform as the government deepens its policy of reducing subsidies, public administration costs in real terms. The effort initiated to stimulate revenue growth needs to be complemented with a serious effort at privatisation.

The future need must be to focus on increasing revenues. The United Front government has made a bold start in that direction by cutting tax rates to encourage higher compliance. Greater investment will help generate the necessary growth in revenues through increases in direct tax revenues and lower the dependence on import tariffs. Adjustments to the supply side constraints will stimulate domestic demand. As the recovery in investment has only just begun, higher rates of revenue collection will begin to reflect in lower public deficit. Revenue as a percentage of GDP in India is low compared to other developing countries. The key factor for success in the government's fiscal management will be determined by the rate of growth in revenues compared to that of its non-development expenditure. In the context of the relationship between the centre and the rest of the economy, it will be difficult for the centre to resolve any of its problems with regard to fiscal management by not devolving power away to the states.

PUBLIC FINANCE: REVENUE

The Indian government's inability to raise revenues and its failure to limit current expenditure has resulted in a chronic revenue deficit. As a percentage of GDP, the revenue deficit was −1.5 per cent of GDP in 1980–81 but −3.0 per cent in 1995–96. In evaluating the prospects for India's revenue deficit there is scope for significantly higher receipts. If the growth of non-plan expenditure remains flat, the deficit should decline from current levels. But, the rate of growth of revenue still needs to be higher than the rate of growth of non-plan expenditure for the government to increase its development expenditure.

Developed countries have been more successful at raising taxes from individuals. Tax revenues, on average, are higher than 19–20 per cent of their GNP. India, like many other developing countries, has been less able or less willing to support the extensive and expensive administration that goes with efficient tax collection. This has resulted in a narrow tax base with the burden of direct taxation falling on a small segment of personal and corporate payers. In addition, the sharing of revenues with the states from personal income tax and excise has led to serious inefficiencies in the allocation of resources. It has also failed to elicit a responsible expenditure behaviour from the states as their expenditure decisions did not have to be accompanied by resource mobilisation.

India needs to implement a more rational and efficient system of taxation across the states. Such a reform in taxation would necessarily involve the cooperation of the states. The entire issue of taxation has been complicated by the revenue sharing arrangements that exist between the states and the centre. The powers of taxation are laid down in the Constitution and the taxes that are allocated to the states comprise mostly of agricultural income tax, land tax, alcohol excise and sales taxes. The rest are assigned to the centre which raises revenues from customs and central excise along with personal and corporation income taxes, including wealth tax. However, the centre has to share its revenue, except for the trade taxes, with the states as decided by the Finance Commissions which are set up every five years. The Tenth Finance Commission recommended that 47.5 per cent of central excise taxes should go to the states along with 77.5 per cent of personal income taxes. The ratios were 45 per cent and 85 per cent previously, resulting in a system of taxation that did not make much economic sense.

The central government's effort to boost tax revenues concentrated on taxes not shared with the states. Thus, corporate taxes have risen in relation to non-agricultural GDP over the last four decades while revenues from taxes on personal income (which is shared with the states) has declined significantly. With reforms an effort was made to redress this situation. The increase in the tax to GDP ratio during the 1980s came from customs duties, a revenue not shared with the states. The central government derived some 80 per cent of its revenue through excise and customs duties while the state governments collected 70 per cent of their revenue from sales taxes. The emphasis on indirect taxation, by both the centre and the states, has been strong. The tax reforms since 1991 aimed at correcting the imbalances in the structure of revenue sources. While direct taxes are the most equitable form of taxation, it is not the most efficient form of revenue collection in a country like India. The Finance Minister in his 1997 Budget has been imaginative in reducing tax rates with the hope of improving compliance and increasing overall revenue. The tax revenue structure is summarised in Table 3.6.

Table 3.6   India's structure of tax revenue (per cent of GDP)

	1990–91	1991–92	1992–93	1993–94	1994–95*	1995–96**
Total tax revenue	16.4	16.7	16.2	15.2	15.3	15.8
Central taxes***	10.8	10.9	10.6	9.5	9.5	9.9
corporate	1.0	1.3	1.3	1.3	1.4	1.5
personal	1.0	1.1	1.1	1.2	1.2	1.4
excise	4.6	4.6	4.4	4.0	4.0	3.7
customs	3.9	3.6	3.4	2.8	2.8	3.2
other	0.3	0.4	0.5	0.3	0.2	NA
States' share of central taxes	2.7	2.8	2.9	2.8	2.6	2.8
Net central taxes	8.0	8.1	7.7	6.7	6.9	7.1
States' own taxes	5.6	5.8	5.6	5.8	5.8	5.9
States' tax revenue	8.3	8.6	8.5	8.6	8.4	8.7

Notes: * Revised estimates; ** budget estimates; *** may not add up due to rounding.
Source: *Indian Public Finance Statistics*, 1995, and *Indian Economic Survey*, 1996–97.

The central government depended for its revenues mostly from trading duties, though they did not foster international competitiveness, and the states from consumption taxes which have been punitively high for industry and the consumer. One of the major aspects of the reform programme has been the shift in the pattern of taxation and revenue collection. But India has a long way to go in boosting revenues from direct, personal taxation. The cost of implementing a western European model of taxation as in the UK or the Netherlands is high. The role that the private corporate sector played in the economic development of East Asian countries is reflected in the high level of corporation tax as a percentage of public revenue in Japan, Malaysia and South Korea (see Table 3.7). India started with developing the Asian model of revenue collection from corporate taxation but was not as successful. Even if India were to catch up with the level prevalent in Korea in the late 1980s, the fiscal deficit would decline significantly enabling the government to increase its development budget. The introduction of the minimum alternate tax (MAT) was aimed at improving corporate tax revenue.

Table 3.7   Revenue from taxation – a comparison (in percentage terms)

Country	Corporate	Individual	Property	Consumption	Customs
Developed economies					
USA	7.0	50.7	8.7	13.3	0
Switzerland	4.9	55.6	6.4	11.8	0
UK	9.6	38.8	11.7	27.2	0
West Germany	7.3	56.1	2.1	20.9	0
France	5.9	53.9	1.9	29.4	0
Japan	22.2	53.7	9.7	11.7	0
Developing Asia					
South Korea	17.4	20.9	1.9	34.0	12.9
Malaysia	23.0	10.0	0.4	18.0	11.9
Thailand	10.0	8.9	2.9	47.4	22.5
Philippines	14.2	7.3	0.5	37.5	24.0
India*	10.6	4.1	1.0	48.1	36.2

Note: Latest available year 1985–88 for all countries except India; * 1992–93; the choice of data is to demonstrate India's position post-crisis.
Source: *The Economist*; Centre for Monitoring the Indian Economy.

While gross domestic savings (GDS) in India had risen to 24 per cent of GDP in 1994, tax policies failed to raise tax revenues at a similar level. The lack of adequate savings in the public sector prevented the government from providing social welfare benefits, thus shifting the burden of providing for the future to the individuals themselves. The withdrawal of the state from such responsibilities has generally accounted for the high savings rate in the Asian economies and has directly influenced social values and culture. In the case of Singapore, the savings rate has been further enhanced by the government enforcing individual contributions towards pension and housing schemes. The mass review of the social welfare system in Europe, which is linked to its cycle of economic development in a global market and the high costs involved in the welfare system coupled with high rates of unemployment not to mention the demographics of ageing in a postwar society, is a reminder of the problems that governments inherit.

The demographics of population growth in India and the dynamics of economic growth are at the opposite end of the spectrum. India has virtually no system of social welfare. It has been argued that labour reforms have not been possible in India because the government is unable to provide any social security. One could argue that the public sector in India, with its employment protection laws and unions, has been one of the best welfare systems in the world. While various governments have not been able to address the issue of excess labour in the public sector, the government has realised that it does not have the resources for social welfare and has attemped to encourage private savings further. Thus, tax incentives have been provided for contributions towards private pension schemes as well as life and health insurance. The liberalisation of the insurance sector will have a revitalising impact on the debt market in India while helping to curb the inflationary impact of deficit financing. Besides, competition will provide better service to the policyholders.

The tax system whose function is to raise resources in an efficient and equitable manner was overloaded with prohibitive rates and saddled with provisions which were aimed at providing various kinds of disincentives and incentives. The result was rampant tax evasion and loss of revenue to the government. Total tax revenue of the central and state governments and UTs was only 16.4 per cent of GDP in 1990–91. According to data available from the Planning Commission, there were an estimated 292.9 million people in employment in March 1990. But, the total number of tax returns including returns from individuals, the Hindu Undivided Family, firms and companies for 1989–90 were under four million of which three million were by individuals. 57 per cent of these returns were in the range of incomes between Rs 20 000–50 000 per annum and 23.5 per cent of returns between Rs 50 000–100 000. This adds up to a high number of employees earning a pittance and/or a high level of tax evasion. Only 217 000 returns were on incomes exceeding Rs100 000 per annum. So much for the theory that India has a middle-class of 150–200 million people. While it was heartening to note from his budget statement that the Finance Minister had 12 million taxpayers, it was disconcerting to realise that it still represented less than 5 per cent of the employed population. It has been estimated there are over 20 million Indians with savings in the Capital Market, a figure significantly higher than the number of taxpayers in the country.

Thus, data on most aspects of the economy is distorted by the 'undeclared' economy. Even in the UK it represents some 12 per cent of the economy. In countries like India it is more than twice the declared economy. Thus, for example, a village school teacher receiving a declared government salary which would be non-taxable due to the low pay and exemptions, would most likely have other sources of 'undeclared' income from private tuitions or from a family business like poultry-farming. It is difficult to bring such income voluntarily under the tax net. In any event, the total income of such a person will not amount to more than Rs 50 000.

This is just one example of how it is not cost-efficient to establish systems to monitor such kinds of tax evasion. The government is conscious of the high level of non-payment of taxes and has tried to encourage retail traders to file an estimated return. Without an efficient collection system, it will be up to individuals to comply. Thus, the government has focused on high-profile income tax raids on individuals and corporates to improve compliance. But, the real challenge lies in altering the mind-set whereby it is less of a hassle to pay tax rather than avoid doing so. Unfortunately, those who comply are often discouraged by the bureaucracy in the system.

In his February 1997 budget, the Finance Minister made an attempt at improving compliance by dramatically reducing tax rates across the board. Personal tax rates in India are now among the lowest in the world at 10 per cent for incomes between Rs 40 000–60 000, 20 per cent on incomes between Rs 60 000–150 000 and 30 per cent for incomes above Rs 150 000. He appealed to the 'residents of large metropolitan cities who satisfy any two of the following economic criteria, namely, ownership of a four-wheel vehicle, occupation of immovable property meeting certain prescribed criteria, ownership of a telephone and foreign travel in the previous year' to voluntarily file their tax returns. Obviously, that was not the case. There is ample scope for increasing the tax to GDP ratio and any improvement will be reflected in lower public deficits and hopefully translate to higher public investment.

Tax Reforms and Government Revenue

The government's income can be classified into revenue and capital receipts. Revenue receipts constitute tax revenues which include direct taxes like corporation and income taxes, and indirect taxes like customs and excise duties, sales tax and non-tax revenues. Capital receipts are government borrowings, internal as well as external, and include other receipts like the proceeds from privatised PEs. In the 1960s, revenue receipts had accounted for 70 per cent of total receipts. This ratio of revenue to total receipts rose above the 75 per cent level in the 1970s and reached 79 per cent in 1979–80. But, by the early 1990s revenues had fallen to 67 per cent of governmental receipts. The decline in the share of revenue receipts in overall receipts started to be evident in the mid-1980s around the time when capital receipts – mainly borrowings both internal and external – began to rise strongly.

The biggest increases in capital receipts were in 1975–76 (after the first oil crisis and a near-severe drought in the country in 1974–75), followed by an increase in 1980–81 (with the second oil crisis) and in 1982–83 (when the country experienced near-severe droughts). As a percentage of GDP, revenue receipts were 14 per cent in 1970–71 and capital receipts 4.6 per cent. By the mid-1980s, revenue receipts had risen to 22 per cent of GDP and capital receipts to 9 per cent of GDP. Revenue receipts as a percentage of GDP have not improved significantly since then (see Table 3.8).

Table 3.8   Total receipts of the government of India

Year	Total* (Rs billion)	Revenue	Capital	Total
		(% of GDP)		
1965–66	52.7	14.6	5.5	20.2
1970–71	80.7	14.1	4.6	18.7
1975–76	185.8	17.9	5.7	23.6
1980–81	333.9	18.1	6.5	24.6
1985–86	805.2	21.6	9.1	30.7
1990–91	1650.6	20.7	10.2	30.8
1991–92	1922.9	21.7	9.5	31.2
1992–93	2121.5	21.7	8.4	30.1
1993–94	2459.8	21.2	9.5	30.7
1994–95 RE	2982.7	21.1	10.4	31.5
1995–96 BE	3328.7	21.3	9.4	30.7

Note: * Includes that of the central and state governments and Union Territories (UTs).
Source: CMIE; *Indian Economic Survey*, 1996–97.

While revenue receipts have risen, they have not risen fast enough to keep pace with the rise in government spending. The difference between revenue and expenditure is met by a combination of capital receipts or government borrowing, both internal and external, and deficit financing. The higher the deficit financing component of capital receipts, the more inflationary is its impact. In 1969–70, the inflationary impact of government borrowing was negligible. By 1980–81 the ratio of government expenditure in excess of revenue as a percentage of revenue had risen to 50 per cent, and by the time of the economic crisis of 1990–91 it had escalated to 60 per cent. The level of deficit financing as a percentage of total expenditure was higher in 1980–81 at 9.4 per cent compared to 6.5 per cent in 1990–91. The extent to which a government has to borrow or resort to deficit financing in order to sustain its economic policies represents the key to its future viability. It also reflects on the quality of the government's gearing. If the gearing is supported by developmental expenditure or other such productive investments, the investment can pay off even though it may still prove to be unsustainable over a long period of time.

With further rationalisation of the tax system and the tax rates coupled with the improvements in the method of tax collection, it is expected that revenue receipts will continue to rise. Various measures have been taken since 1991 to simplify the tax structure and widen its base. There is need to deepen the tax base through better enforcement and scrutiny. But to implement these changes takes time and investments via computerisation of tax records and other such measures requiring increased public spending. The reduction in personal income tax rates has encouraged greater compliance and lower excise duties have boosted domestic demand. The available data during the past few years suggests that the strategy of reduction and simplification of marginal rates of taxation for individuals and corporates is having the desired impact as overall compliance has improved and both personal and corporation tax to GDP ratio has improved since the reforms.

India's past economic policies did not encourage an entrepreneurial culture but rewarded rent-seeking activities leading to the flight of capital, including human capital, out of the country. The liberalisation of 1991 has initiated the return of flight capital as opportunities in the developed world have declined. However, the free flow of capital is not yet a reality. Establishing the foundation for managing such flows takes a combination of bold policy measures and investments to sustain them along with skilled personnel to implement them. Several obstacles remain in facilitating such flows in India. Lack of convertibility on the capital account does not help capital flows nor does the fact that NRIs are not entitled to dual nationality. Lack of development in the banking and taxation sectors mean that investors still encounter a high level of bureaucracy in their investment and tax affairs. The challenge for the government lies in advocating policies that do not reward tax evasion but encourage compliance. The problem is a massive one but policies need to be seen to be investor friendly by being more encouraging and rewarding of both enterprise and compliance.

In 1960–61, tax revenues comprised 52 per cent of income and capital receipts were high at 38 per cent with external borrowing amounting to 15 per cent of receipts of which 6.4 per cent was in the form of concessionary loans. As the cost of external loans went up, the government turned to domestic market loans which comprised 8.6 per cent of total receipts in 1980–81 compared to 3.9 per cent in 1970–71. The major source of tax revenue was excise duties which represented 21 per cent of total receipts in 1970–71 and 37 per cent of tax revenue. Excise duties as a share of revenue rose to 43 per cent in 1990–91 and receipts from customs duties rose to 36 per cent in 1990–91 revealing the extent to which government policies discouraged both consumption and imports. Indirect taxes constituted 80 per cent of tax revenues in 1990–91.

The reform of the tax system since 1991 has been an important aspect of the entire structural reform process in helping to redress the inequities of the tax regime. The strategy has been to move towards a simpler system of direct taxation with moderate rates, fewer exemptions and a wider base. The indirect taxes sector needed overhauling completely and the reform process was aimed to achieve that. Reforms in the sector have come a long way but there is scope for higher revenue realisation through greater rationalisation of indirect taxes. With regard to excise and customs, there has been a drastic cut in the number of end-user notifications which has helped in reducing disputes, misuse and corruption.

Although indirect taxes have been lowered, they still accounted for over 70 per cent of tax revenue in 1996–97 with excise duties accounting for 36 per cent and custom duties 34 per cent. The number of categories of taxes has been reduced along with the peak rates but there is scope for greater simplification. The transformation of the system of credit for taxes paid on inputs, called the Modified Value Added Tax or MODVAT, into a central VAT scheme up to the manufacturing stage remains incomplete. The introduction of a comprehensive VAT is not going to be an easy task in a federation. A modest beginning has been made in extending taxation to include certain services like telephones, non-life insurance, stockbroking, advertising, courier services and radio paging. Rs 9.7 billion was estimated to have been raised in 1996–97 from such sources. India has a long way to go before a full-fledged VAT system of taxation is put in place.

The introduction of lower and simplified tax rates in 1991 led to higher revenue collection with the strongest response coming from personal and corporation tax. But the momentum faltered over the next two years as revenue from customs and excise duties fell due to the domestic recession induced by structural adjustment. The economic recovery in 1994–95 was reflected in higher tax revenues. While tax revenue as a percentage of GDP of the central and state governments and the UTs fell from 16.4 per cent in 1990–91 to an estimated 15.1 per cent in 1994–95, the budgetary deficit as a percentage of tax revenue declined from 13 per cent to 4 per cent over the same period. There is a need to boost tax collection as the excess of total government outlay over current revenue as a percentage of tax revenue declined from 75 per cent in 1990–91 to an estimated 72 per cent by 1994–95. The growth in tax revenue since the reforms of 1991 is summarised in Table 3.9.

Lower growth in customs was one of the reasons for the higher than anticipated fiscal deficit in 1993–94. With the recovery in economic activity and the growth in imports for the years 1994–95 and 1995–96, revenue income improved. Even though the peak rate of custom duty has been lowered, it remains significantly higher than in other developing countries. The broad thrust of the tariff reductions was to provide raw materials, intermediates and capital goods to industry at competitive prices. A major restructuring of tariff rates covering the machinery and metals sector was introduced to encourage higher levels of investment, enhancing the competitiveness of the manufacturing sector. The pace of reduction in import tariffs was calibrated to ensure that it did not impose undue pressure on domestic producers while keeping the revenue stream of the government under some control.

Table 3.9   Growth in tax revenue since 1991 (in Rs billion)

	1990–91	1991–92	1992–93	1993–94	1994–95RE	1995–96BE
Total tax revenue*	877.2	1031.9	1141.6	1219.6	1443.7	1654.35
% change	12.9	17.6	10.6	6.8	18.4	14.6
Income & corporation	107.1	145.8	167.9	191.8	242.5	290.0
% change	9.2	36.2	15.1	14.2	26.4	19.6
Customs	204.4	222.6	237.7	221.9	264.5	295.0
% change	14.5	7.8	6.8	–6.7	19.2	11.5
Union excise	245.1	281.1	308.3	316.9	369.0	427.8
% change	9.4	14.7	9.7	2.8	16.4	15.9
Sales	182.3	215.5	240.3	281.4	302.5	347.1
% change	16.4	18.2	11.5	17.1	7.5	14.7
Others	136.25	166.9	187.3	207.5	265.2	294.5
% change	15.7	22.5	12.2	10.8	27.8	11.0

Note: * Includes taxes of the central and state governments and Union Territories.
Source: *Indian Public Finance Statistics*, 1995.

The major problem in the area of taxation lies in encouraging those running small businesses to comply. Presumptive taxation, apart from its administrative convenience, can raise both equity and efficiency by collecting taxes from those paying nothing earlier. An attempt has been made with a new estimated scheme for small businesses; with a view to encouraging individuals to comply, the assessee is not required to maintain books of accounts or to get accounts audited. This scheme was introduced in 1992–93 to attract those who would normally not have bothered to comply. Computerisation of income tax records has been initiated in Mumbai, Delhi and Chennai, and will be extended to India's major cities before investments can be found for extending it to the whole country. The government has to find the resources to raise its ability to collect revenues.

As the government needed to raise direct taxes, corporate taxes have been deregulated since the introduction of tax reforms. The 1994–95 budget removed the differential tax rates between widely-held and closely-held domestic companies and reduced the basic tax rate for both to 40 per cent. But, companies in India with taxable incomes over Rs 75 000 paid a surcharge of 15 per cent. The effective rate on domestic companies was high at 46 per cent while that for foreign companies was 55 per cent. There was no surcharge for foreign companies. The UF government initiated the abolition of the surcharge by cutting it to 7.5 per cent in July 1996. The surcharge was finally abolished in February 1997 and corporate taxes were reduced for domestic companies to 35 per cent and for foreign companies to 48 per cent. Tax rates on royalty and technical services fees payable to foreign companies have also been reduced to 20 per cent with the hope of enabling greater technological transference. There was a tendency to understate income due to the high tax rates. It is also understandable why firms have resorted to exploring ways of reducing their overall tax liabilities by constantly investing in new projects. The differential tax rates for domestic and foreign companies also does not make much economic sense.

If one studies the balance sheets of various Indian companies, it is not only an interesting exercise in misinformation but the striking feature of many a balance sheet has been zero income-tax liabilities. For those that did pay tax, thanks to various exemptions the effective tax rates paid has been significantly lower than 46 per cent. As firms were being taxed heavily in terms of high import tariffs, excise and sales duties, it encouraged companies to utilise any tax exemptions made available by the government. It was simply a question of tax planning for survival. With high interest rates and high tax rates it is surprising that corporates were able to make any profits at all. A simplified tax structure with lower rates and fewer exemptions should enable companies to be more transparent in their reporting procedures and make their due contribution to the exchequer.

Prior to the economic reforms it was more profitable for Indian corporates to invest their time and energy in getting their various applications for licences cleared in Delhi and resorting to financial engineering that would help them to reduce their tax liability. The entire ethos misdirected genuine individual enterprise and encouraged a high level of tax evasion and corruption. The lack of transparency in the accounting methods of domestic Indian companies has been recognised by the stockmarket and is adequately reflected in their lower valuations. MNCs have been awarded higher valuations reflected in higher price to earnings ratios by the stockmarket as a result of this anomaly. The UF government made an effort to encourage companies that had a zero-tax paying status to pay a MAT to plug this loophole. Greater corporate compliance will boost government revenue.

Taxes on agriculture, which include land revenue and agricultural income tax, as a percentage of the total tax revenue of the centre and the states has declined steadily over the decades from 6.7 per cent in 1961–62 to 0.8 per cent in 1991–92. The situation has not improved with the introduction of reforms. Thus, growth in agricultural taxes has consistently lagged that of total revenue. Between 1961–81, total government revenue grew at an annual rate of 14.4 per cent but agricultural revenue grew at a mere 4.2 per cent. During the 1980s, the rate of growth in agricultural income increased to the 15 per cent level but still lagged behind that of total revenues growth of 16 per cent. While agriculture accounts for 30 per cent of India's GDP, taxes from the agricultural sector account for less than 0.7 per cent of tax revenues. As agriculture also provides the highest employment in the country, it remains a politically sensitive issue for the government. But, reformation of the agricultural system needs to precede tax reforms.

The country's arcane policy framework for agriculture acts as an indirect form of taxation. External trade restrictions and domestic price interventions have been a form of implicit taxation on agriculture which has deterred private investment. The lack of private investment is testimony to the inefficiencies and low return on investment in agriculture. In return for this implicit taxation via minimum support prices for foodgrains and other such crude policy instruments, the farmer does not pay taxes and takes whatever the government has to offer in terms of subsidies in power or fertilisers. Private investment in agriculture has been declining since the 1980s. The policy framework has fragmented domestic agricultural markets, restricted private investment in wholesale trade, storage and agro-processing, thus providing a strong disincentive to invest in the agricultural sector.

Comprehensive tax reform has been an essential plank of India's structural reform and stabilisation programme. Efforts are being made to move the economy towards a tax system which is simple with a wider base and lower rates of taxes. There is a need to deepen the tax base through better enforcement and scrutiny. Better tax administration will promote economic efficiency, growth and equity. Value added tax is on its way and average import tariffs have been reduced to the 25 per cent level which still remains higher than rates in other developing countries. Tariff reduction has perhaps been too carefully sequenced with due priority being given to the task of revenue generation to hasten the goal of reduction in the overall fiscal deficit. The continuing growth in tax revenue from individuals and corporates directly reflects the positive outcome of lower rates of taxation. Taking into consideration the reductions in import tariffs the buoyancy of revenue has been encouraging. The rationalisation in the structure of excise duties continues but it remains the largest source of tax revenue for the states and thus more difficult to reform.

Revenue Sharing between the Centre and the States

More than a third of the total resources of the central government are transferred to the states and the UTs. In 1960–61, net resources transferred from the centre to the states and to the UTs constituted 34.9 per cent of their expenditure and 35.2 per cent of the centre's expenditure. The net transfer of such resources from the centre accounted for 46.4 per cent of the total expenditure of the states and the UTs in 1990–91, and 35.7 per cent of the expenditure of the central government. Thus, the dependency of the states for funding from the centre for its expenditure had risen from approximately 35 per cent in 1960–61 to over 46 per cent in 1990–91. An effort has been made to curb the financial burden of the centre in fulfilling its statutory obligations to the states and the UTs. While it is incumbent upon the states to reduce their own deficits, the centre could demand a reduction in state deficits if it had the political clout to do so. The transfers are summarised in Table 3.10.

Table 3.10 Net resources transferred from the centre to the states and Union Territories

Year	As a percentage of the total expenditure of	
	States and UTs	*Central government*
1960–61	34.9	35.2
1970–71	39.1	30.4
1980–81	34.6	32.6
1990–91	46.4	35.7
1991–92	43.8	37.9
1992–93	43.5	38.3
1993–94	43.7	37.1
1994–95	41.1	37.1
1995–96	40.2	36.2
1996–97 RE	NA	37.4
1997–98 BE	NA	34.8

Source: CMIE; *Indian Economic Survey*, 1996–97; Budget, 1997–98.

Total taxes accruing to the states, as a result of their direct revenue mobilisation within the states and their entitlement to a third of the central government revenue, amounts to over half of the combined revenues of the centre and the states. Thus, the states are culpable for contributing to the overall budgetary deficit. The five-year average of taxes accruing to the states as a percentage of total taxes was 40 per cent in the early 1960s. This ratio has risen to 50 per cent currently. In 1960–61, the combined taxes levied by the states and the centre amounted to Rs 13.5 billion of which 66 per cent was raised by the centre and the rest by the states. Of the amount raised by the centre, 12 per cent was transferred to the states. The final amount accruing to the states in 1960–61 was 46 per cent of total revenues. But revenues accruing to the states rose to a high of 56 per cent of total revenues in 1993–94, and the statutory devolution of taxes from the centre to the states went up from 12 per cent in 1960–61 to over 29 per cent in 1993–94 as well. Since then, the total tax revenues transferred to the states has declined marginally (see Table 3.11).

Table 3.11　　Breakdown of total taxes levied between centre and the states with their distribution ratios

Year	Total taxes (Rs billion)	Total states tax revenue as % of total taxes of centre & states	% of total taxes centre	states	Statutory devolution of taxes from centre to states (%)
1950–51	6.27	43.06	64.59	35.41	7.65
1960–61	13.50	45.93	66.29	33.71	12.22
1970–71	47.52	48.42	67.47	32.53	23.55
1980–81	198.44	52.69	66.41	33.59	28.77
1990–91	877.22	50.93	65.64	34.36	25.24
1991–92	1031.98	51.39	65.27	34.73	25.53
1992–93	1141.66	52.60	65.37	34.63	27.50
1993–94	1219.61	56.13	62.10	37.90	29.36
1994–95 RE	1443.78	54.99	62.22	37.78	27.66
1995–96 BE	1654.40	55.04	62.72	37.28	28.32

Source:　*Indian Public Finance Statistics*, 1995.

These developments imply a greater degree of devolution of power to the states as the states currently raise an estimated 37 per cent of the combined tax revenues but receive 55 per cent of it. It also focuses on the need for the states to implement greater fiscal discipline. It has been a policy to reduce budgetary support to the central PEs with a view to making them increasingly more self-reliant. But no significant adjustment has been attempted in the financial performance of the state public-sector enterprises. Even if the central government were to focus on streamlining the PEs in the states, it would be the responsibility of the state governments to implement it. The only way in which the central government can have any impact on the financial performance of the states is to link the statutory devolution of taxes to improved performance. The present arrangement whereby the centre acts as a sort of development banker to the states by providing them with loans for their infrastructure and other related projects needs to be seriously reviewed.

Thus, adjustments in state finances are important as the centre currently devolves to the states about a third of the tax receipts it collects in addition to the loans and grants it provides to the states. The weak revenue performance of the states transfers the burden of the resulting debt service obligations (of the states) to the centre even though the effective rates of interest on these loans are low. In response, the centre has reduced its lending to the states and raised the cost of borrowing to market levels to impose greater financial discipline. Given the difficult financial position of the states, lower lending from the centre could imply reduced ability of the states to service their debts to the centre. This will impact negatively on the central government revenues even if it is able to deduct at source some payments to the states. The current system of transfers between the centre and the states has not encouraged the need for fiscal prudence at state level.

As mandated by the Constitution, a Finance Commission is set up every five years to recommend transfers between the states and the centre in such a way as to enable each to fulfil their public service responsibilities. In the past, these Finance Commissions have inclined towards filling the revenue shortfall of the states leaving little incentive for the states to improve their revenues through taxation or higher cost recovery. In recent years, the Planning Commission has played a significant role in such transfers. Even in the case of such transfers, it is noticed that states tend to initiate programmes without exploring ways of raising revenues to finance recurring costs. This heavy subsidisation of incremental programmes has encouraged employment growth but it has led to weaker fiscal performance at the state level.

The Tenth Finance Commission (TFC) reporting on 26 November 1994, recommended the phasing out of grants-in-aid which are currently provided to fill the revenue shortfalls at the state level. A combination of loan waivers, provision of grants-in-aid for revenue shortfalls and other such financial amnesty from the centre to the states has been a disincentive for the states to improve their revenue or tackle the problem of a growing wage bill and the proliferation of uneconomic state enterprises. The TFC also recommended a pooling of taxation under which the states would get 26 per cent of the gross receipts of central taxes and that a further 3 per cent is recommended in lieu of additional excise duties. The TFC recommended that this scheme of resource-sharing be brought into force as of 1 April 1996 and be frozen for 15 years. During this period, the Finance Commissions will merely recommend the shares of the different states' devolution and grants-in-aid. The main advantage of such a recommendation is that the centre can be flexible in pursuing tax reforms as such an arrangement removes incentives for favouring one tax over another due to the constraints of sharing revenues.

Unlike a development banker, the central government did not attach conditions to its lending nor was it able to ensure that projects it financed were sustainable. The Eighth Plan indicated that cost recovery rates for economic and social services provided by the states declined steadily and that the fiscal drain to the centre amounted to several percentage points of GDP. On the other hand, vital expenditure programmes like road construction and the building of irrigation systems remained under-funded. It is evident that the problem is not to be resolved at the centre but has to be dealt with at state level. With a minority Congress government at the centre and various regional parties in the states, the centre had no effective mandate to enforce fiscal discipline on the states between 1991 and 1996. This is the greatest challenge that India has to rise up to because reducing the overall fiscal deficit is not simply a matter for the centre. Until a political solution is reached whereby the total public sector deficit is reduced drastically, India will remain vulnerable to macroeconomic instability and sporadic bouts of high interest rates that will have less impact on the fiscally imprudent states, UTs and state PEs but will hurt the small and medium-sized private firms the most. Lower private sector investment can leave the nation on a lower growth path.

The reforms implemented to date including the opening up of the economy to trade and capital flows and delinking reserve money growth to deficit financing have transformed the Indian economy. It will determine the way in which fiscal policy will influence economic activity. Excess demand created by the fiscal deficit will be met by imports that affect the current account and lead to the depreciation of the currency as was acutely experienced in the second half of the financial year 1995–96 when capital inflows declined. A rise in the fiscal deficit will put pressure on the exchange rate and the interest rate, increasing the cost to producers affecting overall investment activity. An open economy is thus more sensitive to the international pricing mechanism and changes in the exchange rate will have a greater impact on domestic inflation. Large fiscal deficits translate swiftly to higher interest rates, lower investment and growth. Lower fiscal deficits thus remain the key to higher investment and growth. But there is no hope of the fiscal deficit being reduced without the participation of the state governments as greater liberalisation in the agricultural sector, reduction in subsidies and privatisation of PEs has to be implemented at the state level.

INFLATION AND MONEY SUPPLY

India's policymakers have demonstrated their ability to avoid the kind of galloping inflation witnessed in Latin America, Africa or more recently in Eastern Europe. India's record on inflation management is relatively good. India's planners share the same aversion to high inflation as the East Asians but have been less successful in managing public finances within a fractured, democratic milieu. The government deployed fiscal, monetary as well as other methods like rationing and price controls to combat inflation. Thus, in the past the connection between inflation and government borrowing was a muted one as the government controlled the prices of goods and thus determined the level of inflation.

The controls may have gone too far in not linking domestic costs to international prices. Many of the controls over industry and the economy were initially introduced during the Second World War to stabilise prices – for example the price of cotton cloth. But the legacy stayed on long after the departure of the British. During the oil crisis of the 1970s the Indian government was fairly successful in managing the price hikes without the macroeconomic instability that affected many other developing countries. Unfortunately in the 1980s cracks appeared in the government's determination to control inflation, and loose fiscal policies resulted in unsustainable budget deficits. Inflation management remains the major policy challenge as increases in government borrowing lead to higher money supply and higher inflation. Since 1991, higher government borrowing has not been the only cause of higher money supply in the financial system.

Since Independence, only on three different occasions has the rate of inflation remained in double digits for more than a period of two years. These occasions were in the early and the late 1970s and the early 1990s. In the 1970s, higher inflation was caused by a combination of failed monsoons and external shocks. In the 1990s, the cause of high inflation cannot be attributed to any of the above factors which would have normally been beyond the control of a country's financial planners. The growth in the fiscal deficit of the government during the 1980s has been an important cause of the build up of inflationary pressures over the late 1980s and early 1990s. The monetisation of the fiscal deficit has a direct role in the increase of money supply and inflation. Over the past decade, 90 per cent of the increase in money supply has been due to an increase in the central bank's credit to the government.

India managed a policy of low inflation through the administered pricing mechanism and maintained a stable currency. The first experience of high inflation was in the mid-1960s due to two consecutive years of drought in the country. But the 1960s was a decade of fairly steady prices globally and inflation became a worldwide problem in the early 1970s, reaching a peak in 1974. Prices went up sharply as a result of a combination of events, the most important being the fourfold increase in the price of oil over the previous year triggering a global recession with high inflation. The gradual collapse of the Bretton Woods agreements on fixed exchange rates aggravated the situation by leading to an outflow of dollars from the USA which resulted in high international liquidity. Poor harvests worldwide also led to sharp grain price increases in 1972 and other commodity prices followed suit. The global business cycle peaked in 1973 creating heavy demand pressures.

India's inflation in the mid-1960s at an average of 11 per cent per annum reflected the government's determination to avoid a high inflationary policy. The severe domestic drought of 1972 and the first oil shock of 1973 led to much higher levels of inflation than the economy had experienced in the past years averaging 18.5 per cent during 1972–75. The uncertain international climate compounded with India's domestic conflicts with its neighbours during the 1960s and 1970s meant that during the 1970s, the price of gold went up by 25 per cent per annum and that of silver by 16 per cent. World inflation peaked again in 1980 in the wake of the second oil crisis. The second oil shock and the near-severe drought conditions in India resulted in an inflation rate which averaged 15.5 per cent per annum between 1979–82. Falling oil prices were partly responsible for the marked decline in inflation in industrial countries after 1986. But, the inflationary pressures in the early 1990s in India were the result of increases in the administered prices of agricultural commodities and petro-goods even though international crude oil prices were actually declining.

The need to align domestic prices with international levels had been recognised. Events like the oil crisis do not by themselves generate sustained inflationary pressures over a long period of time. While it is not clear what exactly causes higher levels of inflation to last over a period of time, monetarists argue that in a relatively open economy sustained inflation is a monetary phenomenon caused by excessive growth in the country's money supply. High inflation tends to be associated with a high growth in money supply but whether they are the cause and effect or simply dual manifestations of the same underlying problem remains unclear. Others take into account the demand and supply of goods and services in the economy which reflect the level of industrial activity in the economy and the accompanying level of infrastructure to match this demand. In any centrally directed economy such factors are irrelevant as the government controls inflation through its pricing mechanism. The success of the government in such a scenario gets reflected in the disparity between its administered prices and the blackmarket prices with the latter always being a better indicator of demand and supply.

During the era of a centrally monitored economy it had been easier to control inflation in India. But in the new economic environment inflation is being controlled through tighter monetary policies. The history of inflation management in China is similar, recording virtually no inflation in the 1970s thanks to the central pricing mechanism. In the 1980s China's inflation was kept under control, but it has been more difficult to continue with such a policy in the 1990s; the central pricing mechanism was no longer available to exercise such control. The key to a successful transition from an inward-looking, centrally monitored economy to a globally competitive one largely depends on the government's ability to control inflation. But inflation management becomes difficult as the variables increase, the effects take longer to surface and the economy becomes more opaque due to inadequate data collection. A comparison of inflation rates is shown in Table 3.12.

Table 3.12   Inflation rates: a comparison

Country	Average annual rate of inflation (%)	
	1970–80	*1984–94*
Brazil	38.6	900.3
China	0.6	8.4
India	8.4	9.7
Indonesia	21.5	8.9
Malaysia	7.3	3.1
Mexico	18.1	40.0
Russian Federation	−0.1	124.3
South Korea	19.5	6.8
Philippines	13.3	10.0
Thailand	9.2	5.0

Source: *World Development Report*, 1995 and 1996.

Countries as diverse as Russia, China and India have had to cope with this painful process of transition, and by any standards India's record has been commendable. The pricing distortions in the Indian context have not been grossly pronounced. Administered pricing accounted for 16 per cent of the wholesale price index (WPI) in India in 1996–97, while the government indirectly controlled the prices of various food items and essential items which constituted 34.4 per cent of the WPI. Thus, through a combination of administered pricing and tight monetary policy, India has delivered a level of inflation that has been commendable. But the link between government borrowing and inflation will become stronger as the economy emerges from the price control mechanism.

Over the entire period since Independence, India has a remarkable record of 6.5 per cent compound annual growth rate in inflation. Over the last 25 years or so, India's inflation rate has been higher at 8.5 per cent which still compares favourably with other developing economies around the world. The price hikes in India have been fairly uniform for all commodities over the past 45 years except in the case of energy which is both import-intensive and import-sensitive. In the 1950s, inflation for all commodities was at 1.5 per cent. Inflation rose to 6.1 per cent over the next decade during which period India experienced two consecutive years of drought. In the 1970s, the oil crisis led to a 13.5 per cent annual rate of growth in the price of fuel and power, but the overall inflation rate for the decade was kept at under 10 per cent. (see Table 3.13).

Table 3.13   Growth in the components of the wholesale price index in India (in percentage terms)

	1950–51 to 1993–94	1950–51 to 1960–61	1960–61 to 1970–71	1970–71 to 1980–81	1980–81 to 1993–94
All primary articles	6.4	0.6	7.3	9.0	8.2
Fuel and power	7.7	2.9	5.0	13.5	9.3
Manufactured items	6.3	2.2	5.3	9.9	7.5
All commodities	6.5	1.5	6.1	9.9	8.1
Additional items					
Gold	9.4	1.7	4.9	25.0	7.9
Silver	9.3	2.0	11.7	16.1	8.3

Source: CMIE.

Measures of Inflation

India's inflation rate is most commonly monitored within the country by the WPI which, based in 1981–82, reflects the changes in the prices of

447 commodities covering all traded goods in the primary, fuel and power and in the manufacturing sectors. The WPI provides a comprehensive coverage of commodities ranging from consumer goods, consumer durables, basic raw materials, intermediate and capital goods.

Retail prices are monitored through the changes in the consumer price index (CPI) for three different groups of consumers – namely, industrial workers, urban non-manual employees and agricultural labour households. The retail price movement is monitored through three different series of data. The basket of commodities for the respective series consist of food; pan and tobacco and beverages; housing, fuel and light; clothing, bedding and footwear; and a number of services classified as miscellaneous. The series for industrial workers CPI (IW), based in 1982, covers 260 commodities. The urban non-manual employees CPI (UNME) index, based in 1984–85, covers 180 commodities. The index for agricultural labour CPI (AL) households covers 60 commodities. The coverage of food articles and products is more comprehensive and their weights are higher in the CPI (IW) and CPI (AL) than in the CPI (UNME). The existing CPI (AL) data series, based in 1960–61, is being replaced by a new series based in 1986–87. The new series will reflect more realistically the structural changes in the consumption pattern of the rural population.

The annual inflation rate based on CPI (IW) is the most commonly used of the three series and it moves in line with the WPI while the volatility of the agricultural labour household's index is an indication of the impact of prices on the bulk of India's population. Agricultural labourers seem to have faced some of the highest levels of inflation within the country and stand to benefit most from lower inflation when the sector is deregulated. One of the main arguments in favour of APM is that it provides stable and low prices for the bulk of India's population. But, evidence suggests that the agricultural sector has experienced some of the sharpest price movements in the economy. Inflation in the agricultural sector is also the key to the political success of governments in elections. Taking the level of poverty into account, keeping prices under control in essential items like rice and wheat through the public distribution system has been the government's key policy. For the first time in the history of the nation, there has been a surplus of foodgrain stocks since 1994 but the government has not been able to reduce significantly the procurement prices of these items for fear of lowering production. Thus, the consumer has failed to benefit from several years of good harvests.

While the level of inflation is an indicator of the health of the economy, higher inflation also influences strongly the voting behaviour in the country. Inflation is therefore the sole economic issue that impinges on the decision of the voter while corruption remains a perennial concern. The economic policies of the government bear the responsibility for the overall rate of inflation. But the various state governments have a role in determining the level of inflation for the different consumer groups within their states. The CPI (AL) usually holds the key to the success or failure of state government's in power.

The Role of Administered Pricing in Determining Inflation

The inflationary impact of the early 1990s was influenced by the administered pricing policy which led to substantial revisions in the prices of certain commodities. There were also clear indications of a build-up of inflationary pressures linked to higher money supply and a weakening fiscal position. An examination of the 447 items that constitute the WPI reveals that only 11 per cent of the commodities included in it accounted for 57 per cent of the inflation during the early 1990s. Rice, sugarcane, wheat, high-speed diesel oil and electricity for industrial purposes consistently contributed to the higher level of inflation.

While administered pricing can balance the inflationary effects of deficit financing to some extent, the indiscriminate use of administered pricing creates a matching blackmarket over a period of time with the net result that the official figures for inflation no longer reflect true price changes. It is to India's relative credit that its centrally controlled economy was reasonably well managed because the effects of decontrol have not been as destabilising as in some other parts of the world. The annual inflation rate rose to 10.5 per cent in November 1990 and peaked at 16.3 per cent in September 1991, averaging 13.7 per cent for the year 1991–92. These numbers compare favourably with the rates of inflation prevalent in various countries in different stages of their transition cycle. However, it has to be noted that the current oil pool deficit estimated at Rs180 billion or 1.2 per cent of GDP is an indication of the extent to which the oil sector has subsidised the price of oil during the past few years. The economic price that elections and the entire democratic process extracts in India has been high. Most governments around the world engage in vote-winning strategies that lead to higher PSBRs. In India, such a burden is placed on all government controlled sectors. Thus, the fiscal burden is significantly higher than the official figures indicate and so is 'real' inflation.

An analysis of the weightings of the major components of WPI (see Table 3.14) and their annual rates of inflation, reveals that food items account for 27 per cent of WPI. This sector is indirectly controlled by the

Table 3.14 Major components of the wholesale price index (in percentage terms)

Items	Weight	1996–97 Jan.–Jan.	1995–96 Jan.–Jan.	1994–95 Dec.–Dec.	1993–94 Apr.–Jan.	1992–93 whole year
All commodities	100	7.6	4.9	11.3	7.6	7.0
Primary articles	32.3	11.7	2.6	14.4	9.5	3.0
of which, food articles	17.4	18.1	2.4	12.9	5.0	5.4
non-food articles	10.1	2.7	2.4	19.0	17.2	-1.4
Fuel, power, light and lubricants	10.7	17.4	1.1	5.3	8.8	15.2
Manufactured products	57.0	3.6	6.9	10.8	6.2	7.9
of which, food products	10.1	7.3	2.1	10.7	10.2	6.7
textiles	11.5	1.9	11.0	14.6	7.6	5.5
Administered items	15.9	14.5	0.9	5.9	9.9	12.4
of which, petroleum crude	4.3	2.3	0.0	5.6	19.4	1.9
POL	6.7	19.6	-0.3	6.5	1.3	18.8
electricity	2.7	11.8	3.6	3.5	26.3	9.8
Seasonal items*	34.4	10.5	2.1	14.0	9.9	4.1
Raw materials#	14.9	2.6	3.0	16.4	16.8	-0.6
Essential commodities**	21.8	13.0	7.9	10.4	12.7	4.4

Notes: * Seasonal items include food articles, non-food articles, sugar, khadsari and gur, edible oil and oil cakes; # raw materials include non-food articles and minerals; ** essential commodities include rice, wheat, milk, sugar, groundnut oil, goat meat, sarees, potatoes, mustard oil, fresh fish and other items.
Source: Indian Economic Survey, various issues.

government as reflected in the management of the supply of foodgrains from stocks. The lowering of import duty on essential items is still up to the government. Besides, adminstered items account for 16 per cent of WPI. Thus, a large component of inflation is determined by the government. With greater liberalisation, the inflation factor for goods and services will begin to be determined more by demand and supply rather than by direct or indirect government price controls.

The contribution of administered pricing to inflation in 1996–97 was higher compared to its level over the previous year mainly due to the General Election in May 1996. The level of contribution of administered pricing in 1993–94 and 1993–92 was also higher at 15.4 per cent and 23 per cent due to a greater level of adjustment required in response to the economic crisis. Since the decontrol of steel, non-ferrous metals and fertilisers (except urea), the major items under price control are POL (except lubricating oil) with coal and electricity. Much of the hike in administered prices came from a rise in the price of coal and the increase in electricity rates charged by the SEBs. The challenge for the government lies in introducing greater competition into these sectors to keep price growth under control. Both sectors, coal and electricity, are among the most inefficient in the world.

The major source of inflation since 1992 has been in the manufactured products sector contributing almost 80 per cent to the WPI in 1995–96, 53 per cent during the two previous years and 63 per cent in 1992–93. The spurt in the prices of sugar, fertilisers, electricity and POL were among the major contributors to inflation in 1992–93 and 1993–94. These sectors were all under price control but with the abolition of controls on sugar and fertilisers (urea), the number of items under administered pricing has been declining. Textiles, within the manufactured products sector, contributed to inflation during 1994–96 due to higher cotton prices. The fuel and power sectors were responsible for 22.6 per cent contribution to inflation in 1992–93 and 17.6 per cent in 1993–94 but their rate of growth declined over the next two years. In 1996–97, the fuel and power sector was responsible for a quarter of price increases.

The level of contribution by primary articles was 14.4 per cent in 1992–93 but shot up in 1993–94 to 30 per cent, and higher still to 41.5 per cent in 1994–95. In 1996–97, primary articles accounted for half the price increase. Primary food articles were responsible for 45 per cent of price rises in 1996–97. This is a sensitive issue as it affects all sectors of society. While the negative rate of growth in the prices of raw materials was encouraging in 1992–93, it also reflected weak industrial growth that year. The stronger growth in the prices of raw materials in 1993–94 and 1994–95 was not only a reflection of stronger domestic demand but also a rise in the prices of commodities internationally. The weak rise in the price of raw materials in 1996–97 indicated a slowdown in industrial production.

The discrepancy in the CPI (IW), which tends to mirror the WPI, is mainly due to the fall in the prices of primary commodities which have different weightings in the CPI and the WPI. Rice, for example, has a weighting of 12.5 per cent in the CPI and 3.7 per cent weighting in the WPI. A group of 30 essential commodities has a 48.8 per cent weighting in the CPI compared to 21.8 per cent in the WPI. While the rate of inflation for agricultural households, as calculated by the CPI (AL), went up from a low of 3.1 per cent in June 1990 to 18.3 per cent by August 1991, and remained at over the 20 per cent level till August 1992, agricultural labourers also benefited most from the policy to rein-in inflation as the General Election became imminent in May 1996.

Much of the spurt in inflation is attributable to primary articles which is heavily weighted in food articles. Wheat and rice are the two main cereals that constitute the bedrock of food reserves in the country. Thus, the procurement of these two cereals constitutes the centrepiece of the government's intervention programme for ensuring availability and price stability of the basic food requirements of the general population in India. Increases in the prices of wheat and rice are also politically sensitive as they cost votes. So, when the price of rice or wheat is increased within the public distribution system (PDS) or when the minimum support price (MSP) payable to farmers for wheat and rice is raised, irrespective of a good harvest or the demand and supply situation, it influences the rate of inflation. The Commission for Agricultural Costs and Prices determines the procurement prices announced by the government. MSPs may either be the same or lower than procurement prices depending on the government's perception of its food reserves. Administered prices, operating under the PDS and the MSP, provide a floor below which foodgrain prices cannot fall irrespective of production and demand.

One of the main functions of the foodgrain stockpile, apart from food security, is market intervention. The discrepancy between foodgrain allocation and offtake under the PDS has led to a growing realisation that the PDS may not be serving the more vulnerable sections of the population. The declining offtake also suggests that, due to better supply and better management of the supply, the price differential between the PDS retail price and the free market price was exceedingly low during 1994–96. This and the increasing burden of government subsidy for continuing the Food Corporation of India's operations has been recognised by the financial planners but no clear policy enunciation has been made for reducing costs and increasing efficiency. Better targeting of subsidies aimed at poverty relief would help in a superior utilisation of food subsidies. Elimination of the food subsidy is considered neither desirable nor feasible. But, there is need to contain the expense of administering the scheme as well as in improving the efficiency of the scheme so that people who need it most can access it. Some policy changes are overdue in this area and are essential to greater liberalisation in the agricultural sector. The government has indicated its intention to meet the objectives of price stability and make essential articles available to the poor.

The central issue prices (CIPs) for the PDS are fixed deliberately below the economic cost of foodgrain production in order to increase the availability of foodgrains to consumers at low prices. These prices are fixed by the central government for the PDS but the 'retail end' prices are determined by the state governments taking into account transportation costs, dealer's commission and other such costs. There are states which fix the retail prices for the PDS even lower than the CIP by providing additional subsidies. The governments of Andhra Pradesh and Tamil Nadu, for example, were operating a Rs 2 per kg scheme for rice and the government of Gujarat had a Rs 2 per kg scheme for wheat in 1994–95. The total food subsidy of the central government used to be Rs 20 billion or 0.6 per cent of GDP in 1987–88. It rose to Rs 55.4 billion in 1993–94, though as a percentage of GDP it was only marginally higher at 0.69 per cent in 1993–94. The food subsidy declined to Rs 55 billion or 0.5 per cent of GDP in 1995–96, and was estimated at Rs 60.7 billion or 0.47 per cent level GDP in 1996–97. It was budgeted at Rs 75 billion for 1997–98. In a period of healthy foodgrain bufferstocks, food subsidy should have been much lower.

The MSP policy for essential agricultural products was aimed to maintain a delicate balance between providing incentives for raising production while protecting the interests of the consumers. The government's agricultural price policy in the new economic environment has attempted to correct the earlier policy bias favouring industry by aiming to bring about a favourable trade regime for agricultural producers in aligning domestic prices with international levels. The agricultural sector needs to take global pricing into account to provide the signals to domestic producers to strive towards global competitiveness. While India is relatively competitive in rice, wheat and cotton; it is not so in edible oils. But what is not fully appreciated is that India's soft wheat fetches a lower price in the export markets compared to the hard wheat which is traded globally and that Indian rice is not particularly in demand in global trade as the Chinese and the Africans prefer different varieties of the same product. India exported 4.9 million tonnes of rice in 1995–96, nearly five times the amount exported in the preceeding two years. This commendable achievement was not a result of a planned export strategy and is not clear if it can be sustained without changes to India's agricultural policy.

India built its programme of foodgrain production since the early 1970s by establishing the MSP mechanism whereby farmers get a remunerative price for their produce by the government and are protected from exploitation by traders. Thus, India's MSP system is the antithesis of a market-oriented mechanism. Better than expected procurement performance has resulted in an increase in foodgrain stocks in the central pool to unprecedented levels (see Table 3.15). While India imported 3 million tonnes of wheat in 1992–93, the stock situation has improved significantly thereafter. The government has to take into account the market realities of excess supply for domestic purposes, mounting public stocks and limited export opportunities in a normal year when announcing procurement prices for foodgrains. Considering the high levels of buffer stock in foodgrains, the government can afford to allow the export of rice and gradually open up agriculture to private sector investment.

Table 3.15   Central pool of stocks (in million tonnes)

1 January	Rice	Wheat	Total
1990	5.65	5.61	11.26
1991	8.66	9.24	17.90
1992	8.63	5.28	13.91
1993	8.52	3.28	11.80
1994	11.17	10.82	21.99
1995	17.24	12.88	30.30
1996P	15.41	13.15	28.56
1997P	12.90	6.90	19.80
Buffer norms for 1 January	7.70	7.70	15.40

Source: *Indian Economic Survey*, 1996–97.

The increased liberalisation in the import of foodgrains has eased supply bottlenecks and, combined with higher domestic stocks of wheat and rice, the environment for overall inflation in the country looks to be manageable in the medium term. Liberal imports coupled with a more active consumer movement can play a substantial role in countering monopolistic and oligopolistic pricing practices by domestic producers. The challenge remains for the government to bring these factors into play so that inflation can fall significantly below current levels. That will take greater political will to implement as it requires changes in various aspects of governmental policy relating to the liberalisation of agriculture and labour along with further reforms in the financial sector, investments in infrastructure both physical and social, and improvements in the general environment for private sector investment. The future course of inflation in India will be linked to the fiscal policy which in turn will be determined by the government's ability to reform various aspects of the economy that impact on government expenditure.

The Impact of Reforms on Inflation and Money Supply

One of the features of the historical management of the money supply in India was that there was no concept of M3, or aggregate monetary resources, until 1969–70. The share of currency and coins with the public declined from 36 per cent before the nationalisation of the banks in 1969 to about 19 per cent in 1994–95. The share of demand deposits also declined following a change in the definition of money supply in 1977–78 when savings deposits in savings accounts which earned interest were re-classified as time deposits. With the change in the bank accounting year from calendar year to financial year in 1988–89, there were sharp and unusual increases in aggregate deposits and credit towards the end of financial years 1988–89 and 1989–90. Foreign exchange assets within the banking sector, which formed a very small portion of M3 in the past, also gained importance since 1991.

Since the 1960s, growth in net bank credit to the commercial sector has been strong. In 1960–61 net bank credit to the government was Rs 24.8 billion or 15.3 per cent of GDP, while that to the commercial sector was only Rs 4.08 billion. Thus, commercial sector borrowing was only 16.4 per cent of government borrowing. Within a decade, net bank credit to the commercial sector had overtaken that to the government. Commercial borrowing was strong in the 1970s and 1980s but since the economic crisis of 1991, it declined during the phase of structural adjustment before recovering again in 1994–95. Industrial capacity under-utilisation, high real interest costs and cheaper means of fund-raising via the capital market were among the salient reasons for this decline. Historically, the two main sources of expansion in M3 were net bank credit to the government and that to the commercial sector. A new development on the monetary front which has influenced money supply since India's liberalisation of 1991 has been the rise in FX reserves.

Prior to the liberalisation of the Indian economy, the link between inflation and money supply was relatively weak and took longer to be reflected in prices. Since the reforms of 1991, the inflationary trend can be ascribed to a relatively higher growth in money supply which contributed to the inflationary effects of administered price revisions in various items like rice, wheat, petroleum and other inputs. Production shortfalls in sugar, cotton, jute and other items also caused short-term supply imbalances triggering price rises. The government's liberalisation effort was rewarded with foreign investment, mostly portfolio investment, which boosted the country's reserves significantly. FX reserves rose from $1 billion in June 1991 to over $19 billion or 8.7 months of imports in 1994. The monetisation of reserves led to an expansion in money supply. Together with increases in administered prices, inflation rose strongly during 1994–95.

The government's inability to operate a tight fiscal policy since 1993–94 meant that the role of curbing the growth in money supply was transfered to monetary policy. The negative effect of such a policy has been noticeable in a lower investment rate due to higher real interest rates. Weak domestic recovery was partly responsible for the decline in investment while the high cost of capital was partially overcome by several Indian companies raising funds abroad. But the small scale industrial sector, denied such access, was squeezed by the high real domestic interest rates. Ironically, one of the major reasons for higher money supply and higher inflation in India during 1994–95 was the increased inflow of foreign portfolio investment which led to a build up of FX reserves. As the portfolio inflows did not translate into higher imports, the RBI intervened by building up its FX reserves rather than allowing the currency to appreciate so as to encourage exports by maintaining a competitive exchange rate.

Slippages in fiscal prudence with higher than anticipated foreign investment flows led to the monetisation of the fiscal deficit and the generation of excess liquidity in the system which was reflected in higher inflation. The future success of the government with lowering inflation will depend on its ability to tackle the stubborn fiscal deficit and control the growth of money supply, including the inflow of foreign funds. Otherwise, intermittent recourse to a tight monetary policy will result in sporadic investment activity. Thus, the overall management of inflation since 1991 has been influenced by a combination of factors including administered pricing, supply-side management by increasing imports of key commodities, operating open market sales from central food stocks and releasing higher levels of food stock through the PDS as well as via tighter monetary policies and, to a lesser extent, fiscal adjustment.

The overall commitment to reducing the fiscal deficit remains the key to lower government borrowing from the central bank which should help in controlling the growth of money supply. A major policy change was attempted in 1994–95 to restrict the growth in money supply by putting a ceiling on the government's access to *ad hoc* TBs issued by the central bank and thus to curb the direct and automatic monetisation of the budget deficit. An agreement was signed between the Finance Secretary, Government of India, and the Governor of the RBI in September 1994 to limit the net issue of *ad hoc* TBs to Rs 60 billion in 1994–95. It was also agreed that similar ceilings would be stipulated for the two following years and from 1997–98 this system would be abolished. The agreement was aimed at providing greater stability in monetary management to help control inflation in the economy. The declining trend in the growth of net RBI credit to the government between 1991–92 and 1993–94 may have encouraged the government to implement such a change.

The ceiling on borrowing from the RBI against *ad hoc* TBs was reduced from Rs 60 billion in 1994–95 to Rs 50 billion in 1995–96, although the 'within-year' (ten consecutive working days threshold above which the RBI was free to sell government securities to bring back the borrowing to the mandatory limit) ceiling on such borrowing was retained at Rs 90 billion to accomodate the mismatch between revenue inflows and expenditure outflows. A sharp reduction in the government's market borrowing in the first half of 1995–96 increased the mismatch and with it the centre's borrowing. The RBI's intention to contain monetary growth is laudable in light of the fact that it has no autonomy of action. The government reneged on its commitment to reduce its exposure to such methods of borrowing. Lax fiscal policy was supported by a stringent monetary policy. The RBI intervened with measures to restrict the growth of money supply by increasing the cash reserve ratio (CRR) and the prime lending rate (PLR) of banks in February 1995. Despite the government's intention to end deficit financing, such a policy was not adhered to and its reversal was responsible for some of the highest levels of inflation in the economy since 1991. With an election looming in 1996, the only way to reduce inflation was through tight monetary policy.

The UF government abolished the issuance of *ad hoc* TBs from 1 April 1997 and replaced it with the Ways and Means Advances (WMA) scheme to severe the link between the budget deficit and higher money supply. In order to proceed with greater fiscal discipline, an acceptable public expenditure management policy dealing with issues of equity and non-discrimination needs to be framed. As the issue of subsidies has been deeply politicised in the past, it was hoped that the establishment of an expenditure management commission would be the first step towards enabling the government to put in place a better expenditure control mechanism. But, it has proven to be difficult even to appoint such a commission reflecting the lack of consensus regarding ways of reducing expenditure in the public domain.

However, the recent report on subsidies, commissioned by the Ministry of Finance to stimulate a wider public debate, is an initial step in this direction.

The other major development influencing the demand for money was the government's shift away from below-market-rate statutory lending by the banks to a more market-based borrowing. Monetary management since 1991 had been aimed at reducing inflation and providing credit support to the private sector. The strong rise in money supply during 1993–95 was curtailed during 1995–97 but the government's contribution to growth in money supply was low between 1991–95. This was unique in the history of India's monetary management that monetary growth was not attributable to the monetisation of the budget deficit. The RBI's net credit to the government grew at 4.7 per cent in 1992–93, 0.9 per cent in 1993–94 and 2.2 per cent in 1994–95. The centre stuck to its agreement with the RBI of not exceeding its borrowing against *ad hoc* TBs, and so during 1994–95 the net increase in *ad hoc* TBs was low. This commitment was reneged on during 1995–96 by the government leading to a 19.6 per cent rise in net-RBI credit to the government.

The shift in the method of financing the fiscal deficit away from *ad hoc* borrowing from the RBI towards more market-based borrowing was reflected in the strong rise of 'bank credit to the government'. The deceleration of money growth, which started in the fourth quarter of 1994–95 and continued over 1995–96, due to a slowdown in the rate of growth of net-FX assets of the RBI, contributed to the lower growth in money supply as well. The rise in bank credit to the commercial sector started in the second half of 1994–95 with the recovery in industrial production. The momentum was lost during 1995–96 and 1996–97 when higher government borrowing in 1995–96 started 'crowding out' private sector demand for credit. Elections tend to be costly in most countries, but the inconclusive outcome of the election in 1996 meant that the new government was not able to rein in public expenditure thereafter due to the lack of consensus on expenditure reform. The decline in net-RBI credit to the government in 1996–97 was encouraging though not the low growth in bank credit to the commercial sector. Growth in bank credit to the government was strong in 1995–96 and less so in 1996–97, thanks to the government borrowing at market rates of interest which has in effect crowded out the private sector. The changes in monetary stock are summarised in Table 3.16.

Money supply growth in India has been overwhelmingly determined by the monetisation of the fiscal deficit. Starting from the third quarter of 1993–94, this phenomenon was replaced by net foreign reserve accumulation by the RBI as the driving force behind the growth in reserve money.

The increase of the RBI's net foreign assets constituted 76 per cent of reserve money increase in 1994–95 compared to a high of 103 per cent contribution in 1993–94. During these two years the government's contribution to growth in money supply was negligible. The surge of portfolio investment into India by foreign institutional investors resulted in capital inflows when the government's fiscal deficit was still high and the current account of the balance of payments was virtually in balance indicating a low level of domestic investment activity. These capital inflows did not translate into imports due to significant barriers to investment by the private sector in areas where investment was required and excess capacity in areas where investment was possible. Public sector investment was not viable as the government's major task was to stabilise the economy by reducing aggregate demand and reducing government spending.

Table 3.16   Changes in monetary stock (% growth)

	1992–93	1993–94	1994–95	1995–96	1996–97*
Net RBI credit to government	4.7	0.9	2.2	19.6	3.3
RBI credit to commercial sector	−14.3	3.6	2.3	4.0	−8.3
Net bank credit to government	11.3	15.6	9.1	15.7	11.4
Net bank credit to commercial sector	15.1	7.8	21.8	16.5	5.3
M3	14.2	18.2	22.2	13.2	10.6
Net FX assets of RBI	20.2	127.1	45.3	−0.8	15.5

Note: * 31 March 1996 to 17 Jan 1997.
Source: *Indian Economic Surveys*, various issues.

In the case of rapid capital inflows, the options available to economic planners are FX reserve accumulation or widening of the current account deficit. The method chosen has implications for the economy. If the later route is exercised, the key is whether the current account is widened through a reduction in domestic savings or through an increase in domestic investment for the road taken determines the future capacity of the economy to service the investment. India's structural adjustment programme denied the option of boosting public spending through a massive infrastructural development programme. The portfolio investments that were made in 1993–94 could not have been utilised by the government as it was the private sector that raised the funds but the private sector was not able to direct it into infrastructural development due to policy barriers.

The government was not equipped with established channels for capital mobilisation overseas while individual companies were more opportunistic in their fund raising. The lag between the private sector's resource mobilisation and utilisation led to the accumulation of FX.

The RBI's response to the relatively large capital inflows was intervention to maintain the exchange rate at Rs 31.37 to the dollar by purchasing all the excess supply of FX at that rate. This resulted in FX accumulation and expansion of the base money which put upward pressure on inflation. India's accumulation of FX reserves in such a manner was an expensive affair as the monetisation of the inflows was not adequately sterilised leading to higher money supply, inflation and an appreciation of the real exchange rate. Sterilised intervention has its own set of constraints as it results in higher domestic real interest rates which can be costly to both the industrial and banking sectors. Thus, capital inflows extracts its price as India's planners learnt after the implementation of reforms.

In countries where capital inflows have coincided with full capacity utilisation rates and rapidly growing investment, there has been relatively little upward adjustment in the exchange rate. But in countries where the capacity utilisation rate has been low and the investment cycle has fallen significantly from its peak, the widening of the current account has been the result of domestic consumption which creates its own cycle of instability for the currency. The major lesson from the Indian experience has been that it can be costly to absorb large volumes of capital inflows not associated with tangible investments when the fiscal deficit is at a relatively high level, import restrictions remain in place and the banking system is in the process of a major restructuring. The capital inflows created instability in the financial system as they were not in the form of FDI but were portfolio investments. In light of that fact, it is significant that it would have been expensive for investors to reverse their investment decision. To that extent, the RBI has not had to deal with the effects of substantial FX outflows.

The fall in RBI credit to the government from January 1994 till March 1995 helped to sterilise the monetisation of FX reserves to some extent, but the process of monetisation itself led to a loss of control over money supply. What was interesting was that despite a sharp decline in net-RBI credit to the government in 1993–94, the fiscal deficit went up strongly. This was the result of the increase in government borrowing from the private sector at market interest rates. The government in financing its fiscal deficit had been shifting away from automatic lending by RBI at below market rates and statutory lending by banks towards a more market based borrowing. The surge in the flow of foreign private savings into the economy and the mobilisation of funds from the domestic capital market explains the relatively low demand for bank credit from the commercial sector in 1993–94. Weak industrial growth in the first quarter of 1993–94 and slowing inflation led to a shift in monetary concerns from controlling inflation to boosting production by the third quarter of 1993–94. Subsequent recovery in industrial production and inflation once again rekindled concerns about the government's ability to manage economic growth without higher inflation by the end of the financial year 1993–94.

The close links between FX markets and short-term money markets was also manifested for the first time since the liberalisation of the exchange rate. The RBI had maintained the level of the rupee at Rs 31.37 to the dollar despite strong capital inflows. However, rising imports due to the industrial recovery and the decline in portfolio inflows resulted in increasing volatility of the currency in the FX markets. In October and November 1995, when market speculation caused havoc on the FX markets, the RBI had to intervene by selling substantial amounts of dollars. Such a manner of intervention helped reduce money supply and led to rises in inter-bank call money rates. The undeveloped nature of the market meant that call money rates continued to escalate to unrealistic levels until the RBI injected funds to stabilise the call market rates.

This constant need to balance growth and inflation remains a challenge for India's policymakers. A tight monetary policy by the central bank can starve the funding needs of the corporate sector and a loose monetary policy can trigger inflationary pressures. High inflation rates in India tend to ruin the prospect of any political party's prospects of returning to power and thus the desire to win the battle of inflation is not simply a question of good house-keeping but also one of survival. A tight monetary policy with a loose fiscal policy also damages the industrial sector's growth. Money supply will increasingly play a key role in determining inflation. Money supply is influenced by the performance of the public sector in its fiscal adjustment, thus linking it to the financial sector and the state of the commercial banking sector's lending to the private sector.

The rising cost of government borrowing in the market has increased pressures on the RBI to accommodate the fiscal deficit which has hindered the progress in the financial sector reforms. Limited flexibility in fiscal policy has encouraged the use of directed credit programmes to achieve development objectives, affecting cash reserve ratio (CRR) and statutory liquidity ratio (SLR) requirements. As money supply is also affected by capital inflows, management of such flows is influenced by both fiscal and monetary policies which in turn determine the level of money supply. Monetisation of large surpluses in the capital account can have the same effect on money supply as the monetisation of a large fiscal deficit. Both call for strong steps to contain monetary expansion which result in high interest rates that affect investment and growth.

INTEREST RATES

It was inevitable in a centrally controlled economy that India had an interest rate regime that was centrally administered. The RBI maintains control over the money supply but, lacking independence, has little control over the credit supply to the government. Thus, when inflation rises due to strong money supply on account of a high PSBR, the RBI steps in with tighter monetary measures which slows down growth on account of the high real interest rate environment. Loss of control over the fiscal situation has meant that interest rates in India have been rising over the past two decades, peaking in 1991 when they coincided with the BoP crisis. India had a plethora of interest rates and part of the reform agenda has been to simplify these multiple rates and reduce the cost of capital for the private sector. The high real interest rates of the past decades contributed significantly to making India a high-cost centre for industry.

One of the major reasons for the high interest rate structure for the commercial sector has been the structure of government borrowing. Until 1991, the government had refrained from developing a proper market for its own debt securities. The low yields on government obligations meant that the demand for such instruments came entirely from institutions forced to hold them. The SLR of commercial banks was fixed by the government at 38.25 per cent as late as 9 January 1993 and the CRR was 14.5 per cent on 17 April 1993. Prior to January 1993 auctions of TBs did not reflect market conditions, and 91-day TBs were sold at yields of no more than 4.6 per cent. In April 1992, the RBI introduced fortnightly auctions of 364-day TBs which facility was subsequently extended to 5-years and 10-years dated securities. Further steps are being taken to develop the debt market with the establishment of primary dealers, improved transactions and custodial systems. While the primary market for government debt has developed comparatively rapidly, the secondary market growth has been slow. The liberalisation of the insurance sector should help in that respect along with developments like the introduction of Indexed Bonds and encouraging FIIs to invest in corporate debt.

The major development since 1991 is the shift towards the government paying market-determined rates for its own borrowing. While in the initial stages of this transition it meant that government borrowing rose sharply leading to higher inflation, in the medium term it will enforce the government to contain its deficit borrowing. However, the simultaneous development of the debt market is necessary for the government to reduce its fiscal imbalance, lower its borrowing from the RBI, and ease the pressure off a tight monetary stance while enabling greater investment flows into the infrastructural sector which is vital for FDI flows into India.

Though the link between high real interest rates, private investment and industrial production was not clearly established in the past, it will become increasingly so as the economy is liberalised further. Most private blue- chip Indian companies borrow at a small premium to the minimum lending rate (MLR), but the bulk of corporate borrowing is at much higher rates. Thus the real cost of capital in India is understated to some extent. An analysis of the impact of real interest rates on industrial production and investment shows that in an era of post-liberalisation it has not had the sort of influence on private investment decisions as one would normally expect. The resilience of the manufacturing sector, in spite of the high real cost of capital, was clear. Post-1991, the private sector's easier access to cheaper capital via the capital market enabled the private sector to carry on with its investment activity. Also, industrial production figures are dominated by the public sector. The history of real interest rates is summarised in Table 3.17.

Table 3.17   History of real interest rates in India *vis-à-vis* industrial production and domestic private investment

Year	MLR[1]	WPI-MP[2]	RIR[3]	IPI[4]	GDFC[5]
1986–87	17.5	3.9	13.6	9.2	−0.8
1987–88	16.5	7.2	9.3	7.3	23.9
1988–89	16.0	9.4	6.6	8.7	36.4
1989–90	16.5	11.3	5.2	8.6	13.3
1990–91	16.5	8.4	8.1	8.3	15.5
1991–92	16.5	11.3	5.2	0.6	13.5
1992–93	19.0	7.9	11.1	2.3	15.1
1993–94	19.0	6.2	12.8	6.0	13.1
1994–95	15.0	10.8	4.2	9.4	15.2
1995–96	16.5	6.9	9.6	11.7	18.1

Notes: [1]MLR – minimum lending rate; [2]WPI-MP – wholesale price index for manufactured products; [3]RIR – real interest rate; [4]IPI – industrial production index; [5]GDCF – gross domestic capital formation for the private sector. Percentage change year-on-year in nominal terms.
Source: RBI; CMIE; *Indian Economic Survey*, 1996–97.

The stronger levels of industrial production in the late 1980s also coincided with the highest levels of real interest rates in the economy. One explanation is that inflation for all commodities in the WPI was actually higher than inflation for manufactured products leading to better price realisation for the manufacturing sector. The lower levels of industrial production despite lower user cost of capital has been the result of weaker domestic demand in the economy since the implementation of structural adjustment and stabilisation. In July 1991, the government's highest priority in the short term was to stabilise the economy through expenditure switching and contraction of aggregate demand. To stabilise demand, the government tightened monetary policies and made it a key objective to reduce the fiscal deficit of the central government. While the lower cost of capital will prove beneficial to manufacturing industry in the long term, it did not have much impact on industry immediately after the government's reforms because India's past industrial policies had left a legacy of capital stock which had been underutilised and that allowed significant rises in production levels without a matching addition to capacity.

Since 1992–93, due to the gradual decline in the rate of inflation and the relatively rapid growth of money aggregates, nominal interest rates started to decline. The RBI had its own reasons for keeping the MLR high; mainly to maintain a high spread for the banking sector as their healthy profits would contribute towards their recapitalisation. The MLR was also the RBI's major monetary policy instrument. But a high MLR led to the stagnation of bank credit to the commercial sector. It encouraged the corporate sector to raise capital in the domestic and international markets as it also coincided with the abolition of the Controller of Capital Issues (CCI) in 1992. Most Indian companies had not been able to raise equity capital at anywhere near market prices during the regime of the CCI. With a buoyant stockmarket and strong demand for equity stock both at home and abroad, Indian firms issued shares to fund their future growth plans. This explains the higher investment in 1995–96 despite a rise in the real interest rate.

The faltering recovery of the economy in 1992–93 was reflected in the decline in bank credit in 1993–94 (see Table 3.18) as real interest rates went above 10 per cent in March 1993. In response to a decline in real interest rates in 1994–95, bank credit grew strongly over the same period with the recovery in demand for credit and a rise in investment and production. Thus, a reduction in real interest rates can be a strong instrument in stimulating the economy. And the reverse is the case when real interest rates rise as is evident in the provisional figures for 1996–97. The reform of the monetary mechanism is an essential factor of financial sector development. The liberalisation of the economy involves greater deregulation of interest rates and less directed lending. Priority sector lending as a share of gross bank credit was high in 1993–94 due to strong demand from the small-scale sector. Export credit was also buoyant. Interest rates on post-shipment credit in rupees for over 90-days have been decontrolled to help exporters. Changes in other instruments such as the cash reserve ratio (CRR), the statutory liquidity ratio (SLR), and treasury bill (TB) rates have had the effect of reducing the implicit tax on the banking system as a result of their enforced lending to the government.

Table 3.18   Distribution of gross bank credit (variations in Rs billion during period indicated)

(last reporting Friday)	1991–92	1992–93	1993–94	1994–95	1995–96	1996–97*
Gross bank credit[#]	79.7	211.3	97.2	401.3	347.1	– 38.7
public food procurement	1.6	20.7	41.6	13.7	−24.8	−13.6
gross non-food credit	78.2	190.6	55.5	387.6	372.0	−25.1
priority sectors	25.1	44.1	40.5	102.8	92.3	7.0
agriculture	14.1	18.1	12.5	27.8	31.0	8.5
small-scale industry	9.7	18.8	25.9	50.2	42.5	−10.1
other priority sectors	1.3	7.3	2.1	24.9	18.8	8.6
medium & large industries	25.8	115.5	−7.7	168.1	184.4	−16.3
wholesale trade[**]	2.4	8.2	3.6	24.2	22.4	−13.3
other sectors	24.9	22.9	19.2	92.5	72.9	−2.5
Export credit[***]	11.1	50.6	17.3	79.7	46.4	−40.2

Note: Data relates to 47 commercial banks accounting for over 90 per cent of bank credit; [#] data includes bills rediscounted with RBI, IDBI, Exim Bank and other approved financial institutions; * 1997–97 figures are from April–September and are provisional; [**] excluding credit for food procurement; [***] also included in non-food credit.
Source: *Indian Economic Survey*, 1996–97.

Amendments in the Banking Companies Act have been made to permit public sector banks to raise capital through public issues. The lack of discretion in their lending was reflected in the poor management of public sector banks which reported losses of Rs 47.8 billion in 1993–94, a –29.5 per cent decline in their net profits for the year. Though their income went up by 33 per cent, provisioning for bad debts had to be increased by 48 per cent which accounted for their poor financial performance. Policy measures to increase the efficiency and the profitability of the banking sector were heavily overdue as the efficiency of the sector is integral to sustaining the liberalisation programme. The deregulation of interest rates in the banking sector along with the other changes has helped to replace physical control of monetary variables by instruments based on market incentives. However, unless fiscal prudence is strengthened by the government, monetary control remains the major route to reducing inflation. While the government is withdrawing gradually from using the various instruments of monetary control to rein-in inflation, it has resorted from time to time to the traditional methods of exercising monetary discipline in combating inflation.

Decades of non-commercial orientation of the financial sector with directed lending, loan waivers and rising non-performing assets made it difficult for lending institutions to adjust to a market environment with tighter prudential requirements. The greater discretion that Indian financial institutions now exercise in the composition of their overall portfolio has brought about a more efficient allocation of their financial resources. Commercial banks' enforced holdings of government debt has been reduced and subsidised credit to priority sectors as determined by the government has been rationalised and its cost to the financial system reduced through an increase in rates. Thus, a decline in provisioning for bad debts following a reduction in non-performing assets and the generation of larger spread due to better asset and liability management have been the reasons behind the banking sector's return to profitability in India since 1993–94. While the initial years of change have set the pace and agenda for continuing reform, the momentum of restructuring of the financial sector needs to be accelerated. An efficient financial sector is fundamental to the economy.

CONCLUSION

Despite significant progress in the external sector since the introduction of reforms in 1991, fiscal progress has been unsatisfactory. The government has found it easier to initiate revenue reforms, including the taxation of trade and services along with that of personal and corporate income, but has found it politically inexpedient to proceed with expenditure reforms. The momentum of reforms on the revenue front needs to be deepened in terms of simplification and uniformity as well as in expanding the tax base. Personal income taxes have been significantly lowered to reduce tax evasion and other rent-seeking activities. Higher government spending should be directed towards investment in the relevant infrastructure to deal with revenue collection. The government's major task remains the reduction of its fiscal deficit. Thus, expenditure reform should be high on the government's priority list.

Various options are available to achieve the reduction in expenditure through cuts in subsidies and their better utilisation, cuts in the excess public sector employment and automatic rises in real pay, and privatisation of PEs. The government has maintained the level of non-plan expenditure in many of these areas as a percentage of GDP. The participation of the states is vital to make it viable but no real dialogue has begun to achieve that. The effects of deeper fiscal reforms are many and will benefit most sectors of industry and society. Its effect on the real cost of capital along with the pricing of goods and services, not to mention greater flexibility on the part of the government to increase its investment in infrastructure and the social sectors, will lead to an overall adjustment of the various distortions that currently exist in the economy. India's past policies created a high level of distortion which has stood in the way of greater economic efficiency and productivity.

Unless reforms are implemented swiftly, the risk of delays and the pain associated with it can take a greater toll on government finances. The initial years of reform have actually hurt the poorer sections of society and as such has given economic reforms an unpopular start. The poor management of the distributional aspects of economic reforms by the government is also to blame. While the poorer sections of society need to be compensated, the delay in implementing reforms is not going to help matters. In fact, the poorest will not be affected in any way by structural changes in public employment or privatisation of uneconomic public sector undertakings. The bitter pill of expenditure-management has to be swallowed for the fiscal deficit to be curtailed. Greater liberalisation of the economy and the withdrawal of government funding from sectors of the economy that can function in a more efficient and accountable manner will enable the government to do a better job in empowering the poor.

The other aspect of expenditure reform that could possibly facilitate change, is establishing mechanisms for evaluating returns made on public investment. It is accepted that the bulk of government expenditure is for the greater public good and thus evaluating returns is more complex and, in any event, can be abused by the government. However, making international comparisons will enable to initiate an informed debate in the country and will help to introduce change. Improving the level of literacy will contribute to raising the level of economic debate in the nation. India's politicians represent the various interest groups in the country which have depended on the government's largesse, be it in the form of a license or a subsidy. Thus, it has been difficult for any party to undermine its own grassroot support. Creating lobbies in favour of deregulation or generating an environment universally supportive of reforms will take time. But time alone will not be able to introduce change except in the form of a crisis. Implementation of reforms and a greater awareness of the nature of the reforms will help usher in an awareness of global practices in the long term.

From the standpoint of the performance of the stockmarket, high real interest rates tend to discourage private sector borrowing and investment which has a depressive effect on the economy. Tight liquidity is also not a healthy environment for the performance of the market. During 1995–97, Indian corporates were reduced to issuing bonds yielding 18–20 per cent as real interest rates rocketed to 12–14 per cent. Companies had to borrow at nominal rates that were over 20 per cent. Inflation was around 10 per cent. In the case of small to medium-sized companies, the real interest rate was often more than 15 per cent. In such a scenario, the differential between returns on equity and those on fixed rate bonds necessitated a downward adjustment in the market which made equity investments unattractive. The amounts raised by corporates at extremely attractive terms via equity issues in 1994 and 1995, both domestically and abroad, were not fully invested until 1995–96. Thus, the investment schedules of major firms were not affected as was evident from the import figures of 1995–96. While an element of consolidation was necessary the following year, industrial investment and production was affected by the high cost of capital during 1995–97. Until Indian companies are able to deliver a reasonable return on their cost of capital, the stockmarket will reflect that state of affairs.

Since the stifling interest rate scenario of 1996, the gradual reduction in the real cost of capital will help stimulate economic activity. The sharp decline in bank credit seen during 1996–97 should reverse in 1997–98 as real interest rates fall below 7–8 per cent. The structural transformations in the Indian economy has led to a rise in the investment rate from 23.6 per cent of GDP in 1993–94 to an estimated 27.4 per cent of GDP in 1995–96. Private sector investment has risen from 13 per cent to 18 per cent over the same period. Complemented by the steady inflow of FDI and FII at \$4 billion, the economy has delivered growth at 6–7 per cent over the last few years. Greater investment in technology and an awareness of increasing investment in the social sectors, particularly in primary education, is set to establish a more viable basis for longer term growth. The agricultural sector's strong performance in 1996–97 will boost demand from the rural sector.

The Indian economy has the potential to step up its rate of growth to the 8–10 per cent level. But, it will not be achieved unless the government is able to address the factors that continue to restrain higher levels of productivity growth; namely high fiscal deficits, low public savings, low investment in infrastructure and in the social sectors, lack of reforms in agriculture and trade, an undeveloped financial sector and the limited role of the private sector. The lack of mechanisms for assessing public sector investment and comparing it with international levels of achievement must hinder achieving higher returns. An intelligent understanding of global practices often results in informed choices.

4 How is Investment to be Financed?

INTRODUCTION

India's policymakers discouraged private consumption by restricting and imposing high tariffs on the import of consumer goods to encourage savings. While it is worrying to contemplate the consequences of an American-style consumerism becoming a way of life in India, it is deplorable that the Indian consumer has paid too high a price for the nation's past policies. The American consumer financed the growth of Japan and the East Asian countries. The rising level of consumerism in Asia today is contributing to international trade and supporting growth in the region. However, the resources of our world, including economic ones, are finite. Thus, the challenge for the next century lies in allocating these resources efficiently so that wealth creation is more equitable.

India's savings rate has risen from 10 per cent of GDP in 1950 to 25 per cent in 1995, but the growth in public savings has been poor. It has declined from a high of 4.9 per cent in 1976–77 to 1.9 per cent in 1995–96. The reforms of 1991 aimed to stem the decline in public savings and to increase public investment in the infrastructural and social sectors. The development potential of foreign savings has been accepted in principle, although in reality such flows remain restricted due to various policy constraints. This chapter analyses the benefits of implementing policies that encourage higher domestic savings while improving the framework for the transfer of foreign savings into areas of the economy where investment is vital to sustaining growth.

To accelerate the growth of GDP from the present 6–7 per cent level to a sustainable 8–10 per cent level over the next decade will require investment to rise from the current 25 per cent level of GDP to over 30 per cent; or to levels seen in East Asian economies. The bulk of this investment has to come from private sources. India cannot depend on foreign savings to fund more than 15–20 per cent of its required capital expenditure. Even this will not be forthcoming unless the right policies are perceived to be in place. Thus, a rise in domestic savings is vital to India's development. Increased public savings is crucial to improving investment in infrastructure and the social sectors which will provide the foundation for growth. Successful privatisation of infrastructure takes time and can rarely replace public spending. Similarly, India cannot aspire for real prosperity without investing in its people, particularly its poor, for which public investment is essential. In the long term, the level of domestic savings will determine India's rate of growth.

DOMESTIC SAVINGS

India's small and indifferent domestic base for the production of consumer goods, with the lack of a social welfare system, meant that private savings received a major boost at the expense of consumption. The private household sector has been the largest contributor to GDS while the contribution of the private corporate sector has been modest. India's private consumption expenditure has been heavily weighted towards food. In 1992–93, expenditure on food accounted for half of private consumption. As a rise in real per capita consumption is the key to an increase in the standard of living, a significant increase in its growth rate is also an indicator of increased savings. Real per capita private consumption increased at the rate of 1 per cent per annum during the 1960s and the 1970s, and accelerated to 2 per cent in the 1980s. Per capita consumption as a share of per capita income declined from 83 per cent in 1960–61 to 64 per cent by 1990–91, reflecting a significant rise in private savings (see Table 4.1).

Table 4.1   Structure of India's private consumption (% of total)

Items	1960–61	1970–71	1980–81	1990–91
Food, beverages & tobacco	60.4	63.4	58.8	53.9
Clothing & footwear	8.9	8.6	11.2	10.7
Rent, water, fuel & power	18.1	14.3	12.6	10.8
Furniture & furnishings	2.3	2.6	2.8	3.4
Transport & communications	2.9	3.2	5.1	10.6
Others	7.4	7.9	9.5	10.6
Per capita consumption (Rs)*	310	602	1462	4003
Per capita income (Rs)*	372	793	2008	6246
Per capita consumption as % of per capita income*	83.3	76.0	72.8	64.0

Note: * Figures based on current prices.
Source: Centre for Monitoring the Indian Economy.

The rate of growth in the savings of India's public sector has been poor. It improved in the second half of the 1970s, reaching its highest level of 4.9

per cent of GDP in 1976–77, but declined significantly in the 1980s. One of the goals of the reform programme was to curtail the growth in public expenditure. The savings rate of the public sector declined to a low of 0.6 per cent in 1993–94. Although a recovery was perceptible in 1994–95, any major restructuring of the public sector that could induce a perceptible reversal in the rising trend in public expenditure has not been attempted. The path to greater public investment is through increased public savings. The implementation of legislation, with possible political ramifications, has held back higher public savings.

India's gross domestic savings (GDS) is significantly lower than in East Asian economies where government policy has been more successful in generating higher savings by implementing policies that encouraged higher returns on savings and investments. Thus, one of the simplest examples of how government policy did not support higher savings in India was the low real rates of interest on private bank deposits prior to the liberalisation of interest rates. In countries with very high inflation rates, the savings rate tends to be low as the value of savings decline rapidly in an inflationary environment. A low level of inflation along with a reasonable real rate of return on savings encourages superior savings as has been the case in many Asian countries. While India has a fairly successful financial sector and one of the largest capital markets in the developing world, real rates of return on savings in bank deposits are unattractive hampering savings in financial assets as the growth in GDS rate is directly linked to real interest rates.

The comparatively higher levels of currency holdings in domestic savings implies that, with increasingly positive and inflation-adjusted rates of interest, the flow of savings from currency into bank deposits will accelerate over the years. The undeveloped banking system has restricted the use of credit as an acceptable mode of payment for the household sector. In spite of the low real rates of return on bank deposits, it comprised 28 per cent of the savings of the household sector in 1991–92. The high proportion of physical assets (like property, gold and silver) as an essential constituent of household savings illustrates a variety of reasons from the inefficiency of the financial sector to the lack of any form of social security. India's black economy has been a huge drain on the real economy as undeclared funds could not find their way into financial savings. They ended up in physical assets like gold, jewellery or property and encouraged private expenditure of all kinds from lavish weddings to other forms of entertainment or gifts creating a culture that transformed bribery and corruption into socially acceptable behaviour. What is not reflected in the official data is the amount of savings-capital that found its way out of the country through various 'unofficial' channels. The share of declared physical assets as a portion of household savings is only an indicator of the undeclared hoardings of physical assets. It has been estimated that India's private savings in gold alone amounts to $100–120 billion. The steady devaluation of the rupee greatly encouraged the buying of gold and silver as a hedge against inflation. Household savings are summarised in Table 4.2.

Table 4.2   Gross financial savings of India's household sector (% of total)

	1970–71	1980–81	1991–92
Currency	16.8	13.4	12.3
Bank deposits	35.7	45.8	27.6
Non-banking deposits	3.2	3.1	3.5
Shares and debentures	3.2	3.4	6.1
Units of UTI	0.7	0.3	14.9
Claims on government	5.0	5.9	7.4
Life insurance	9.8	7.6	10.4
Pension funds	23.2	17.5	18.5
Other*	2.4	3.1	−0.8
Total	100.0	100.0	100.0

Note: * Trade debt
Source: Centre for Monitoring the Indian Economy.

The government has made several sporadic attempts to convert black money into white by launching various amnesty schemes. One was declared by the Finance Minister in his 1997 budget. But a complete overhaul of wages and taxation along with other aspects of Indian bureaucracy will be required to discourage corruption and tax evasion. In reducing personal income tax rates, the Finance Minister has attempted to reduce tax evasion. The government needs to set an example by laying down clear guidelines on the funding of political parties to be able to prosecute individuals effectively. The stockmarket scam of 1992 is an example of how inadequate regulatory and legal framework resulted in a failure to achieve any serious convictions for the violation or misappropriation of funds. Greater transparency in the entire process of economic policymaking will also help reduce speculative action and encourage individuals to keep their savings in financial assets.

It is worth pointing out that in 1960–61 the country's financial savings outstripped savings in physical assets. But, this trend was reversed by 1970–71 as financial savings fell to 40.5 per cent of household savings compared to 59.5 per cent in physical assets (see Table 4.3). While various factors contributed towards such a development, government policies were such that it would have been imprudent to keep savings in financial assets alone. It was during the 1960s that India's savings rate improved but a larger portion of household savings got diverted towards investments in physical assets. This phenomenon coincided with the first substantial devaluation of the currency and the beginning of a kind of economic insecurity among Indians that reflected government policy. It was also the era of the mass exodus of Indians who left for the labour-starved countries of Europe and America in search of better economic opportunities. It also reflected government policy to the extent that the private sector's savings went into property and housing as the government's role in that area was largely non-existent.

Table 4.3   Savings of India's household sector
(as % of total savings of the household sector)

Items	1960–61	1970–71	1980–81	1990–91
Financial Savings	58.9	40.5	39.4	42.9
currency	18.7	10.2	7.4	5.9
deposits	1.4	7.8	13.7	7.8
shares/debentures	8.7	2.8	2.0	7.1
govt. bonds	7.4	–0.4	2.6	6.4
life insurance funds	6.5	5.6	3.9	5.0
pension funds	16.3	14.5	9.7	10.6
Physical Assets	41.1	59.5	60.6	57.1

Source: Centre for Monitoring the Indian Economy.

An analysis of the savings rate versus the investment rate since the late 1950s reveals the extent of India's dependence on capital inflows to sustain its gross domestic capital formation (GDCF). The reliance on external capital peaked at 3.8 per cent of GDP in 1957–58 or at 26 per cent of investment. The share of external inflows to finance investment declined to 0.5 per cent of GDP in 1970–71. Between 1975–76 and 1977–78, savings overtook investments. But, the oil crisis of the 1980s coupled with the lack of adequate policy response meant that the significant achievements of the 1970s were virtually lost during the 1980s. The government made a conscious policy effort to steer clear of overseas financial dependence. But, the share of net capital inflows required to fund domestic investment rose to 3.1 per cent of GDP by 1988–89 and the savings and investment gap rose to 12.7 per cent of GDCF. Net foreign capital inflows peaked at 3.4 per cent of GDP in 1990–91, the year before the economic crisis, representing 12.3 per cent of investment. An effort was made since the reforms to lower this resource gap but it has been achieved at the cost of investment rather than

through increased public savings. The savings and investment gap (S – I) is
summarised in Table 4.4.

Table 4.4   India's savings and investment gap (% of GDP)

Year	Public sector	Private corporate sector	Household sector	GDS	GDCF	S–I gap	S–I gap as % of GDCF
1950–51	1.8	1.0	7.7	10.4	10.2	+0.2	NM
1960–61	2.6	1.7	8.4	12.7	15.7	–3.0	–18.9
1970–71	2.9	1.5	11.3	15.7	16.6	–0.9	–5.5
1980–81	3.4	1.7	16.1	21.2	22.7	–1.5	–6.8
1990–91	1.0	2.8	20.5	24.3	27.7	–3.4	–12.3
1991–92	1.9	3.2	17.7	22.8	23.4	–0.5	–2.3
1992–93	1.5	2.8	17.7	22.1	24.0	–2.0	–8.1
1993–94	0.6	3.6	18.9	23.1	23.6	–0.6	–1.5
1994–95	1.8	3.9	19.2	24.9	26.0	–1.0	–4.0
1995–96E	1.9	4.1	19.5	25.6	27.4	–1.8	–6.6

Source: *Indian Economic Survey*, 1996–97.

The gap between savings and investment is also the key to gauging a
country's dependence on external savings for sustaining its economic development. By 1994–95, the savings–investment gap was at 4.0 per cent of
GDCF and represented 1.0 per cent of GDP. With a rise in gross domestic
savings, GDCF has risen without a high dependence on external capital
inflows. As the import of consumer goods continues to be severely restricted, India's imports are mainly to sustain domestic investment activity. To what extent India's future private consumption will be directed
towards the imports of consumer goods is difficult to predict at this stage of
its development. The possibility of a decline in the savings rate and a deterioration in the resource gap cannot be ruled out. With greater investment
by MNCs in the country, the domestic production of consumer goods is
expected to keep pace with the demand for such products. The rise in private consumption expenditure will affect the gross domestic savings. But,
if public savings were to improve to levels seen in other East Asian countries, the resource gap will not rise with higher private consumption as disposable incomes also tend to rise with economic prosperity.

Role of the Private Corporate Sector

The increasing role of savings in the private corporate sector's investment activity needs to be emphasized as much as the decline in the savings
of the public sector in funding its investment. In 1970–71, the savings of

the private corporate sector accounted for 14 per cent of its investment while that of the public sector was high at over 44 per cent. By 1994–95, the ratio had risen to 26 per cent for the private sector; but for the public sector it had fallen to 20.6 per cent. The private corporate sector has depended increasingly on internal resources for its investment activity as the real cost of capital has been high and equity financing was equally prohibitive prior to the abolition of the Controller of Capital Issues in 1992.

Savings tend to fall during times of crises as in 1967–69 (droughts and wars), or in 1975–77 (the first oil crisis) and in 1990–91. But during the 1980s, savings of the private corporate sector declined as it was a period of relatively buoyant economic activity. While the ratio of savings to investment increased in the 1990s, part of the explanation lies in the lower rate of investment growth. The combination of a reform induced recession and the existence of unutilised capacity in the manufacturing sector meant that investment declined in the aftermath of reforms. But, the private sector's role in investment has been rising since 1993–94, accounting for an estimated 66 per cent of India's GDCF in 1995–96. The public sector was designed to play a dominant role in GDCF but its poor savings record hampered its ability to invest. The capital intensive growth in PEs became increasingly unsustainable as they generated lower savings. By 1990–91, public sector savings accounted for only 10 per cent of public sector investment.

The increase in government borrowing from the banking sector resulted in a 'crowding out' of the private sector. The curtailment of the role of the private sector in India's development was thus a direct result of policy rather than the private sector's failure to invest. An effort has been made since 1991 to allow the private sector a greater role in economic development through higher levels of investment while encouraging the growth in public savings. The implementation of policy changes that will support such activity has taken longer than anticipated to be put in place, but a recovery in the investment activity of the private sector along with increased savings in the public sector, albeit at the cost of investment, is evident. The role of the public sector cannot and should not be reduced overnight. But, its investment focus should shift more towards human development aspects of growth rather than economic aspects. The concern of the government since 1991 has been to reorient expenditure in such a way as to contain the fiscal deficit which has affected private investment negatively. The role of the private sector is summarised in Table 4.5.

Depreciation contributed to the savings of the private corporate sector and has been responsible for boosting its investment activity. Depreciation and taxation allowances accounted for 10 per cent of the private sector's capital formation in 1990–91. One of the results of such a policy was the complex shareholding structure of companies, mostly in the form of conglomerates, as these structures were created by the main shareholders in the company, usually a family group, to exploit the loopholes in India's company law. With the onset of liberalisation and the increasing role of the private retail investor, the policy framework for the protection of the rights of minority shareholders needs to be established clearly. Thus, changes in company law are required to make the prospect of investing in India more investor-friendly.

Table 4.5	The role of the private sector in India's savings and capital formation

Year	I	II	III	IV	V
1960–61	19.2	37.2	64.4	79.4	56.6
1970–71	14.4	44.6	77.1	81.5	63.7
1975–76	12.0	44.0	78.2	77.6	59.6
1980–81	13.7	39.6	78.1	83.8	54.0
1985–86	15.6	28.7	74.7	83.7	58.5
1990–91	18.0	10.4	84.1	95.8	56.0
1991–92	23.3	21.0	89.4	91.6	58.0
1992–93	18.6	17.2	85.5	93.1	63.0
1993–94	27.4	6.5	95.1	97.6	55.4
1994–95	25.9	20.6	89.0	92.8	58.6
1995–96E	22.8	23.6	86.4	92.5	66.0

Notes:
I	Savings of the private corporate sector as a percentage of the gross capital formation of the private corporate sector.
II	Savings of the public sector as a percentage of the gross capital formation of the public sector.
III	Savings of the private corporate sector and the household sector as a percentage of the total gross domestic capital formation.
IV	Savings of the private corporate sector and the household sector as a percentage of the total gross domestic savings in India.
V	Capital formation by the private sector as a percentage of gross domestic capital formation.
Source:	*Indian Economic Survey*, 1996–97.

The exploitation of the depreciation and taxation policies by the private corporate sector also created an extraordinary situation whereby some of the largest Indian companies paid no taxes by a skillful use of these allowances. Such incentives encouraged investment and discouraged savings. Thus, the growth in the savings of the private corporate sector declined while the depreciation rates grew. The provision of such incentives prompted managements to channel funds through various corporate accounts that made analysis and detection difficult. The rationalisation of corporate structures in India is heavily overdue. With the introduction of the changes in company law, it is expected that corporate restructuring in India will provide some interesting investment opportunities. The UF government attempted to address the tax loophole by imposing a minimum alternate tax (MAT) in the face of stiff opposition from vested interest groups in 1996. In 1997, by reducing corporate taxes the pressure has been eased to withdraw MAT.

In India until recently the government borrowed heavily from the banking sector at highly concessional rates. That was detrimental to the economy and every few years necessitated a currency devaluation. The private sector, both corporates and households, were thus forced to subsidise the capital intensity of the public sector. The rate of return on public investment was low and the incentive to save was also non-existent as there was no system of reward for greater efficiency or savings. As the government reduces its borrowing and puts in place policies that reward savings and investment, it will spur revenue collection leading to a virtous cycle of lower public borrowing and higher public investment.

Contribution of the Banking Sector

One of the landmarks in the development of banking in India was the nationalisation of the banks in 1969. Deposits grew at 7 per cent per annum in the 1950s and at 13 per cent in the 1960s. Recognising the need to boost that growth rate, the government responded by nationalising the banking sector. The number of bank branches grew exponentially between 1969 and 1980. The State Bank of India & Associates had 2462 branches in 1969 but had expanded to 12 903 branches by 30 June 1996 with over half of these offices being located in rural centres. The nationalised banks had 4553 outlets among them in 1969, but had 31 055 offices by June 1996. The total number of commercial bank branches grew from 8262 in 1969 to 62 881 in 1995.

During the 1970s, the growth rate of bank deposits was 20.5 per cent and it settled down in the 1980s to 17.6 per cent per annum. An analysis of the comparative rates of growth in the deposits of commercial banks and their investment in government securities' allocation of bank credit during 1981–91 reveals that deposits in the commercial banking sector rose 5.3 times, bank credit by 4.3 times while the enforced investment in government securities went up 7.6 times. As the return on TBs was low, commercial banks were unable to provide a real rate of return to the depositers. Despite that, bank deposits grew at 17.6 per cent between 1981–91. The liberalisation of the banking sector since 1992–93 has meant that these anomalies are being

corrected, albeit at a very slow pace. With the rise in real interest rates on
deposits, it is expected that the momentum of growth should be higher
between 1991–2001. The rate of growth of deposits is shown in Table 4.6.

Table 4.6   Growth of deposits in scheduled commercial
banks in India

Year	Incremental change (Rs bn)	Exchange rate	Deposit inflow (US$ bn)
1985–86	131.33	12.24	10.73
1986–87	172.34	12.78	13.49
1987–88	153.15	12.97	11.81
1988–89	289.07	14.48	19.96
1989–90	282.81	16.65	16.99
1990–91	293.33	17.94	16.35
1991–92	372.94	24.47	15.24
1992–93	390.17	30.65	12.73
1993–94	521.44	31.37	16.62
1994–95	536.30	31.40	17.08
1995–96P	502.19	33.45	15.01

Source: *Indian Economic Survey*, 1996–97.

While the rate of deposit inflow to the banking sector in India has been
impressive, with better inflation-adjusted returns on deposits, it is hoped that
India's savings rate will rise further. The savings rate has been boosted with
higher real interest rates than in the past with a shift in personal savings from
physical assets into financial assets. Consistently superior macroeconomic
management is necessary to bolster confidence in the government's ability
to avoid crises paving the way for a rise in financial savings. In spite of the
low real rate of interest on bank deposits, the addition to deposits in the banking system has ranged between $15–19 billion every year since 1988–89, with
the exception of 1992–93 in the aftermath of the economic crisis. However,
the cost of capital to industry has remained high as government borrowing
continues to 'crowd out' the private sector.

One of the lessons learnt from the various East Asian countries is the role
of government in underpricing capital to achieve rapid industrialisation.
The underpricing of capital was managed by tight fiscal policies and an
outward orientation in trade so that economic efficiency and international
competitiveness was maintained. The lesson to be borne in mind from the
Indian experience is that the government tried emulating that but, in following a policy of central allocation and import substitution, created an
anti-export bias that fostered inefficiency and corruption. Thus, the government had to keep on increasing its borrowing to support its inefficient

PEs with the result that the public sector fiscal deficit remained high and, with it, the cost of capital to the private sector.

While international trade tends to encourage competitiveness, one of the disadvantages of international banking is that credits get channelled principally to those undertakings where governments have been able and prepared to provide the kind of guarantees that international banks demand. In many countries it has resulted in the excessive growth of the public sector. Such lending also tends to generate greater debt liability for the recipient country. In India until recently a high portion of the allocation of bank credit was controlled by the government. The combined credit advances to agriculture and other priority sectors by the public sector banks went up from 14.6 per cent of total bank credit in June 1969 to 36.8 per cent by March 1995, having declined from over 38 per cent in March 1994. The share of priority sector lending in bank credit also varies from state to state ranging from 67 per cent in Haryana and 59 per cent in Bihar to 37 per cent in Gujarat and less than 20 per cent in Maharashtra in March 1995.

As a result of such policies, the private sector's access to capital has been severely restricted. The private sector thus learnt to make the best use of capital. While returns on public sector manufacturing investment in India has been low at under 5 per cent, private manufacturing has yielded fairly respectable returns of 20 per cent or more. Like most other institutions in India, the banking sector became highly 'political'. Banking systems around the world have been used for political gains and India was no exception. But political interference was largely responsible for declining efficiency and productivity across the public sector.

Table 4.7   The growth of credit and deposits outstanding in India's commercial banking sector

Year	Credit/deposit ratio (%)	Incremental credit/incremental deposit ratio (%)
1970–71	79.3	81.21
1975–76	76.8	90.85
1980–81	66.8	61.53
1985–86	66.5	59.92
1990–91	60.3	57.17
1991–92	56.0	32.62
1992–93	56.6	60.89
1993–94	52.2	22.18
1994–95	55.3	75.77
1995–96P	58.6	87.93

Source: Centre for Monitoring the Indian Economy; *Indian Economic Survey*, 1996–97.

The decline in the rate of increase in credit since the 1970s compared to the rate of growth of deposits in the commercial banking sector resulted in the incremental credit to incremental deposit ratio falling steadily from over 90 per cent in 1975–76 to 57 per cent in 1990–91 (see Table 4.7). One of the major reasons for the slower rate of growth in bank credit to the private sector was the mandatory investment in government securities by the commercial banks. Thus, bank credit available for the private sector declined in the late 1980s. The dramatic collapse in the incremental credit to deposit ratio after 1991 reflected the bunching of several factors after the economic crisis of 1991.

The structural adjustment programme led to the contraction of demand in the economy which exacerbated the existing low capacity utilisation rates for the industrial sector. The need for lower investment rates in industry also coincided with greater equity-raising from the capital market by the corporate sector. The high real cost of capital in the banking sector, despite the low credit to deposit ratios, encouraged the corporate sector to raise equity finance as the stockmarket was buoyant and it was possible to issue shares at near market prices domestically. Thanks to greater overseas demand for Indian corporate paper, some of the more established Indian companies were able to issue their shares at a premium to their domestic prices to FIIs. The lower borrowing requirements of the Indian private sector between 1991–92 and 1993–94 was thus reflected in the commercial banking sector's lower credit to deposit ratios. As FIIs' investments declined and industrial investment accelerated, private sector demand for bank credit increased.

The banking sector's ability to provide cheap credit to the private sector is thus greatly influenced by government policies. Higher deposit mobilisation coupled with greater discretion in asset allocation should ensure in the future that the distribution of outstanding credit in the banking sector is done judiciously with a view to increasing reward while reducing risk. Bank credit to the private corporate sector comprised of 64 per cent of commercial banks' resources in the mid-1980s. This ratio fell to 52 per cent by 1993–94 as a result of a weaker demand for credit from the corporate sector. Also, the rate of return on government securities became more attractive as the government started paying market rates for its borrowing. The banking sector's investment in government securities was the highest in 1993–94 at 32 per cent of its overall resources. The higher cash balances with the RBI in 1993–94 and 1994–95 reflected the central bank's policy of monetisation of the FX inflows into the country creating a greater demand for rupees from the RBI.

One of the salient features of the distribution of bank credit is the rise in consumer banking in India. The share of 'individuals' in outstanding bank credit in the country increased from less than 10 per cent in June 1980 to 16 per cent by March 1992. The rise in the share of personal loans and professional services from 2.2 per cent in 1980 to 9.4 per cent in 1990 reflected the rise in private enterprise which was unleashed by the reforms introduced during Rajiv Gandhi's government. This sector of private borrowing was quite distinct from that of the small-scale industrial sector which declined from 18 per cent of bank credit in 1980 to 13 per cent in 1992. The growth in personal loans soon after the economic crisis of 1991 gives us an insight as to how these loans were deployed. It is clear that during this period of India's economic restructuring, outstanding credit to industry had declined. However, the liberalisation of the economy awakened the dormant stockmarket of India. Between January 1991 and June 1992, the Bombay Stock Exchange Index of 30 shares went up over four times, rising from the 1000 level to over 4400. The stockmarket lured the private investor, attracting a large share of individual savings and personal credit. But the collapse of the market thereafter, coupled with the bad delivery of shares, dealt a severe blow to the retail investor's confidence in the market mechanism.

India's stockmarket 'scam' of 1991–92 was a serious setback in enhancing the role of retail investors in the development of the economy. Those retail investors who were naively sucked into the market at the top in 1992 have not been able to recoup their losses. On the other hand, bank deposits have offered greater security and, more recently, decent returns. The opportunity cost to the uninformed investor has been high but no higher than the cost involved in gambling, betting or buying a lottery ticket. Investing is not gambling and investors need to learn that lesson. The Indian market was transformed into more of a casino than a vehicle for serious investment.

The higher deposit rates due to the high levels of inflation combined with the liberalisation of the banking sector has not helped investment in equities. Nor has the secure returns on corporate bonds yielding inflation-adjusted returns. With fixed-term returns of 15–18 per cent being offered to individual depositors with inflation rates around 10 per cent, there is little incentive to enter the risky business of investing in the stockmarket where settlement problems still persist. Greater fiscal prudence by the government will help in a low inflationary environment. But, better market systems need to be put in place to protect the small investor. The establishment of the first depository was a welcome step in aligning the Indian capital market with other developing markets in the world.

The Importance of Financial Sector Reforms

For the government to bring about a successful transfer of savings from physical to financial assets, three basic conditions need to be fulfilled: a stable and low inflation rate, tax incentives to save in financial assets and an established regulatory authority. A higher inflation rate will keep interest rates high and discourage investments in stocks and shares although it will boost bank deposits and other fixed-term savings. But tax incentives to invest in the corporate sector as is the case with personal equity plans, single-company PEPs and exemptions on capital gains tax up to a specified limit in the UK for example, and other such exemptions, should encourage a rise in individual savings in equity-related products if actively introduced in India. India is already one of the largest equity-owning countries in the world; but as a percentage of the adult population the ratio is low at under 10 per cent. Thus, there is scope to attract a higher portion of individual savings into financial assets.

The introduction of an open market in financial products should introduce greater competition and superior service to the customer. But it will also increase the risk of exposing the individual investor to the vagaries of such a system. Hence the critical need for better regulation of financial markets. The growth in insurance products, personal pensions and mortgage-related instruments should attract a significant portion of India's savings into the financial sector. There is potentially a huge debt market in India with government securities, public sector and corporate bonds even though trading is severely restricted as the money market is effectively an inter-bank market. Average daily activity in the debt market has been as low as $10–15 million or about a tenth of the volume of the equity market. The development of a long-term debt market, in both government and corporate debt, will be important for financing infrastructural development as well as in reducing inflationary pressures on the economy.

The combined stimulus of liberalisation and foreign involvement in the growth of the insurance sector in India will impact upon the funds pooled for investment by the insurers. Given India's current low insurance density, compared to other East Asian countries and India's growing middle class, any increase in insurance density will mobilise substantial funds that could be made available for infrastructural development. In the UK, for example, during 1994–95 approximately 30 per cent of the government's securities were held by insurers. Thus, the presence of a well-developed debt market assists not only in increasing funds for investment but also reduces inflationary pressures in the economy. If the Indian government is to avoid the inflationary path of financing its deficits, it must be able to float debt instruments in the market.

The investment profile of the country's biggest insurer, the Life Insurance Corporation of India (LIC) reveals the extent to which the LIC invests in government securities. Thus, liberalisation of the insurance sector should release funds for the private corporate sector and other commercial activities without affecting the government's ability to finance its deficits. The LIC is required to invest 75 per cent of its funds in central and state government securities and in socially-oriented sectors. Only 25 per cent of its funds are allowed in corporate sector investments. In 1995–96, the LIC invested Rs 64.85 billion in central government securities, Rs 11.39 billion in state government securities and other government guaranteed marketable securities, and a further Rs 18.41 billion went towards socially-oriented loans. The Rs 34.06 billion that was invested in corporate investments represented a trebling of investment in that sector since 1993–94. On 31 March 1995, Rs 427.03 billion rupees or 76 per cent of the LIC's funds were invested in government-related securities, with Rs 81.08 billion invested in such instruments during 1994–95. A general insurance company in India is permitted to invest up to 25 per cent of its assets in other than government approved investments. The government guidelines also stipulate that 45 per cent of the accretions be invested in socially-oriented sectors. This limit used to be 70 per cent prior to 1 April 1995. Thus, the fiscal deficit remains the major obstacle to freeing up allocation norms for provident and insurance funds which could be directed more commercially.

While India has had a functioning stockmarket for most of this century, the Capital Issues (Control) Act of 1947 meant that the pricing of capital issues was in the hands of the Controller of Capital Issues (CCI). In the past, getting an allocation in a placement of shares by an established company was like winning a lottery because the issues were grossly underpriced and assured an attractive rate of return to the investor. In other words, the investor took no risk at all while the company issuing the shares faced significant dilution as the new shares were usually issued as par value or at a slight premium to par value rather than at market value. But the market did not take cognisance of earnings per share figures, return on equity or on capital employed. Indian price to earnings ratios have been linked more closely to the standing and reliability of the management in the market as that determines the reliability of a company's declared earnings as well as its stated returns on capital employed.

The crucial role of the capital market in servicing the investment needs of the country has been recognised. Steps were taken to enhance that role by setting up the requisite regulatory authority to oversee that process. Reforms with regard to market-determined pricing of new issues, the flotation of Euroissues, foreign institutional investment in domestic stocks, private mutual funds along with the privatisation of PEs have radically altered the scope of the capital market. The Securities and Exchange Board of

India (SEBI) is the regulatory body armed with statutory powers to protect investors and regulate all financial intermediaries. The stock exchanges are preparing for a substantial growth in business. India's capital market has achieved enormous growth since the early 1980s. The share of the primary market in channelling private savings into investment in the private sector has never been more buoyant.

It was not until the abolition of the CCI in 1991–92 that the private corporate sector was allowed 'free pricing' in its equity issues. The total number of capital issues in the domestic market more than doubled between 1991–92 and 1992–93 (see Table 4.8). The total amount of money raised through public issues has also seen significant growth since 1991–92. The net contribution of funds raised through capital issues to gross domestic capital formation went up from 5.6 per cent in 1988–89 to 11.1 per cent in 1994–95, having peaked at 12.7 per cent in 1993–94 as capital formation was relatively weak that year. Liberalisation has enabled the capital market to play a significant role in transferring private savings into investments, but the rate of growth of private corporate sector investment has been lower than the rate of growth of capital-raising by companies. Hence, the rise in the ratio of funds raised to gross domestic capital formation as the funds raised by the private corporate sector could not be invested in areas of the economy that needed investment due to the lack of an adequate policy framework.

An analysis of the distribution of capital raising by the corporate sector, both private and public, reveals the shift from bonds and non-convertible paper to equity issues once the office of the CCI was abolished. The high level of issuance of bonds by PEs prior to the securities scam was reduced considerably thereafter. Many of the PE-bonds were treated as sovereign securities due to the state ownership of these enterprises. The greater flexibility and enterprise of the private sector is also reflected in the greater fund-raising activity by the private sector than by the public sector. The major mode of capital issuance was through public issues (see Table 4.9).

The deregulation of the mutual funds sector was also reflected in the increased capital-raising activity by the private sector mutual funds which rose from 8 per cent of the total in 1988–89 to 16 per cent in 1993–95 (see Table 4.9). The development of the mutual fund industry has been a recent phenomena in India starting in October 1986. The mutual fund sector is dominated by the Unit Trust of India (UTI) and the public sector banks. The entry of the private sector in the mutual fund sector is even more recent; permission for private mutual funds was issued in late 1993. There were 31 mutual funds, excluding the UTI, registered with Securities and Exchange

Table 4.8   Funds raised via public capital issues in India (Rs billions)

	1988–89	1989–90	1990–91	1991–92	1992–93	1993–94	1994–95	1995–96
Number of issues	253	379	351	497	1034	1143	1666	1725
Amount raised	54.6	122.8	110.5	145.9	167.5	243.7	276.2	208.0
As % of GDS	6.5	11.9	8.7	10.4	10.8	12.9	11.6	7.4
As % of GDCF	5.6	10.7	7.6	10.1	9.9	12.7	11.1	6.9

Source: Indian Economic Survey, various issues.

Table 4.9 The distribution of capital issues (%)

	1988–89	1989–90	1990–91	1991–92	1992–93	1993–94	1994–95
By Type of Securities							
Equity	19.4	15.4	38.4	45.8	66.8	60.9	74.5
Convertible debentures	32.1	42.8	23.0	25.5	24.9	21.9	17.9
Non-convertible debentures	5.5	18.7	5.3	1.0	5.0	8.3	6.3
PSU bonds	43.0	23.0	33.3	27.8	3.3	8.9	1.4
By Mode of Issue							
Public issues	46.0	36.1	43.9	48.4	56.1	50.1	54.9
Rights issues	24.9	27.6	21.6	23.5	38.6	33.8	24.9
Private placement	29.1	36.3	34.5	28.2	5.3	16.1	20.2
By Ownership							
Private sector	54.5	55.1	39.9	37.1	63.3	54.3	74.6
Public sector	37.7	36.2	35.4	27.8	4.8	26.2	6.9
Public mutual funds	7.9	8.7	24.7	35.1	31.9	15.8	15.6
Private mutual funds	0.0	0.0	0.0	0.0	0.0	3.7	2.8

Source: Centre for Monitoring the Indian Economy.

Board of India in December 1996. Of those registered, 10 were in the public sector and 21 in the private sector with 17 mutual funds having foreign participation in their asset-management companies. The role of mutual funds in acting as a conduit for savings into investments has been an established feature of the Indian market. But, like most consumer products in India, there has been limited choice. Due to the slow pace of change in the financial sector as in the rest of the economy, the consumer has not benefited from technological upgradation or improvements in the quality of service in the sector. The level of service taken for granted in most developed countries is simply unheard of in most parts of India.

Table 4.10   Capital raised by mutual funds in India

Year	Total (Rs bn)	% of GDS	% of GDCF
1989–90	10.72	1.0	0.9
1990–91	27.29	2.1	1.8
1991–92	51.29	3.6	3.6
1992–93	97.00	6.2	5.7
1993–94	74.93	3.9	3.9
1994–95	42.75	1.8	1.7
1995–96	65.08	2.3	2.2
1996–97*	21.67	NA	NA

Note: * April–December.
Source: CMIE; *Indian Economic Survey*, 1995–96 and 1996–97.

While the retail investor in India continues to operate in the primary market, mutual funds offer the best solution to holding a diversified portfolio as secondary market broking services are not easily available. With the establishment of a central depository and electronic broking, it is expected that this trend will change enabling a more active participation from the retail sector. Equally, with greater competition in the mutual fund industry, the private investor stands to benefit from better performance and lower charges. Despite the elimination of barriers to entry in the mutual fund industry, the UTI continues to dominate the market (see Table 4.11). The performance of domestic mutual funds has not been encouraging during 1995–96 and 1996–97 aggravating the decline in investor confidence in such vehicles. The high real interest rate environment is not beneficial for equity investing.

Foreign mutual fund specialists have not been able to make any significant impact in the domestic market. Apart from Morgan Stanley Asset Management, no other FII has been able to raise funds with any success. Various FIIs, from Alliance Capital to Templeton, have set up domestic

mutual fund capabilities without much success in their fund-raising activities as most lack any long-term track record in the management of Indian
investments. Morgan Stanley raised about $300 million locally in India in
January 1994. Domestic market conditions since March 1995 have not
been conducive for equity investments and have affected fund-raising activity. It is inevitable, though, that the UTI will have to contend with some
serious competition in the future. The good news for the local investor is
that with the entry of major global players, the mutual fund industry will
benefit from greater competition.

Table 4.11   Mutual funds' ownership of market capitalisation

Mutual funds	Market value of total investments* (Rs billion)	% share of total market capitalisation
Unit Trust of India	596.19	13.09
Canbank	28.27	0.62
State Bank	28.02	0.62
Life Insurance Corp.	15.03	0.33
Bank of India	12.94	0.28
General Insurance Corp.	7.05	0.15
Indian Bank	4.47	0.10
Punjab National Bank	0.83	0.02
Private Funds	21.26	0.47
Total	714.05	15.68

Note: * As on 31 March 1995.
Source: ING Baring Securities (India) Pvt Ltd.

The development of the National Stock Exchange (NSE) has provided
the necessary impetus for change in the country's oldest and largest stock
exchange, the Bombay Stock Exchange (BSE). The NSE provides screen-
based, computerised trading and market-making along with short settlement cycles backed by a central depository system. The Over-the-Counter
Exchange of India started operating in October 1992 and its main objective
is to promote small companies (equity base of less than US$1 million).
Intermediaries are also gearing up for change via corporatisation,
recapitalisation and forming strategic alliances with international investment banks in order to rise to the changing needs of the global marketplace.
A national clearing and depository system is being put in place. All this has
contributed to a rapid rise in the market capitalisation as a percentage of
GDP since 1991 (Table 4.12).

It is clear that the Indian capital market has come a long way since 1875
when it was set up as 'The Native Share and Stockbrokers' Association'.
There are 21 stock exchanges today with over 7200 companies listed country-

wide and some 4700 companies listed on the BSE alone. The turnover ratio of the BSE at 15.6 per cent is significantly lower than most of the East Asian markets like Malaysia (58.7 per cent), Thailand (60.9 per cent) and Korea (174.1 per cent). But, it is higher than that of other developing markets like South Africa (8.5 per cent) or Chile (9.5 per cent). In order to provide the market with greater depth it is important that the number of participants increase. India's 'big-bang' initiated with the liberalisation of the financial sector in 1991–92 which constituted an essential aspect of reforms as efficient financial intermediation is the key to development. The policy aim is to improve the operational efficiency of the financial system whereby it is able to take on its role as an efficient allocator of economic resources.

Table 4.12   Market capitalisation as percentage of GDP

Year	%
1989–90	12.1
1990–91	20.6
1991–92	57.4
1992–93	25.1
1993–94	49.7
1994–95	48.2
1995–96	45.8

Source: ING Baring Securities (India) Pvt Ltd.

Financial services constitute an important constituent of any developing country's infrastructure and are crucial to rapid economic evolution. The extent to which India's industrial sector is represented in the total market capitalisation also gives us an idea of its role in the evolution of that sector in the economy. As deregulation in the service sector has already begun and in some areas the policy framework for private investment is already in place, the service sector is poised to attract a significant portion of new investment based on its huge potential for growth. Indian legislation in the name of a social democratic regime had not allocated any major role to the private sector in the development of the service or the infrastructural sectors of the economy. Even in the industrial sector, the private sector was offered a limited role as the public enterprises (3.5 per cent) and government departments (11.8 per cent) constituted over half of the industrial sector. The socialist bias of the policymakers meant that the unregulated small-scale sector was also represented and its contribution to GDP was 6 per cent. The private sector's role was thus confined to 7 per cent of GDP in 1991–92.

India's Privatisation Initiative and its Impact on Savings

India's capital market reflects less than 10 per cent of the economy. The composition of India's market capitalisation is set to change significantly over the next decade as it begins to reflect the full spectrum of the economy. As the process of liberalisation deepens, the market is set to benefit from privatisation as well as from greater market orientation of the economy. The current wave of liberalisation in the developing world is a reversal of a trend in the 1950s when governments intervened in their economies with a view to accelerate the development process by investing in key industries such as finance, raw materials, transportation, telecommunication and heavy industry. Soft budget constraints with an emphasis on political goals like providing employment and subsidising user costs resulted in a grossly inefficient public sector. As the PEs became unsustainable, governments started to sell these oversized and inefficient public sector companies by privatising them.

The Indian government's privatisation programme has been slow to materialise. An attempt was made to divest up to 20 per cent of government holdings in various PEs to introduce competition, efficiency and accountability to the PEs while raising funds for investment and reducing public expenditure and encouraging wider public ownership of equity. A large portion of India's initial disinvestment of PEs was made to the UTI and other public sector mutual funds as it would have been difficult to get a reasonable price in the market for such a placement. As the ownership of PEs remained with the government, it was difficult to get substantial private investment. While there may be no justification for divesting shares of PEs at greatly reduced valuations to FIIs, the problem was mainly in assessing the price that the market would be willing to pay.

Such an impasse arises when private investors are unsure of the future direction and policy environment in sustaining the privatisation effort. The absence of adequate economic and institutional framework in the shape of a competitive private sector, effective regulatory bodies and appropriate economic policies can mar the success of any privatisation effort. Thus, large-scale privatisations must form part of a comprehensive reform plan for only then can it contribute to the economy. It is often the case that the absence of the infrastructure to support the privatisation effort leads to its failure. Thus, governments get caught in a kind of privatisation trap even as the process is meant to create that infrastructure. The experience of the Indian government has been no different as it has been unsuccessful in benefiting from its own policy of opening up the stock market to FIIs.

A combination of inadequate policies, bad market sense and ill-informed choices meant that the government failed to place the equity of its more successful PEs with FIIs. The failure of the high-profile overseas placement of Videsh Sanchar Nigam Limited (VSNL) is a case in point even though the government has been successful since then in divesting its holdings in VSNL along with other PEs like Indian Petrochemicals Corporation Limited, National Aluminium Company Limited, Steel Authority of India Limited and The State Bank of India to FIIs. A strong privatisation programme gives a signal that the government has become open to private enterprise and that foreign investors can anticipate an improved regulatory environment. A sustained privatisation effort thus leads to a rapid rise in investment inflows not only directly related to the sale of the PEs but indirectly by attracting additional investments to refurbish and improve the existing assets which studies have shown to have been as high as 90 per cent of the value of the original investment.

In India, the privatisation effort has been faltering. The government has not divested more than 49 per cent of its holdings in any of the PEs. There are over 245 PEs with an equity capital of over Rs 580 billion in government hands. This is not taking into account the various government departments whose scope for economic activity is much larger than that of the combined PEs. The government is keen to obtain a fair price for its divestment and yet it will be difficult to secure that in the domestic context. While privatisation proceeds could help with the fiscal situation, the failure of the government to raise even the amounts budgeted for is an indication of the lack of political will to implement its plans. Since June 1992, the share of the PEs in India's market capitalisation has improved to approximately 38 per cent. This is set to improve with the government's ongoing privatisation effort.

The evolution of India's stockmarket will be a test of the efficacy of market forces as a means of equitable economic growth. If the introduction of the market mechanism ends up not benefiting a significant portion of the economy, its reign will be short-lived. While the redistribution in market capitalisation has begun, its contribution to poverty alleviation is far more difficult to quantify. Having defined the Indian market's limitations, it must be pointed out that no industry accounts for more than 12–15 per cent of market capitalisation. The top 40 business houses account for less than a third of the market and the public sector represents just over a third. The top 220 companies account for 85 per cent of market capitalisation and there are over 1250 companies whose market capitalisation is less than $5 million.

The outcome of India's policies to date has led to a rise in savings though not in the public sector. Thus, India's savings rate remains low compared to other East Asian countries. Among the world's 'super-savers', Singapore saves around 48 per cent of its GDP, Korea 36 per cent, China 39 per cent, Hong Kong 35 per cent and Taiwan 28 per cent. One of the factors contributing to this accelerated growth in savings has been the high contribution of government savings. Asian governments have contributed over 15 per cent to national savings during 1983–92, compared to India's paltry 2 per cent. During this period in both Africa and Latin America, where the overall savings rate has been low, the public sector made significant contributions to national savings; 5 per cent in Africa and 15 per cent in Latin America. The relationship between GDP growth and savings is a circular one. Increase in per capita GDP raises the level of savings which in turn spurs GDP growth. In India, an increase in public savings will boost overall savings which will contribute to higher investment and growth. Given the link between growth and savings, higher growth should translate into higher domestic savings through improved government budgets and higher private savings.

FOREIGN SAVINGS

Capital flows to developing countries have been rising steadily over the past decade. In the early 1980s, until the international debt crisis, private capital flows to developing countries were mostly in the form of syndicated bank loans. In the 1990s, developing country governments and corporations, both public and private, have been raising resources in the international capital markets by issuing securities. The rise in portfolio investment along with FDI meant that in the early 1990s half of the external financing of developing economies came from private sources and went to private destinations. Net capital flows to developing countries grew from $75 billion in 1988 to over $230 billion in 1995. Most of this growth in capital flows occurred in 1990–93, when flows doubled from $100 billion in 1990 to $207 billion in 1993.

Such a shift in private resources was made possible due to the improvements in the macroeconomic performance of the developing countries along with the massive restructuring of their economies which enabled the private sector to play a dominant role. The growth in world trade has also helped in the rise in private capital flows to developing economies. Emerging markets (EMs) have been of interest to a wide group of non-bank investors mostly interested in maximising the returns on their portfolio investments without significantly enhancing their risk profile. Greater integration of the world via global communication networks and developments in information technology has resulted in up-to-date market information being available in financial centres around the world. Investors are thus able to respond to these changes by taking a more global approach to their asset allocation. However, capital flows to EMs represents a marginal share in the capital resources and the GDP of the industrialised countries. Thus, the $207 billion capital flow to EMs in 1993 represented 1 per cent of the GDP of the OECD countries and 5 per cent of the OECD's gross domestic capital formation.

The monetary developments in the industrialised nations, particularly the decline in the short-term interest rates in the US, also contributed to this capital outflow. The diversification benefits of EM investments in a global portfolio by increasing reward-to-risk ratios have been established. It would be reasonable to assume that substantial outflows will occur over the decades from the industrial countries to the developing countries as they make the necessary adjustments in their demographic transition. Assuming that over this period the working population of the industrial countries remains unchanged, the fact that a relatively larger portion of the population is getting closer to the retirement phase of their life will imply that their investment needs will decline while their savings will rise. Private savings in developed countries has also had to rise to compensate for inadequate government pension.

It is feasible to assume that the industrialised countries will choose to run current account surpluses with a view to accumulating foreign assets whose superior income could help pay the pensions of an ageing population. The other major consideration for the industrial countries is the problem of immigration. Capital flows will ensure that the incentives for economic migration will be curtailed. In fact, it might even reverse the cycle as the shortage of technical skills in the developing world can be supplied from the surpluses in the industrialised one. Such a scenario, however, will not materialise if the industrial nations are forced to inflate their way out of unemployment, under-employment and the attendant social problems.

From the developing countries' standpoint, with growing populations and ever-increasing demand for capital investments compared to their ability to save, such capital inflows can prove beneficial. The main advantage for the recipient of these equity flows is the greater risk-bearing by the investors themselves and the reduced cost of capital unlike the syndicated bank lending of the 1970s. Other benefits include better incentives for investment management under private-to-private flows which result in the development of the domestic capital markets and greater resource mobilisation at lower costs.

Despite the increasing capital flows to developing countries, the foreign financing of investments in EMs has made only a marginal contribution to their fixed investment, particularly in Asia (see Table 4.13). In the case of India, the economic liberalisation in 1991 facilitated foreign inflows but they did not amount to more that 6–7 per cent of gross domestic capital formation during 1993–95 when gross domestic investment in the country was not particularly buoyant. The experience of Asia suggests that high levels of domestic investment and economic growth rates are sustained by higher levels of gross domestic savings. The lower rate of dependence on foreign investment among East Asians in financing the later stages of their development made them less vulnerable to shifts in capital flows. But their lower exposure to such risks also attracted higher capital inflows.

Table 4.13   Foreign financing of investment in emerging markets

Region	Percentage share of investment	
	1981–89	*1990–94*
Africa	14.8	22.2
Asia	1.7	1.5
Latin America	5.3	10.2
Middle East & Eastern Europe	8.6	15.6
All Emerging Markets	6.0	5.8

Source: IMF: *World Economic Outlook*, May 1995.

One of the major concerns for developing countries in an environment of higher capital inflows is the real appreciation of the exchange rate if the rate of capital inflow greatly exceeds the investment needs of the country which hinders the growth rate of the economy via lower exports. Thus, limiting the current account deficit to a sustainable level becomes the key aim of economic policymaking. The enhanced role of the private sector does not imply that the government has no further responsibility in providing adequate institutional framework for channelling such flows. The other issue that needs to be spelled out clearly is whether such capital flows are being directed towards the most productive investments.

The problem in answering such a question lies in defining which sectors of the economy stand to benefit most from such capital infusion. As most capital transfers are at the private level, and the private sector's role in crucial areas of the economy like infrastructure or education and health remains restricted, the question often asked is 'are these capital flows serving the development needs of the economy?' However, if the government can relieve itself of its commercial responsiblities which can be taken over by the private sector, the government can then focus on human development issues. Thus, foreign capital flows can indirectly serve the development needs of the economy. The entire question of social sector development is a complex one when it comes to the issue of funding and equity as government funding comes out of private resources.

Despite the major developments in the integration of global finance, there is no single source that research can access to arrive at an accurate database of fund flows. One can only depend on approximate figures and broad trends. Net portfolio investment in developing countries registered a fourfold rise between 1983–89 and 1990–93. The performance of the stockmarkets of developing countries also accelerated this phenomenon. The combined market capitalisation of the 32 developing countries' stock markets followed by the International Financial Corporation increased from $67 billion in 1982 to $770 billion by the end of 1992, a staggering elevenfold increase. Capital inflow was partly responsible for this growth in market capitalisation. The capital flows are summarised in Table 4.14.

Table 4.14 Capital flows to developing countries (US$ billion)

Annual averages	1977–82	1983–89	1990–93
Net foreign direct investment	11.2	13.3	34.2
Net portfolio investment	−10.5	6.5	26.8
Long-term capital flow	42.1	−5.7	−5.9
Short-term capital flow	−12.3	−5.3	38.7
Total net inflow	30.5	8.8	93.8

Source: International Monetary Fund.

In the past, thanks to an overregulated investment environment, foreign direct investment (FDI) into India was among the lowest in the world. Asia received 44.5 per cent of FDI into developing countries between 1988–91; India received 0.5 per cent reflecting its share of global trade. As investment tends to follow trade, it is expected that India's share of FDI will improve with its increasing share of global trade. With greater economic liberalisation and improvements in the country's infrastructure, it is anticipated that the impediments to FDI flows into India will also disappear.

Cross-border equity flows have grown substantially since the mid-1980s (see Table 4.15). The trend towards increasing internationalisation of equity investment is so clearly established now that approximately 10 per cent of all quoted stocks worldwide are today in the hands of non-domestic investors. The steady rise of investment in EMs has meant that when total global flows declined, the portion allocated to EMs remained high as was the case in 1990. Unfortunately, these funds had no way of being invested in India as direct foreign portfolio investment was permitted in September 1992. Apart from

Investing in India

a successful record of policy reforms and macroeconomic performance, appropriate institutional structures need to be in place for the management of foreign capital flows. In India, the role of foreign investment was acknowledged at a time when the country was recovering from an economic crisis.

Table 4.15   Net cross-border equity flows to markets (US$ billion)

Market	1986	1987	1988	1989	1990	1991	1992	1993	1994
North America	19.8	20.3	−3.7	13.8	−15.9	9.6	−4.0	32.3	6.3
Europe	33.4	29.7	22.8	47.1	15.3	23.4	24.8	68.5	29.1
Japan	−15.8	−42.8	6.8	7.0	−13.3	46.8	9.0	20.4	45.5
Emerging markets	3.3	5.9	3.5	10.1	13.2	15.8	21.2	62.4	39.9
Pacific Rim	3.4	6.0	2.5	3.4	3.9	4.7	11.0	40.1	16.0
Latin America	0.2	0.4	0.7	7.0	10.0	11.2	9.6	20.0	14.9
Other emerging	−0.3	−0.6	0.3	−0.3	−0.7	−0.1	0.6	2.3	9.0
Rest of the world	1.2	3.5	3.5	8.6	3.9	5.1	0.9	12.8	−1.8
Total	42.0	16.4	32.9	86.6	3.2	100.6	51.9	196.4	119.0
Emerging markets as % of total	8.0	35.8	10.6	11.6	413.8	15.7	40.8	31.8	33.5

Source: ING Baring Securities (India) Pvt Ltd.

There have been significant changes in the Indian capital market since 1991–92; both the economy and the industrial sector have recovered from the economic crisis without the need for any major foreign equity flows. But the overall decline in gross domestic capital formation (GDCF) since the economic restructuring indicates that there were severe bottlenecks to private investments. As already indicated, the government sector dominated corporate management and with it the investment decisions in all major sectors of the economy. Foreign investment in India is summarised in Table 4.16.

Table 4.16   Foreign investment in India (US$ million)

	1990–91	1991–92	1992–93	1993–94	1994–95	1995–96
FDI	97	135	313	586	1314	1929
FII	0	0	0	1665	1503	2009
Euro-equity & others	5	4	242	1984	2078	205
Total foreign investment	102	139	555	4235	4895	4143
As % of GDCF	0.1	0.2	0.6	0.9	1.7	2.1

Source: *Indian Economic Survey*, 1996–97.

As the objective of India's structural adjustment was to reduce the high expenditure of the government and open up areas of the economy to private investment, it is not surprising that GDCF declined in the public sector. India's private sector has responded well to economic reform, planning a strong economic expansion led by investment and export growth. While obstacles to private investment remain, the private sector has sizeable investment plans in infrastructural related areas like telecoms, petrochemicals, oil exploration and power. FDI approvals into India have shown a major advance since 1991 but actual inflows remain low due to delays in implementation in policy changes.

The Development of an Off-shore Indian Market

The problems associated with investing in India's local stockmarket and the demand for Indian equity by FIIs led to the evolution of an off-shore Indian market. Changes already implemented in the regulatory and supervisory structures in the securities and exchange practices in various developed countries also helped Indian corporates to make public offering of their shares in the stockmarkets of developed countries. The passing of Rule 144A and Regulation S of the SEC in the USA had ushered in the use of American Depository Receipts (ADRs), Global Depository Receipts (GDRs) and other equity-related vehicles that could be used by non-US firms to raise capital in the US.

The concept of the ADR was structured by Morgan Guaranty Trust Company in 1927. These are equity-based instruments which are publicly traded in the US stock market. Each unit of an ADR can represent a multiple or a fraction of underlying shares. ADR holders have all the rights of shareholders. The GDR is similar to an ADR except that it can be listed in several securities exchanges around the world. It was introduced by Citibank in an attempt to increase the investor base for raising capital. GDRs are traded under a global book entry settlement system through Euroclear and CEDEL, among others.

Reliance Industries was the first Indian company to issue equity to FIIs by placing its GDRs in the international market in May 1992 at the height of the domestic stockmarket scam. Reliance raised US$150 million to finance a gas cracker. Morgan Stanley acted as their advisers cum investment bankers. The stockmarket in India collapsed as the scam began to unwind and FIIs were left with significant losses on their initial Indian investment. Thus, the Indian GDR market was virtually stillborn and it was not until November 1993 that Aditya Birla came forward with GDRs for his flagship company, Grasim Industries. Mr Birla placed his company's shares with FIIs at a small discount to the local market price. Grasim Industries gave investors exposure to India's largest producer and the world's second largest producer of viscose staple fibre. The company also produces cement and sponge iron. The GDR issue of Grasim was offered at a price to earnings ratio (P/E) of 12 times for a company with an established record of 15–20 per cent earnings per share (EPS) growth. Taking into account inflation and return on capital employed in India, the stock was being offered at a reasonable valuation to foreign investors.

By March 1997, well over 50 Indian companies had raised $6–7 billion via the issuance of GDRs and convertible bonds. It is interesting to note that as the market advanced, so did FIIs' appetite for Indian equity. Foreign investors were no longer worried about the high valuation of Indian shares. In fact, Mr Birla himself was able to command a premium on the domestic market prices of some of his later GDR issues; such was the demand for Indian equities. FIIs were prepared to pay a premium on top of an inflated share price in the domestic market taking the view that GDRs attracted no capital gains tax in addition to dispensing with the settlement risk associated with dealing in the local market. The total market capitalisation of the off-shore instruments for investments into India in December 1996 amounted to approximately $12 billion comprising of GDRs ($4–5 billion), Convertible Bonds ($1–2 billion) and Country Funds ($5–6 billion). This cumulatively represents less than 10 per cent of India's market capitalisation.

FIIs were allowed to invest directly in the local market in September 1992. But neither the Stock Exchanges nor the country's major providers of custodial services foresaw the problems that would arise as a result of FII investment. The failure to implement the necessary improvements in custodial services to facilitate the flows which started in July 1993 meant that by January 1994, FIIs were facing significant settlement risks in investing in local shares. The fact that local investors had faced settlement problems for decades was of no consolation to FIIs who had the option of taking their funds elsewhere. The off-shore GDR market developed in 1994 as a result of the continuing demand for Indian paper by FIIs and their inability to access it directly.

A form of forward trading, called *badla*, was manipulated by the GDR issuers for enhancing their share prices before the issue, as the pricing of a GDR was linked to the domestic price of the stock. The small number of investment players in the market made such blatant rigging of prices easy to implement and detect. Apart from the UTI, most of the other fund management companies have been recent entrants, thus the natural volume of trading in equities is low. The *badla* market was initially devised to keep the wheels of the market running without incurring a huge cost to the individual participants. *Badla*, like any other system in India, was open to abuse and severe protestations by FIIs led to SEBI's decision to abolish *badla* as well as to improve the overall market mechanism. However, since *badla* was not substituted by any other version of options' trading in the market, it meant that the market ground to a virtual standstill when FIIs withdrew from the market. The SEBI banned *badla* in March 1994, a month before VSNL's privatisation issue. Having paid fancy prices for some second-rate Indian companies, FIIs refused to pay up for India's overseas telecommunication provider.

Thus, India's international privatisation experience was quite different to that of other developing countries. In 1990, the Chilean government had raised $98 million by selling a part of Telefonos de Chile. In 1991, Argentina raised $364 million by issuing GDRs in Telefonica de Argentina. In May 1991, Mexico carried out the largest single issue of ADRs when the government privatised 15 per cent of TELMEX for $2.4 billion. In the first half of 1993, 75 per cent of equity portfolio flows to Argentina's privatised state oil company, YPF, came from foreign investors. YPF raised $3.04 billion in total. Between 1988–93, 69 transactions involved portfolio equity investments for a total of $10.6 billion or 11 per cent of total privatisation revenues for the developing world. During 1988–93, 671 of the 2279 privatisations in developing countries involved foreign investors. In terms of sales volume, foreign investment amounted to $33 billion or 34 per cent of the total revenue generated by privatisation. FDI was the main mechanism through which foreign investors participated in most of these privatisation programmes, contributing $22.5 billion. South Asia, dominated by India, was not the beneficiary of these funds.

Several dedicated country funds for India were also launched in 1993 and 1994 to capitalise on the surge in demand for Indian investments. Most EM portfolio investors were caught underweight in a rising market and were prepared to pay a price for enhancing their short-term returns. However, with *badla* banned and the inevitable slowdown in the flow of funds into EMs after the Mexican crisis and the reversal of the global interest rate cycle in early 1995, the magic of an ever-rising Indian stockmarket was no longer working.

The correction of the Indian stockmarket began in September 1994 with news of Reliance Industries' decision to place some shares privately with the UTI, followed by the merger of the company with two of its subsidiaries in a share swap that was not perceived to benefit Reliance's shareholders. This was a swift reminder of the risks of investing in India. This lesson was followed by the plague in Surat which cast a shadow on the prospects for export growth and highlighted the poor infrastructural development in the country. It also coincided with the uncertainty surrounding the prospects for the central government in the aftermath of the Congress Party's massive defeat in the November 1994 elections in Maharashtra, the state that had benefited most from India's liberalisation.

The collapse of the Mexican market had a profoundly negative impact on all EMs. Most foreign investors became sellers of emerging market funds. India's General Election which was due by May 1996 did not help investments into the country by various firms who recognised India's long-term potential but saw no short-term reason to get invested in the market. The inconclusive outcome of the elections did not inspire confidence in the ability of the 13-member coalition government to be able to address the difficult policy issues ahead. Last but not least, the spectacular performance of the US and UK markets through 1995 to 1997 made it unnecessary to take the risk of investing in EMs.

If cheap capital is critical to cost reduction for companies, then it is clear who the short-term winners are, provided the money raised via GDRs and convertible bonds is invested efficiently by the management of these firms. Some of these companies had succeeded in raising foreign capital that amounted to more than their domestic market capitalisation. India is destined to become a major consumer of goods and services and substantial investments will be required to keep increasing capacity, productivity and distribution facilities to meet these demands. It is inevitable that Indian companies will be opportunistic in their fund raising activity. Minority shareholders' rights are not respected by the majority shareholders who also happen to be the 'promoters' or the families who own and manage these companies. As FIIs are allowed to own up to 30 per cent of a company, there is hope that these irregular practices can be curbed via FII intervention. India is underowned internationally, and if both investors and corporates behave in a more responsible manner, both parties could benefit in the long term.

It is true that in the initial stages of liberalisation of any EM, the return of flight capital tends to be motivated by short-term speculative motives rather than long-term, fundamentally driven investment motives. This behaviour was noticeable in the flow of non-resident Indian (NRI) funds into India prior to the economic crisis of 1991. But, FIIs have also proven to be quite speculative in their investment behaviour. The development of the GDR market has been interesting to the extent that it is an off-shore, unregulated market, where the closing prices of GDRs vary between market-makers. India appears to have succeeded in exporting its market inefficiencies abroad. The problem with the Indian GDR market continues to be wide margins and a lack of transparency in dealing. Less than half the GDRs are traded via the Stock Exchange Automated Quotation System, making it difficult to get information on volumes traded or prices at which they trade in or closed at. But the volumes traded on SEAQ for the Indian GDRs are so poor that it would take days to complete an institutional order of less than a few million. The advantages of dealing in the GDR market are that there are no settlement and custodial problems that arise when trading in the local market, and no capital gains tax which is, by itself, a significant advantage. While these factors may encourage speculative trading activity in the GDR market, the risk is mostly transfered to the investor.

Equity investments are beneficial to the recipient nations as there is the least disruption when capital flows out of the market. In India, a 30 per cent capital gains tax for investments held under a year is to ensure that the incentive for withdrawing funds in the short term is reduced. It also acts as a disincentive for the investor in the first place as portfolio investors today have a short-term investment horizon, particularly in EM investments. The trading bias of most portfolio activity results in speculation rather than in long-term investing. In fact, a long-term investment is usually classified as a short-term one that has gone wrong. All fund managers prefer to keep their options open to reverse any investment decision without being penalised for it. Thus, the strategy of issuing GDRs by Indian corporates can be counted among India's major successes in implementing reforms though it has failed to benefit the development of local brokerage firms who lacked the resources for setting up international distributional capability. Instead, the local brokers opted for joint ventures with major distributors as with DSP and Merrill Lynch, Batlivala & Karani and James Capel or ICICI Securities and JP Morgan.

In the Indian market where the free-float of stock is low and illiquidity is a problem, the GDR route offered the ideal panacea to all parties. Considering that the funds raised went directly to the corporates' bank account and not into inflating share prices, GDRs acted like FDI. The major difference being that the foreign direct investor has a pretty good idea of the value of the intended investment and is in it for the long haul compared to the portfolio investor in India who unfortunately did not have a clue to the real value of investments made. It has been proven that economic models that successfully priced assets from industrial countries have failed to price assets traded on developing markets. Thus, while high returns can be achieved very quickly in volatile markets, losses can also be incurred by the inexperienced FII.

Despite the shift in risk and responsibility to the investor, what any developing market needs to promote is the mature, professional, long-term investor. But an analysis of the level of competence of the average portfolio investor dealing with India reveals an alarming lack of experience, even a lack of understanding of the fundamentals of the companies invested in. It is a reflection of how India is perceived among global investors. One of the major criticisms made by fund managers is the lack of reliable information about the companies they invest in. The 'head of emerging markets' of a major investment company in the UK is of the opinion that stock selection is unproductive in EMs as estimated earnings projections can be unreliable and that one is better off analysing global liquidity flows and getting the asset allocation decision right. While there is some truth in that argument, the world's most successful investors have been those who understood the companies they invested in and held on to their investment for years. These investors felt comfortable with the risks they took only because they 'knew' the potential value of their investments. But, this level of confidence comes only with years of knowledge of investing in a country, particularly in the company concerned.

The level of understanding that a long-term investor, like a foreign direct investor or a venture capital investor, has in a market or a company needs to be cultivated. While Indian corporates came diffidently, were taken aback with the thirst for Indian paper and responded by issuing their equity abroad, there was little time or consideration for building relationships with their prospective investors and understanding each other's long-term objectives. Building investor confidence is not something that Indian corporates are good at doing at home. What India needs is more fund managers who understand the companies they invest in and stick with their chosen investment candidates over a full investment cycle. To achieve that level of rapport, both parties have to be more forthcoming in sharing information. Quarterly corporate reporting along internationally acceptable accounting standards would be a start. While equity portfolio capital does not necessarily bring with it the access to foreign technology, techniques and markets that FDI does, it helps channel funds to the private sector and has superior risk-sharing value than debt.

Dedicated country funds do not directly benefit the companies that they invest in unless the investment is made via a share issue directly to the company. But they can help in the growth of the domestic mutual fund industry which in turn can help mobilise domestic savings into private sector investments. In December 1996, there were over 50 specialist foreign funds which invested in India and about 10 funds that invested in South Asia. There are plans for several more to be launched. Most asset management companies with global investment management capability have invested in India, some have launched dedicated India Funds. The notable exceptions are Fidelity, Mercury and Gartmore among others who have not launched their own branded India Funds. The list is also notable for the absence of major European investors, particularly the Swiss. There were some 427 FIIs registered with SEBI but less than 150 have been actively investing in India. Settlement and custodial problems initially prevented major global mutual fund specialists from making a high allocation to India in their Asian or EM Portfolios. As settlement constraints eased, political uncertainty took over making investing in India more of a risk than before.

With the world's sixth largest economy, India has been struggling to attract a decent allocation in EM funds when, with the right economic policies, India could have been part of global international funds. India's weighting in international equity portfolios does not reflect the size of its economy nor its potential for growth. With sustained economic reforms, India could attract a larger portion of foreign investments, of both FDI and FII. If India persists in its reform path by addressing tighter fiscal discipline, introducing greater tariff cuts, liberalising the labour market, restructuring its PEs and investing heavily in the country's infrastructure and human development, there is every reason to believe that the flow of investments into the country will accelerate.

India was unable to reap the benefits of substantial portfolio inflows due to the combination of factors that prevented it from receiving such capital flows. These factors were mainly in the form of barriers to portfolio investment but others like poor credit ratings after the crisis, high and variable rates of inflation, the limited size of the stockmarket in terms of the free float of shares, the absence of a solid regulatory and accounting framework and investor protection also made it difficult for pension fund trustees to direct their investments into India. India was not even part of the Emerging Markets' Index prior to 1993. Restrictions on foreign ownership and taxation on capital gains and dividends which were not harmonised with other EMs and industrialised countries were also perceived as odds stacked against the outsiders.

The changes made in all the areas mentioned above since 1992–93 helped India attract a higher asset allocation by 1994. The continuation of reforms will also ensure a continuing higher allocation to India. Thus, on the demand side for Indian securities, the major hurdle inhibiting FIIs are the regulatory impediments imposed by the country as well as the restrictions imposed by the trustees of these institutions. Similar restrictions are also in place on pension funds and life insurance companies in India. Since India is in need of capital for its development, it makes sense for Indian pension and insurance assets not to be invested abroad, but these same assets should be deployed to a greater extent in private equity rather than in government securities.

Portfolio investment in India depends not only on the domestic constraints in India but also the industrial country regulations. India represents 5–6 per cent of global emerging market portfolios. In most Asian portfolios, there is no specific allocation for India. At best, it is no more than 2–3 per cent. It is therefore up to India to address these issues and implement whatever changes that are deemed necessary to encourage wider investment in India. On the supply side of Indian securities, foreign institutional fund managers have been concerned with restrictions on direct entry, the illiquidity of the market, poor accounting practices, high transaction costs, lack of screen-based trading, an unreliable settlement system, an onerous registration process, inadequate custodial facilities and a high capital gains tax for investments held under one year. Like other EMs, India also suffers from a shortage of well managed, large capitalised companies (see Table 4.17).

Table 4.17   Distribution of market capitalisation

Market capitalisation ($ million)*	No. of companies
> 5000	2
1000–5000	19
500–1000	19
250–500	26
100–250	70
50–100	109
25–50	184
5–25	727
1–5	1678
< 1	2421

Note: * As on 30 September 1996.
Source: ING Baring Securities (India) Pvt Ltd.

The problem of overheating of the market on small foreign inflows acts as a deterent to allocating any significant amount of funds to the Indian market. In other markets where excess funds found their way in, the inherent undervaluation of the market also disappeared. In the case of Mexico, foreign investment rose from $4 billion at the end of 1990 to $21 billion by the end of 1992; it represented 19 per cent of the market capitalisation of the Bolsa Mexicana de Valores. This was reflected in the valuation of the shares in the market which changed from being an extremely attractive investment in 1990 to a speculative one by 1994. In India, the amount of funds required to destabilise the market is significantly less. The risk for any serious, long-term investor in such markets become unmanageable, forcing them to quit.

The rapid increases in the market capitalisation and valuation as a result of the domestic speculation that was unleashed in India after the economic liberalisation of June 1991 in anticipation of foreign investment inflows resulted in what is referred to as the stockmarket 'scam' of India in 1991–92. *Badla* or margin trading, along with an inefficient settlement system, encouraged an unprecedented level of speculation in the Indian market that took the BSE Index from the 1000 level in 1991 to 4400 by mid-1992. The market was totally liquidity-driven and had lost touch with its economic fundamentals. Anecdotal evidence suggests that individual stocks went up in multiples of the index's appreciation. This is also evident in the turnover figures on the Bombay stockmarket that rose from Rs 6.6 billion on average every month in 1987–88, to Rs 60 billion in 1991–92. Thus, it took less than $2 billion dollars of direct investment in the stockmarket over a period of a year to overheat the market, thanks to the limited free float and the low trading volumes.

To be able to absorb global capital flows, the Indian stockmarket needs to develop further through greater participation of domestic mutual funds and FIIs. With increasing privatisation and capital issues in both domestic and overseas markets, the critical mass required for a higher level of sustainable foreign investment should be achieved. Thus, it is conceivable that there will be periods when demand and supply of stocks will be such that India's market capitalisation will increase without a significant appreciation in the market index. Large-scale privatisations and corporate fund raisings via GDR issues can satisfy the demand for Indian investments. Thus, during 1995–96 and 1996–97 (up to December), FIIs invested some $2 billion dollars over each period. However, this did not translate to any real appreciation in the level of the market index. The index level had declined marginally and market capitalisation in December 1996 stood at Rs 4774 billion compared to Rs 4862 billion in December 1995. But during 1993–94 and 1994–95, annual FII investments of around $1.5 billion resulted in the doubling of the market capitalisation.

CONCLUSION

With the development of the global pension fund industry, pension assets around the world amounted to $6860 billion in 1993. The pension fund industry is set to grow exponentially with the demographic shift in the world's other major asset, its people, along with the rise of economic prosperity among the Asians. Pension funds are already one of the largest providers of capital to the developing world. With the growth in the pension fund industry as well as the rise of the private sector in engineering economic growth around the world, the global flow of portfolio capital is set to increase significantly.

The question is not just whether portfolio flows to developing countries will be large enough to contribute to their financing needs in the future, but how best to utilise that amount which is available for investment. Even a small shift in increasing portfolio investments directly into India or indirectly into the EM universe will have a significant impact on the Indian market. It is crucial to ensure that the resources thus mobilised are used to enhance the overall growth potential of the country. The question of the volatility of capital flows has as much to do with the external aggregate shocks the country experiences as well as the macroeconomic policies pursued by the developing country. Given the increasing integration of international financial markets, the task of maintaining financial competitiveness in the international arena is a challenge that India must face. Thus, market oriented domestic policy reforms must aim at maintaining a sustainable level of growth to keep foreign savings in the country.

For India to be able to absorb a higher level of foreign portfolio investment would imply better infrastructure, a sustainably higher level of domestic investment and a more efficient capital market. There is scope for India to improve its desirability as a destination for foreign portfolio investment. Apart from tighter macroeconomic policies, measures might embrace improvements in infrastructure which include not only physical infrastructure like roads, availability of power supplies, telecommunications and transport but also a cheap, skilled and disciplined labour force along with a developed financial services sector. The challenge for the government is to establish the framework to facilitate the private sector to invest more freely in the economy so that the government can focus its own investments towards sectors like education, health, family planning and increasing access to opportunities for developing human capital.

Since the introduction of liberalisation, foreign investment flows into India have risen sharply. So have the amount of funds raised in the domestic market through capital issues. The rate of growth in funds raised by the private sector far outstripped its ability to invest it in the economy. The argument that the private sector was 'crowded out' by high government borrowing did not apply until after 1995–96 when finance from non-banking sources declined and deposit growth rate was inadequate to meet the upsurge in demand for funds from the banking system by the government and the commercial sectors. While financial sector reforms have been initiated, greater fiscal consolidation is necessary to reduce real interest costs in India. The level of savings by the public sector needs to be improved as well.

The opening up of the economy to private enterprise has not yet proven to be the driving force behind the country's economic dynamism, because initially unused capacity rates in industry remained high enough not to warrant a significantly higher level of investment. Equally significant is the fact that areas of the economy that need substantial investments, like infrastructure, are still struggling to attract the funds due to inadequate policy framework for private sector participation. The sooner the government, including state governments, get policy reforms in place the better it is for investment flows into requisite areas of the economy.

Thus, what has held back investment and growth has not been so much the non-availability of funds but the implementation of policies to channel funds that were available. The entire question of the efficient utilisation of funds, their capital to output ratios is another matter and is not under consideration at this point. A small portion of the funds raised by the private sector was used in reducing outstanding debt but otherwise most of these funds were initially deployed in rent-seeking activities instead of being invested in the economy. The private sector has shown great enterprise in its fund raising ability and it is upto the government in channelling this enterprise to develop the economy.

To what extent India will be able to utilise the availability of savings, both foreign and domestic, to unleash the potential for sustainable growth in the country rests almost entirely on the political willingness of the government to implement policies towards that goal. The argument for greater financial deregulation is to facilitate international capital inflows so that the Indian economy can benefit from integrating with the global economy. Only when India is ready to liberalise on the capital account will its economy be able to capitalise from the benefits of private savings, including foreign savings, in boosting investment growth where such investment is desirable.

The risks of volatile capital flows are well-documented and can severely affect the real economy. By restricting its capital flows, India has minimised any negative impact of outflows on the real economy. India's banking, regulatory and capital market mechanisms are very much in their infancy and are not resilient or mature enough to cope with volatile capital flows. Thus, while capital market development is vital for channelling savings and investment, it cannot precede or be considered in isolation from further liberalisation in the trade and financial sectors or the development of infrastructure along with greater fiscal reforms.

The political uncertainty over the past two years coupled with a series of high-level corruption scandals and raids by law-enforcement authorities involving some high-profile individuals and companies in India has made foreign investors nervous about the prospect of channelling their assets into such an unstable environment. The inability of the government to implement any serious expenditure reforms along with the high real interest rate scenario has made it difficult for companies to raise funds, equity or debt. While many FDI projects are on hold, the depressed level of the market also offered a golden opportunity to some overseas investors looking for stakes in medium-sized Indian corporates that were finding it difficult to finance their investment plans.

This venture-capital-type funding has been vital to the survival of India's small business houses which have been worst affected by the high interest rate environment over the past couple of years. But most foreign fund managers either lack the expertise or the time required to monitor these high-risk investments even though the rewards can be significant. Sometimes, the risk can be beyond the control of the individual company itself and in a country where there is no timely legal redress, the cost to the investor can be high if mistakes are made. The government is encouraging such investments by allowing venture capital funds to invest up to 20 per cent of their corpus in the equity of any single company.

Understanding the risks involved in investing in India and being able to manage them effectively implies greater cooperation between investors and corporates concerned. Investors either have the option of trading the market volatility or devoting their time to identifying managements and building up an investment-oriented relationship with them. Equity investors are no different to bankers and need to be able to evaluate their credit risk appropriately. In a newly-liberalised market, where both investors and the companies involved are in the process of learning, the secret of successful investing is to 'know the risk'. Correctly assessing one's risk is what investing is all about. If an investor learns to manage the risk of investing in India, the reward will look after itself.

5 The Challenges Ahead

INTRODUCTION

The challenges ahead for India's planners are manifold ranging from improving the physical infrastructure, increasing investment in the social sectors, liberalising agriculture and deepening financial sector reforms to facilitate the flow of private investments. Non-competitive market structures and inadequate incentives have widened the gap between 'best practice technology' used internationally and that prevalent in India. In a competitive global environment, reform is an ongoing process. The government aims to step up investment in all the sectors, from agriculture to infrastructure. But that will involve reforms in the legal, administrative and regulatory framework relating to existing corporates, labour, tax, land and competition laws. Perhaps the most important challenge is that reforms need to be introduced without destroying the social fabric of the nation or aggravating existing levels of pollution.

Due to the limited scope of the book, it is not possible to examine the panorama of challenges ahead for India. The aim of this chapter is to highlight some of the salient issues that can hinder India's development. Much depends on the willingness of governments to define the future course of liberalisation to assist the private sector in implementing its investment schedules. The signals that have issued over the past few years have been mixed leading to delays in private investment flows, preventing the benefits of reform to trickle down to the weaker sections of society. Reforms were to benefit the entire community but the decline in investment in infrastructure since 1991 has not contributed to job creation. Central assistance to the states and Union Territories of Rs 24.7 billion during 1996–97 for expenditure on basic minimum services, or allocating Rs 25 billion for the Rural Infrastructure Development Fund, does not translate to increased job opportunities for the poor.

The development of infrastructure is capital-intensive and involves a long-term investment horizon, but it provides employment for a large section of unskilled and semi-skilled labourers. Any policy framework in the Indian context that could have utilised the availability of cheap labour for greater development of infrastructure over the past few decades would have contributed to the economy not only through higher tax collections but also through lower transport and power costs. It is clearly important to do so as investment in physical infrastructure has been both inadequate and inefficiently implemented. Without appropriate infrastructure there can be no sustainable growth.

The potential for the privatisation of infrastructure investment and services has increased tremendously over the decades but the role of the public sector will continue to be vital. The government has reduced spending in infrastructure due to its fiscal constraints. The performance of the infrastructural sector in 1996–97 has been poor, registering a decline in crude oil production and power generation. The non-availability of funds with lack of evaluation and implementation of projects has led to major time and cost over-runs. At the end of December 1996, the average time over-run was 18 months and the average cost escalation was 29 per cent resulting in an additional burden of Rs 31 billion in 189 central-sector projects alone. One of the policy challenges ahead of India is to set transparent guidelines for the allocation of risk to attract private sector investment into infrastructure which can bring with it superior skills in project implementation and management.

The supply side constraints that the economy has encountered over the past decades partly reflects the inability of Indians to afford goods and services at cost. As this state of affairs was created via a complex system of subsidies and a centrally-determined pricing mechanism, the government has only its own policies to blame for the low growth in real per capita income. Enabling the private sector to play a vital role in infrastructural development did not undermine the role of governments in East Asian countries in running high budget deficits through public expenditure programmes on the development of transportation, power generation and distribution, shipping and telecommunications, oil refining, oil and gas exploration. India's lack of an integrated approach to its infrastructural development has held back growth.

The strategic importance of the social sectors in achieving the long-term objectives of equitable economic growth in a low-income country like India cannot be emphasized enough. The development of social sectors like education and health is crucial for sustaining higher rates of growth in an increasingly integrated world economy. While steady growth has led to improvements in social indicators such as life expectancy, infant mortality and literacy rates along with the decline in the incidence of poverty, the level of development in the social sectors remains poor. There is concern that the fiscal stabilisation programme of 1991–92 and the ensuing liberalisation of the economy has been achieved at the cost of human development.

Official estimates indicated that the proportion of the population living below the poverty line rose in the initial adjustment period from 17.4 per cent in 1990–91 to 20.3 per cent in 1992–93. Over this period the incidence of urban poverty rose at a higher rate than rural poverty but it was estimated that the poverty level declined to 18.9 per cent in 1993–94. It has also been noted that shortfalls in resource mobilisation at the centre translated to a declining investment in the development of human capital in the states. While this was true during the years of the crisis, since 1993–94 social sector programmes have been strengthened and reoriented in favour of the weaker echelons of society.

Despite India's major achievements in agriculture, its share in the global trading of agricultural commodities is less than 1 per cent. Agriculture is protected, making a large segment of it inefficient. This has had a negative effect on India's ability to boost exports and to attract private investment into the sector. India's new economic policy did not attempt to dismantle the controls in the agricultural sector although the process has been initiated. Various policy changes like the lowering of import duties on capital goods for greenhouses, plant and machinery for food processing industries, easier credit for export and market pricing for produce has boosted agricultural exports. Indian agricultural products are beginning to get globally competitive but the changing environment for agriculture means that India has to invest more on developing its share of world trade. Public investment in agriculture has been steadily declining, but it is encouraging to note that private sector investment has been rising, albeit slowly.

Heavily subsidised availability of fertilisers and electricity and the implicit taxation through trade restrictions and domestic price interventions created a system of distortions in the agricultural sector which impeded private investment from flowing into the sector. The level of public expenditure on agriculture has been high, but returns on investment have been declining steadily since the 1980s. Economists have long argued that the institutional framework of India's agriculture has been the main obstacle to higher productivity growth and employment generation. A large number of small and marginal farmers have found it beyond their means to employ new technologies due to lack of access to affordable finance while a small segment of farmers with greater political access have continued to exert an undue influence on policymaking and appropriated to themselves a substantial portion of the benefits accruing from the subsidized inputs that the government has provided.

The escalation in subsidies has not only been inequitable but has prevented investment in the agricultural infrastructure which would have been for the greater good. The resources presently devoted to current expenditure on subsidies for agricultural inputs could be better spent on the creation of assets by investment in rural infrastructure like transport, storage and effective rural credit support. While the thrust of the agricultural credit policy is to provide timely and adequate support to small and marginal farmers, the problem of loans overdue has seriously inhibited credit expansion. The waiver of agricultural loans in 1990 aggravated the problem of loan recovery which improved from 54 per cent in 1992 to almost 60 per cent in 1995.

There is tremendous potential for injecting greater efficiency into sectors that are vital to India's development. The key lies with governments, both at the centre and in the states, to be imaginative in their efforts to unlock the growth potential of the economy. Some states are ahead of the centre in implementing their restructuring plans in certain sectors like the power sector in Orissa. But the centre has not made a concerted attempt at reforms in infrastructural development, in agriculture or in the social sectors on a national basis. As the contribution of the public sector has been curtailed in the aftermath of liberalisation, there is urgent need to facilitate the flow of private investment into vital areas of the economy.

IMPROVING INDIA'S INFRASTRUCTURE

The public sector's role in developing India's infrastructure since the 1950s has been considerable but the gap between demand and supply has been unacceptable. A comparison to other countries is shown in Table 5.1.

Table 5.1   India's infrastructure – a comparison

Country per capita	Electricity production (Kwh 1992)	Commercial energy consumption*	Telephone main lines+ (no of connections)	Paved roads#	Railways (traffic units**)
India	373	243	8	893	488
Brazil	1570	691	89	929	61
China	647	647	10	NA	847
Malaysia	1612	1711	112	NA	30
Mexico	1381	1577	80	1019	73
South Africa	4329	2253	89	1394	804
Thailand	1000	770	31	841	75
Turkey	1154	955	160	5514	65

Notes: * Kg of oil equivalent in 1994; + figures for telephone main line connections are for 1000 people in 1992; # figures for paved roads are in kilometers per million persons in 1992; ** figures for railways are for rail traffic units per $000 GDP in 1992.
Source: *World Development Report*, 1995 and 1996.

The cause for this woeful state of affairs was inadequate investments as much as the misutilisation of available resources. The absence of private sector investment despite declining public spending is also to blame for this lack of development. According to the India Infrastructure Report presented by an expert group on the commercialisation of infrastructure projects headed by Rakesh Mohan, investment has to rise from the current annual level of 5.5 per cent of GDP to 7 per cent by 2000–01. In absolute terms, investment needs to be stepped up from the present $17 billion annually to $30 billion by 2000–01. As a large portion of this funding is expected to come from private sources, there is urgent need to establish the legal and regulatory framework to expedite such transfers. The report has been fairly conservative in expecting 15 per cent of total capital requirements for infrastructure to come from external sources leaving the remaining 85 per cent to be raised domestically.

The strategic role of the capital market in mobilising domestic savings for investment in infrastructure can only be realised with greater liberalisation of the insurance sector and rapid development of the debt market. Thus, reforms are necessary to enable life insurance, provident and pension funds to invest in long-term debt instruments with longer maturity periods as that is essential for infrastructural projects. The debt market in India remains undeveloped despite its tremendous potential for growth. When measured in terms of the outstanding value of debt instruments, the size of the traditional debt market was estimated at Rs 3000 billion and the untraded debt market at Rs 600 billion. A large part of household savings flow into fixed-income securities. The evolution of the debt market is fundamental to financing India's infrastructure.

Private investment in infrastructure is estimated to rise sevenfold from Rs 120 billion in 1995–96 to over Rs 800 billion in 2005–06. The pattern of financing will also shift from predominantly public investment in infrastructure to higher private/foreign participation. Public sector investment is expected to rise from the current Rs 475 billion to Rs 1000 billion in 2005–06. As budgetary support is expected to remain unaltered, the increase in funding has to come increasingly from internal revenue generation which is estimated to rise from the current 40 per cent of requirements to 50 per cent of requirements in 2005–06 (see Table 5. 2).

As the level of infrastructure is directly related to a country's global competitiveness, the development of infrastructure has a significant impact on FDI. India's inability to attract a higher level of FDI is the result of infrastructural bottlenecks that such capital encountered. The reforms since 1991 aimed to better utilise the existing infrastructure, while laying the foundations for the liberalisation of the sector, so that the momentum of export growth and economic recovery was not held back in the interim period. The entry of the private sector will inject competition, efficiency and accountability along with better risk-sharing. It will help induce market orientation in the pricing and distribution strategies of the PEs.

Table 5.2   Financing requirements for infrastructure (% GDP)

	1995–96	2000–01E	2005–06E
Infrastructure investment	5.5	7.0	8.0
Other investment	20.5	22.4	23.5
Total capital formation	26.0	29.4	31.5
Private sector investment	16.0	19.4	21.5
Private sector % in infrastrucutre	20.0	36.0	44.0

Source: *The India Infrastructure Report*, 1996.

To enhance foreign investment in infrastructure, the government has allowed automatic approval of foreign equity up to 74 per cent in key industries such as electricity generation and transmission, non-conventional energy generation and distribution as well as in the construction of roads, bridges, railbeds, ports and harbours. Industries in which automatic approval has been given for foreign equity participation upto 51 per cent have been expanded to include support services to the transport sector. Telecom projects have also been classified as infrastructure and thus qualify for all the exemptions available to investments in the sector. The government has granted a five-year tax holiday on certain infrastructural projects like the building of roads, bridges, airports, ports, railway projects, water supply, sanitation and sewerage projects and set up the Infrastructure Development Finance Company to provide long-term finance to the sector. To encourage private savings to flow into infrastructure, tax exemptions of various kinds have been offered. The Asian Development Bank has provided a loan of $300 million for the Public Sector Infrastructure Facility whose role is to promote private sector participation in the development of infrastructure.

Reforms have been introduced to several sectors relating to infrastructure, but they need to be developed further. The Air Corporations Act of 1994 enabled private air transport companies to operate in the domestic sector. The repeal of the Air Corporations Act of 1953 opened the way for the restructuring of the financial as well as the organisational systems of both Air India and Indian Airlines. The Foreign Investment Promotion Board (FIPB) permitted a 40 per cent foreign holding in private Indian airlines. This opened the way forward to joint ventures including that of Kuwait Airways and Gulf Air in a combined 40 per cent stake in Jet Airways,

India's sole profitable private carrier. Other joint venture partnerships are in the offing. Private investment has also been allowed in the development and maintenance of airport infrastructure and in the handling of materials in major domestic airports.

In the power sector a package of incentives to attract private investment was announced which included a reduction of import tariffs on power equipment, a tax holiday on new power projects, a guaranteed rate of return on investments made, and provision of counter guarantees by the central government for a set of 'fast track' projects. Competitive bidding is now mandatory for all new private power projects. FIPB guidelines suggest permitted foreign equity shares upto 100 per cent in road projects, tourism, petroleum industries and power generation. In the POL sector, the government allowed imports and distribution of certain products like domestic liquified petroleum gas and kerosene by the private sector at market prices to stimulate new investments. Private and foreign companies are now allowed to invest in oil exploration and production in joint ventures with the Oil and Natural Gas Commission (ONGC) or Oil India Ltd (OIL) and in the refining of POL. The domestic market in lubricants has been opened up to foreign collaboration.

The new National Telecom Policy opened up the sector for private participation in basic telecom services and allowed foreign equity ownership up to 49 per cent. In the area of postal services, the government has allowed private distribution of postal stationery on a commission basis. Following the new policy of liberalisation, the railways have introduced reforms in their marketing, simplified rules and procedures in key areas and introduced commercially viable policies. In ports, the private sector is being encouraged to participate in the leasing of port equipment, setting up of private ports by coast-based industries, ship repair, maintenance and transportation within ports. In the road transport sector, octroi duties were abolished by various state governments to facilitate domestic trade. To promote private sector investment in the development of roads, several amendments were introduced in 1994–95 to the National Highway Act enabling large firms to enter the sector, levy a toll on road users and borrow from financial institutions. In spite of these changes, the speed of reforms remains slow as the time lag between policy implementation and the physical availability of the additional infrastructural capacity is usually several years.

The Energy Sector

The government's investment in the energy sector rose from 18 per cent of its plan outlays in the 1960s and 1970s to 30 per cent in the late 1980s. But the rate of production has failed to match the growing energy needs of the economy. Lack of resources was only part of the problem; inadequate policies were mostly to blame. The higher rate of economic growth in the 1980s translated to an increasing deficit in the demand and supply of energy. In the Eighth Plan the outlay for the energy sector was Rs 1155 billion or 26.6 per cent of the Plan outlay. The recognition that development of commercial energy was becoming increasingly capital-intensive meant that 10 per cent of the energy sector's investment in the Eighth Plan came from the private sector.

India's commercial energy production has risen from 58.6 million tonnes of oil equivalent (Mtoe) in 1970–71 to an estimated 217 Mtoe in 1994–95. There has also been a significant shift in the pattern of energy supplied with the share of commercial fuels increasing from 26 per cent in 1955 to 60 per cent by 1990. Non-commercial fuels, comprising of firewood, crop residue and dried animal waste, account for 14 per cent of world energy consumption and for a third of developing countries' energy consumption, but they account for 40 per cent of India's final energy consumption. In view of the perennial shortages and restrictions imposed on users of commercial energy, the past trends of consumption do not represent the growth in demand but only in availability. Like most sectors of the economy, growth has represented supply rather than demand. A comparison with other countries is shown in Table 5. 3.

Table 5.3   Commercial energy consumption

Country	Per-capita energy use (kg of oil equivalent)		Average annual growth rate of energy consumption (%)		Energy imports as a % of merchandise exports	
	1980	1994	1971–80	1980–93	1970	1993
India	137	243	4.7	6.7	8	36
Brazil	595	691	8.4	3.7	13	11
China	421	647	7.4	5.1	n.a.	6
Indonesia	169	393	12.5	7.5	30	6
South Korea	1087	3000	11.1	9.5	16	18
Malaysia	692	1711	8.4	9.8	10	4
Mexico	1453	1577	10.3	3.1	6	4
Philippines	277	364	5.3	3.5	14	19
Thailand	259	770	6.8	10.5	16	9

Source: *World Development Report*, 1995 and 1996.

India's need for oil and gas is estimated to rise significantly by 2010. Coal has been the main source of primary commercial energy not just for direct use in industry but indirectly through conversion into power. Coal and lignite represented 70 per cent of energy production in 1990 having declined from 79 per cent in the 1970s after the discovery of oil in Bombay High. India's pattern of energy production and usage has thus gone against a worldwide shift from liquid fuel towards natural gas, hydro and nuclear power. Energy consumption in India rose from 64.9 Mtoe in 1973 to 201.9 Mtoe in 1993, over half of which was used by the industrial sector, a quarter by the transport sector, 14 per cent by the residential sector and 9 per cent by agriculture. The level of energy consumption in India is extremely low but its growth has been higher than the rate of growth of the economy. GDP grew at 3.5 per cent in the 1970s while energy consumption grew at 4.6 per cent. In the 1980s, GDP growth was 5.6 per cent compared to energy consumption growth of 6 per cent. With modernisation and technological development, the energy intensity of India's growth will decline.

Per capita energy consumption is expected to rise by 145 per cent by 2010 at which level it will still be significantly lower than the current per capita consumption of 3640 Mtoe in Japan and 7759 Mtoe in America. Japan has become one of the most energy efficient countries today due to its dependence on oil imports. It is estimated that the total demand for oil and gas in India will rise to 227 Mtoe by 2010 with a shift towards a higher demand for hydrocarbons. What is significant in India's energy usage is the high level of conservation and distribution losses as a percentage of total energy supply which stood at 20 per cent. If these conservation and distribution losses can be reduced or eliminated, India's level of energy deficiency would improve. Even if the level of imports were to be maintained, then the country's per capita energy usage could improve without any deterioration in the BoP position.

Oil and gas accounted for 30 per cent of India's commercial energy production in 1990 and, including oil imports, represented 40 per cent of energy supply and 56 per cent of energy use in the same year. Energy imports as a percentage of merchandise exports rose from 9 per cent in 1970 to 23.6 per cent by 1995–96, reflecting the extent of India's dependence on imports. Energy imports as a percentage of total energy consumption has remained unchanged at 20 per cent between 1980 and 1994 implying that India will need to continue to import a fifth of its energy consumption. It is estimated that oil and gas will account for 42 per cent of India's commercial energy usage by 2010 compared to 38 per cent in 1993. The implication is that no more than 27 per cent of India's requirements can be met out of indigenous production. The remaining portion has to be imported. To service these imports, India has to enhance its export ability. But to sustain a 15 per cent export growth involves the availability of energy and other related infrastructure which need to grow at higher levels.

The transport sector accounts for half of India's oil consumption. While improvements in automotive technology have helped, the surge in demand for automobiles and other vehicles has led to higher oil consumption. There has also been a shift in the kind of energy used by the transport sector from coal to oil due to the shift from rail to road transport. In agriculture, energy efficiency has been difficult to implement due to a combination of subsidies and obsolete technology. Obsolescent plant and technology has been the main cause of energy inefficiency in the public sector but a cost-plus pricing formula in the industrial sector has added to the inefficiency factor. The impact of this higher cost of energy on the competitiveness of manufacturing has been recognised but measures to rectify the problem remain slow in being implemented. Switching to more fuel-efficient boilers has yielded some energy savings. The conservation of electricity has been attempted on a massive scale in the public sector but the problem lies mainly with the management of the State Electricity Boards (SEBs). While the short-term priority of the energy sector is to improve efficiency through the reduction in conversion and distribution losses as well as by maximising capacity utilisation rates, the medium-term objective is to substitute POL with other renewable sources of energy. There is also a shift in the industrial structure from energy intensive industries like iron, steel and petrochemicals to less energy-intensive industries such as electronics and the manufacturing of machinery which should help in the long term.

It is estimated that less than half of India's households have an electricity supply and that 70 per cent of this consumption is for basic lighting and fans. In addition to the electrification of rural areas, the increase in disposable incomes will be the key driving force for greater demand for power. A higher penetration of household electrical appliances will also put enormous pressure on power supply. The annual growth rate of electricity consumption in the household sector between 1981 and 1994 was 12.8 per cent. The household sector accounts for a third of India's oil consumption but efficiency improvement in that sector has been marginal. The developments in the services sector will lead to the concentration of power demand during the peak office hours. With higher economic growth, demand for electricity is set to rise.

The Power Sector

The central government utilities with the SEBs own about 96 per cent of India's power sector. Private sector sales of power were less than 5 per cent of consumption though the private industrial sector has become more self-reliant through power generated in captive plants. The government has long recognised the need for private investment and allowed private power companies in Bombay, Calcutta and Ahmedabad to enhance their generating capacity. The new power policy received an overwhelming response from independent power producers (IPPs) but by January 1997 only eight projects with an aggregate capacity of 4950 Mw or less than 6 per cent of existing capacity had been finalised. The policy to encourage greater private investment resulted in increasing interest by investors but various policy bottlenecks meant that project implementation was unduly delayed. By January 1997 there were only three new private power projects under construction with planned additional capacity of 1164 Mw, the largest being the Dabhol project with a capacity of 740 Mw.

The under-utilisation of available resources is also reflected in the external assistance portfolio in which the total undisbursed balance of assistance in the power sector was Rs 171.6 billion in March 1995. The thrust towards greater private sector participation resulted in 124 applications for power projects seeking clearance from the Central Electricity Authority for a total capacity addition of 67 281 Mw involving investments worth Rs 2465 billion by March 1996. Power generation in 1995–96 was 380 billion Kwh, a rise of 8.3 per cent over the previous year. But, during April to November 1996 the growth was 3.4 per cent. Although the power sector has been considered a priority sector, additions to capacity have chronically fallen short of 'planned' targets. The installed capacity on 31 March 1995 was 83 288 Mw. Thus, during the first four years of the Eighth Plan, capacity addition was 14 799 Mw or 48 per cent of the target for the Plan period. During 1994–96 there was a significant improvement in meeting targets for capacity addition, but the failure to meet targets has plagued the industry since the 1950s. Nearly half the addition to capacity in 1995–96 was in the central sector, 42.5 per cent was in the state sectors and the remainder in the private sector. Lack of funds, delays in project implementation which are normal in the public sector were made worse by the announcement of the power policy for private participation. Thus, several projects that were scheduled for commissioning did not receive timely funding from the states.

India's reliance on thermal power, accounting for 79 per cent of generation in 1995–96, has resulted in higher unit cost due to a longer gestation period for thermal plants and the higher cost of fuel. Thermal plants are better suited to providing base-load power demand while hydro-plants tend to be efficient servers of peak demand. Capacity addition in the thermal sector has led to thermal plants being increasingly used to satisfy peak demand. This has contributed to a lower plant load factor (PLF) and reduced the marginal output of the thermal plants. The average PLF for all thermal plants improved from a low of 52 per cent in 1985 to 63 per cent in 1995–96. PLF varied from 72 per cent in the private sector to 70 per cent in the central sector and 58 per cent in the SEBs. There were major differences within the SEBs with Andhra Pradesh, Tamil Nadu and Rajasthan achieving PLFs above 70 per cent and Bihar and Orissa around 20 per cent. It is estimated that an improvement of 1 per cent in the national average PLF could be the equivalent of a fresh capacity addition of 500 Mw. As the effort to improve efficiency under existing constraints has been made, it is unlikely that the PLF can be raised significantly from current levels without new investments via renovation and modernisation programmes.

The responsibility for the transmission of electricity rests with the central and state governments which make bulk transfers from the generating plants to the state-owned distribution grids. The SEBs are responsible for planning capacity additions, operating state generating plants, regulating the private utilities, distributing electricity and collecting revenues. The critical area in the power sector is thus the performance of SEBs as the state governments are responsible for fixing the price of electricity and are in a position to offer political patronage through the power subsidy to the agricultural sector. The SEBs act as agents of the electoral machinery rather than operating as independent business units. Official estimates suggest that generation costs went up from 22.5 paise per Kwh in 1974–75 to 110.22 paise in 1991–92, but average realisation rose from 18.82 paise to 85.5 paise leading to a rise in revenue shortfall in recovering costs from 16 per cent to over 22 per cent. By 1994–95, the average tariff per unit sold had risen to 133 paise but the cost per unit at 160 paise left a 17 per cent deficit.

Under the Electricity Supply Act of 1948, the SEBs were required to adjust their tariff in such a manner that net after-tax profits were not less than 3 per cent of the value of net fixed assets at the beginning of each year. State governments have the authority to fix higher rates of return but most SEBs did not increase tariffs in line with the costs of generation. This provision was to become operative from 1985 but the SEBs are yet to comply with this statutory stipulation. Since 1985 only two SEBs, Andhra Pradesh and Tamil Nadu, have shown a consistent financial surplus. There are three SEBs with after-tax returns above 3 per cent. The financial deficits incurred by the SEBs are due to the heavily subsidised tariff rates for the agricultural sector and the domestic sector which together account for 45 per cent of electricity sales. The India Infrastructure Report (1996) suggests a 10 per cent revision in tariffs annually on top of inflation, but the government has been reluctant to raise user-charges in various sectors of the economy. The introduction of 50 paise/unit from agriculture could have raised Rs 26.8 billion or 0.2 per cent of GDP in 1995–96.

The low tariffs for agriculture and domestic sectors are partially compensated for by higher ones for the commercial and industrial sectors but they do not make up for the total amount of the subsidy. Such a policy led to a fall in electricity consumption by the industrial sector from 70 per cent in the 1960s to 34 per cent in 1994–95 making this level of cross-subsidization unsustainable. The skewed electricity tariff system whereby one sector of the economy benefits at the expense of the other is prevalent throughout Asia except in Hong Kong. But it is most noticeably weighted against industry in India. In China, for example, the industrial and commercial sectors benefit at the expense of the household sector. A World Bank study comparing electricity tariffs across a group of Asian cities, conducted in 1993, confirmed such disparities in the pricing of electricity. It is worth noting that the medium-sized industrialist in Bombay paid the highest tariff according to this study.

In 1996–97, the cumulative gross electricity subsidy to the agricultural and domestic sectors in India was estimated at Rs 195 billion compared to the cumulative surpluses from the commercial and industrial sectors at Rs 75 billion. The state government 'subventions' (contributions made by the state governments mainly for rural electrification) accounted for a further Rs 40 billion resulting in a loss or 'uncovered subsidy' of Rs 80 billion which translated to a −17.7 per cent return on net fixed assets. The stipulated 3 per cent return would have fetched Rs 122.7 billion. The average return on assets was estimated to improve to −16 per cent in 1997–98. The drain on the finances of the SEBs has resulted in growing debts owed to the central power corporations. On 28 February 1995, the SEBs' total dues outstanding to the central power corporations was Rs 57 billion with Uttar Pradesh and Bihar accounting for half of it. The gross subsidy for the agriculture and domestic sectors has gone up from Rs 74 billion or 1 per cent of GDP in 1992–93 to Rs 195 billion or 1.8 per cent of GDP in 1995–96. It was expected to rise to Rs 218 billion in 1997–98.

The other factor responsible for the financial losses of the SEBs is the losses arising from transmission and distribution (T&D). These losses improved from a peak level of 23 per cent to 20.9 per cent in 1994–95, but they remain over twice the international average of less than 10 per cent. Chronic under-investment in the T&D network has left the network overstretched. It has not been cost-efficient to build high-tension transmission lines to transfer electricity to villages with low consumption requirements. Power is transferred by extended lower-voltage lines designed for distribution over shorter distances. Such a mismatch has resulted in the high rate of losses. The irony in India's T&D losses thus lies in the very aim of the government to provide 100 per cent rural electrification. A 1 per cent reduction in T&D loss would result in a saving of capacity of some 800 Mw. Along with high T&D losses, India's generation losses are also among the highest at 7.9 per cent compared to other Asian countries.

According to an Asian Development Bank study, 45 per cent of India's power investment should be dedicated to its network. Like the shortfalls in capacity addition, the accumulating shortfalls in the annual addition target for the T&D network has created an inadequate network. In 1995, the shortfall was 40 per cent of the target. With electricity now reaching 86 per cent of villages, the T&D burden rests on improving the high-voltage transmission between the states and the regions. When peak demand drops in one state or region, the excess needs to be transferred as power cannot be stored. India's inability to manage power better stems from the lack of a national grid. In 1989, the Power Grid Corporation of India was incorporated with a view to establishing a national grid by the year 2000. If a national grid is functional by then, India could save a substantial amount of electricity.

The Central Electricity Authority estimated capacity additions required from 1996–97 to 2006–07 at 111 500 Mw. This would require investments worth Rs 6244 billion at fixed prices. Assuming that current inefficiencies can be substantially reduced, additional capacity requirements over the next decade would still be around 84 000 Mw needing investments around Rs 5000 billion. Unless investments are made, the power sector cannot support the future needs of the economy. An annual capacity growth rate of 9 per cent against a demand growth rate of 7.5 per cent to sustain an economic growth of 6–7 per cent appears to be conservatively estimated. At the end of the Seventh Plan, the energy gap was at 8.5 per cent and peak shortage was 17.7 per cent. In 1995, supply fell short of demand by 8 per cent and that of peak demand by 16.5 per cent. The maximum demand in 1995 was 57.5 billion Kwh compared to an installed capacity of 81.1 billion Kwh. While these figures suggest a reserve capacity of 30 per cent, actual available capacity during the year was 48 billion Kwh resulting in a peak deficit of 16.5 per cent. If these trends in electricity generation, demand, fuel mix and PLF continue, the peak deficit is estimated to rise to the 29 per cent level while the energy gap will persist at 10 per cent.

The government aims to finalise a national energy policy to overcome the existing constraints to reforms in the power sector. Getting the private sector to invest in India's power sector will require providing them with a higher degree of security than has been available. Private funding will be crucial to sustaining the growth in power generation. A Common Minimum National Action Plan for power has been adopted to address the investment needs of the sector. But to take the plan forward will require policy measures covering pricing, regulatory and other aspects of structural reform that involve total commitment from all political parties in the country.

The Oil Sector

Demand for petroleum products in India has been rising at 8 per cent per annum, a rate faster than domestic supply. Oil and gas accounted for a third of India's commercial energy production in 1995. With oil imports, it represented 40 per cent of the country's energy supply and 60 per cent of energy use that year. Consumption of oil and natural gas in India has been low at 77 Mtoe compared to 157 Mtoe for China. But, demand for petroleum, oil and lubricant products (POL) in India is set to rise with higher economic growth and could have serious implications for India's balance of payments position.

Petroleum products account for a quarter of India's import bill. The POL group has an 11 per cent weighting in the index for inflation. A 10 per cent rise in POL prices leads to 1 per cent rise in inflation. The current oil pool deficit suggests that the government has the unpleasant task of having to revise the oil price upward annually, contributing to inflation over the medium term. The sharp rises in POL imports reflected increases in the demand for hydrocarbons with higher economic growth combined with a fall in domestic crude production and a hardening of international oil prices. India's long-term energy policy thus remains crucial to the success of its reform programme.

The petroleum sector is also vital to the economy in earning revenues. As estimated in the Public Enterprises Survey of 1994–95, the sector accounted for 11.8 per cent of the government's total investment of Rs 1724 billion in its PEs on 31 March 1995. But, the share of the petroleum sector in the net profit of the profit-making PEs has been high, accounting for half the profits in 1994–95. The sector also accounts for the bulk of the government's tax revenue from excise and customs duties, corporation tax and dividends. The Indian Oil Corporation (IOC) alone contributed Rs 56.7 billion which amounted to 20.7 per cent of the contribution made by all the PEs or 0.6 per cent of GDP. The strategic importance of the sector to the economy has kept the exploration and production of hydrocarbon resources under government control. To meet the demand for POL in the future, the exploration and production (E&P) sector will require massive investments in the range of Rs 1800–3400 billion which is clearly beyond the resources of the Oil and Natural Gas Commission (ONGC) and Oil India Ltd (OIL).

As the pricing and distribution of POL is controlled by the government, its failure to link domestic pricing to international ones has resulted in undermining the profitability of Indian refiners. A comparison of net margin per barrel illustrates this point with India at 0.6 per cent compared to 1.6 per cent for companies in northwest Europe and 3.9 per cent in Singapore. India's Oil Coordination Committee controls imports of crude oil, refinery product mix, pricing and distribution of POL. The Administered Pricing Mechanism (APM) is the crux of the regulatory framework aimed at insulating domestic prices of POL from the volatility of international prices and providing a uniform pricing structure across the country. To manage demand more effectively, a complex method of cross-subsidisation was used via the Oil Pool Account (OPA).

The APM was created to insulate refiners from volatility with an assured 12 per cent post-tax return on net worth. But the absolute return on net worth for the downstream oil companies depended on other variables like crude throughput, fuel mix, fuel loss, depreciation and tax allowances. The OPA was meant to be self-balancing but it remained in deficit as the pricing structure was out of line with cost increases. With the APM, the government was able to control inflation by allowing the oil pool deficit to absorb that cost. The deficit is not financed by the budget but by the oil companies, mainly the IOC, and was estimated to rise to Rs 155 billion by the end of March 1997. The oil price adjustments necessary for the reduction of the oil pool deficit has become a 'political' issue as price rises affect most sectors of the economy. But, rises in the oil pool deficit puts a strain on the contributing companies whose ability to invest is greatly hampered by the populist decision of the government. The outstanding amounts of the oil companies from the oil pool deficit pushed up their borrowing requirements from around Rs 175 billion in December 1996 to a staggering Rs 230 billion by the end of March 1997. Under the APM, total subsidies on POL were estimated at Rs 184 billion or 1.3 per cent of GDP in 1996–97.

Low domestic crude prices, inability to access the capital markets and restrictions on acquiring global oil equity have hampered the exploration efforts of the upstream oil companies. It is hoped that the deregulation of crude prices should lead to a rise in domestic realisations for the oil companies generating cash flows for fresh exploration. Despite liberalisation and the general delicensing in the industrial sector, companies in the oil sector have not been free to make their own investment decisions. India's proven reserves of 0.8 billion tonnes, at current rates of production of 560 000 barrels a day, is estimated to last for 29 years against the world average of 44 years. As no new major discoveries have been made in the last few years, there is cause for concern that India's oil reserve creation is falling short of target, particularly if current rates of production go up. The government has thus stepped up its exploration activity aiming at a substantial jump in reserve accretion through the Accelerated Programme for Exploration. Private participation has yet to produce any tangible progress in reserve additions. Lack of quality data and adequate information availability along with the perception that ONGC had refrained from giving out the better blocks may have dampened private interest in exploration activities even though India's terms of production sharing are considered to be among the best in the world.

India's hydrocarbon production peaked in 1995–96 at 35 million tonnes. ONGC produced 90 per cent of the total crude and the rest was produced by OIL and other joint venture companies. The production of crude oil during April to October 1996 recorded a 10 per cent decline over the previous year. Frequent power cuts, water cuts and other environmental constraints accounted for the decline. Accretion to reserves continue to fall short of production while production itself has been declining. India's dependence on imported crude remains high; more than half the total crude throughput was imported during 1992–94. The import of POL at 47.7 million tonnes in 1995–96 represented 20.5 per cent of the total value of imports. Since 1990–91, India has imported over half of its total crude oil requirements and about 20 per cent of its POL resulting in the total oil import bill accounting for 20–25 per cent of imports.

Lack of an adequate domestic refining capacity has resulted in the need to export the crude oil produced domestically. India's refining industry currently has a total crude processing capacity of 60.4 million tonnes per annum. The average capacity utilisation rates of India's 13 refineries was 103.9 per cent in 1995–96. To increase refining capacity, significant new investments have to be made. Despite substantial shortages in POL, there has been no major greenfield refining project undertaken in India since 1982. While the cost difference between expanding existing capacity and setting up a grassroot refinery project had led the government to take the cheaper option, the scope for capacity addition at existing sites is limited. The government is keen to increase the number of participants by encouraging creation of fresh capacity through joint ventures which would entail having to set up greenfield projects. With increasing demand for POL, imports of refined products have risen.

Lack of adequate environmental laws in India has led to higher demand for middle and heavy distillates and reduced the need for secondary processing. Indian refineries's secondary processing intensity, which measures the size of secondary processing relative to crude distillation capacity, is low at 21.7 per cent compared with an average of 35 per cent for international oil majors. The crude oil from the Bombay High is light with a low sulphur content, thus eliminating the need for further secondary processing. The demand for middle and heavy distillates has been high at over 82 per cent since the 1970s. With higher levels of pollution, it is simply a matter of time before stricter legislation is introduced for protecting the environment, increasing the demand for lighter distillates. The government has already introduced the use of unleaded petrol from April 1995 in the four metropolitan cities and at selected highways to contain pollution. It has been decided to introduce unleaded petrol in all the state capitals and UTs by December 1998 and throughout the country by the year 2000.

Economic growth has stimulated demand for POL which has grown at 5.7 per cent between 1984–94, a rate of growth that is lower than the 7.3 per cent growth seen in Asia. Supply has not kept pace with demand leading to higher imports. India's demand for POL is skewed heavily towards the middle distillates but limitations in domestic refining to meet such demand has led to the imports of middle distillates like kerosene and diesel which account for 95 per cent of the total imports of POL. The transport and household sectors dominate the total demand for POL accounting for 85 per cent of the total demand in 1984–85 with transport taking the major share at 56 per cent. A decade later in 1994–95, the pattern of usage was still dominated by the transport sectors at 50 per cent and the household sector at 14 per cent of total demand. The industrial sector's demand for POL has risen to 25 per cent with agriculture using 9 per cent. The commercial transport sector, including small transport operators, the railways and the agricultural sector, use high-speed diesel. Gasoline is used for personal transport. Kerosene is used for cooking by the vast majority of households with liquefied petroleum gas (LPG) replacing kerosene among the middle classes. The highest rate of growth in the demand for LPG over the past decade at 15.4 per cent illustrates better living standards in the country.

The mismatch between India's refining capability and consumer demand is felt most acutely in the northern region which accounts for almost half of the total deficit. India's current refining capacity of 60 million tonnes per annum (Mtpa) is expected to increase to 135 Mtpa to meet the estimated demand of 102 Mtpa of POL by 2001–02. With the contribution from the private sector, India's total refining capacity is estimated to rise substantially from current levels. As the additional capacity is expected to be commissioned only after 1999–2000, the current deficit situation is likely to get worse. As part of India's liberalisation plan in the hydrocarbon sector, the government has allowed 11 private sector parties to set up a total refining capacity of 60 Mtpa of which 6 projects with a total capacity of 23 Mtpa are for export-oriented units only. This is in addition to the expansion in the existing refineries or the joint venture companies that are being put up by the public sector.

The government set up a restructuring committee to develop a comprehensive long-term hydrocarbon policy. This study group submitted its report entitled 'Hydrocarbon Perspective – 2010' in February 1995 recommending decontrol of the hydrocarbon sector, replacing the APM with a market determined pricing mechanism. Private investment is required for enhancing reserves via access to state-of-the-art technology, the extended recovery of oil in existing fields as well as in accelerating exploration efforts and acquiring oil equity globally. The creation of refining capacity and marketing infrastructure, along with the development of port facilities and pipeline capacities, will be beyond the scope of the public sector alone. The Oil Industry Restructuring Committee's report calls for decontrol over a six-year period. To ensure India's energy security for sustainable economic growth, it is necessary to liberalise the energy sector.

Transport and Communication Sectors

The progress made by the public sector in the development of transport and communication facilities has been poor. Supply has lagged demand to such an extent that India's per capita usage falls significantly below that of other developing countries like China or Indonesia. The national highway system is bursting at its seams, coastal shipping has stagnated despite the extensive coastlines and airlines provide mainly passenger services. The arrears in the railway's track renewal programme runs to thousands of kilometres. The bulk of the domestic airline fleet is over 16 years old. Several state transport buses should not be on the roads. While 44 per cent of India's fleet in overseas trade was less than five years old in 1975, barely 5 per cent is of similar age currently. Public sector investment in the transport sector as a share of the total planned expansion declined from 23 per cent in the first three plans to 15.9 per cent in the Fourth Plan. It fell further to 12.6 per cent in the Sixth Plan and was at a similar level during the Eighth Plan period. An integrated policy approach to transport is not in place while the lack of technological upgradation remains a major concern.

One of the stumbling blocks for private sector participation in India's infrastructural development stems from the fact that economic costs were not used as the basis of pricing recommendations. Socio-political exigencies have been used as an excuse to keep public sector transport prices below cost. In the railways for example, such distortions have been largely resolved with regard to freight rates but passenger rates need to be revised upwards to reflect true costs. Uneconomic public road transport fares have also held back growth in the sector and fuelled the boom in an unregulated private sector. An attempt was made in the Eighth Plan to dismantle the direct and indirect transport subsidies and give the private sector a greater role.

The Railways

India boasts of one of the largest railway networks in the world but a large portion of the network growth was achieved in the early decades after Independence. The transport of bulk commodities like coal, cement, fertilisers, foodgrains, raw materials for steel plants and POL account for 85 per cent of the total freight traffic with coal itself representing 47 per cent of the total. In 1995–96, the revenue-earning freight traffic moved by the railways was 390.7 million tonnes, a 7 per cent rise over the previous year. The number of passengers carried rose from 1.3 billion in 1950–51 to an estimated 3.9 billion in 1994–95. The electrification programme has been given the highest priority to save on energy costs, which constitute around 20 per cent of the total expenses of the railways. However, its progress has been slow as electrified networks still account for less than 20 per cent of the total route today.

Experts have suggested a shift towards rail transport from roads for long-haul freight routes as that would prove to be energy efficient as well as environmentally friendly. But user preference has been shifting in favour of transportation by road which is more demand-responsive although more costly. The National Policy Committee in the early 1980s had anticipated a split in which the railways would carry 72 per cent of the long-distance freight traffic and the rest would go by road. But, the lack of a policy aimed at the customer produced exactly the opposite result with road transport accounting for an estimated 60 per cent of freight and 80 per cent of passenger traffic. This trend reflects the shortage of capacities on railways and very high traffic density on major routes. Developing an intermodal transport system with greater cooperation between railways and road might help to lower overall transport costs to the economy. But international experience shows that the choice of mode of transport is best left to the user. In India, as in the rest of the world, shippers prefer trucking to rail transport. Multimodal freight transport in India can be improved significantly with improvements in roads and in the legislation relating to the Transportation of Goods Act 1993.

The focus of action for the Eighth Plan period included replacement and renewal of overaged assets, increase of terminal and rolling stock capacities, gauge conversion and electrification. But, the resources required to implement these target plans were simply not available. The government has also reduced its budgetary support to the railways from 75 per cent of the railways plan outlay in the Fifth Plan to 42 per cent of outlay in the Seventh Plan and further down to 19 per cent of outlay during the Eighth Plan. This decline in budgetary support has adversely affected the railways plan for the acquisition of locomotives, coaches and wagons. In the wake of such budgetary cuts, it was imperative that the railways should have been allowed to function more as a commercial undertaking rather than as a public utility service.

Alternative methods of financing, including direct access to the capital markets via the Indian Railways Finance Corporation, have been introduced. However, such sources of finance, including market borrowings, have become more expensive with higher interest rates and more uncertain. Thus, the railways has suffered from a higher level of under-investment as internal savings have not been adequate to compensate for the decline in budgetary support. The level of internal savings in the railways and communications sector has been rising since the Sixth Plan, but obviously the level of investment required has been substantially higher. The restructuring of the railways in the wake of reforms in 1991 has helped in increasing savings. The railways have been forced to depend on internal savings which were estimated at 66 per cent of expenditure in 1994–95. While revenue receipts from both passenger and goods traffic as a portion of gross receipts has remained virtually unchanged between 1990–91 and 1995–96, earnings from other sources have risen. The outcome is that net revenue as a portion of the gross traffic receipts of the railways has risen since 1991. But, with increased outlay on account of the Pay Commission recommendations and growing lease rentals, internal revenue generation has fallen increasingly short of the required investments.

The railways employ around 1600 000 workers, the largest number for any public sector undertaking in the country. A comprehensive plan for human resource development to upgrade skills, retrain workers and achieve higher productivity growth has been initiated by introducing management training, implementing strategies for the improvements in performance as well as in the productivity of assets. The United Nations Development Programme (UNDP) is assisting in matters of organisational development and system changes to improve efficiency, productivity and quality. The project focuses on areas like total quality management, information systems, workforce motivation and restructuring. The railways aim to build more integrated automatic operation control systems for superior utilisation of tracks, tractions, terminals and trains. Signalling and telecommunications systems are being revamped with the application of computers with networking capabilities. Staff productivity has improved but there is scope for further improvement.

Roads and Road Transport

With a network of 2.7 million kilometres, India can boast of the third largest road network in the world, except that half of this constitutes unsurfaced roads and even the surfaced roads have extremely poor riding quality compared to other developing countries. Thus, covering a distance of 300 km per day in a commercial vehicle in India would be considered quite an achievement, while covering over twice that distance per day would be considered fairly comfortable in most developed countries. Railway crossings, octroi posts and other tax barriers along with inadequate capacity, insufficient road breadth and surface thickness are common complaints on Indian roads. In addition, there are the problems associated with security, pollution and the lack of facilities on main roads.

India's road network, like other physical infrastructure, has deteriorated due to inadequate investment and maintenance. It is estimated that 20 per cent of the national highways need widening from their current single-lane status, 50 per cent of the two-lane roads have to be strengthened and 30 per cent need to be four-laned, while selected corridors on the national highways need to be converted to expressways. The national highways network of 34 298 kms constitutes less than 1.5 per cent of the total road network, a decline from 4.6 per cent in 1961. But from 1951 to 1994 the average annual growth in road traffic has been 8–10 per cent. Much of the recent expansion of the road network has been in the rural areas but 50 per cent of India's villages still do not have all-weather roads.

Surfaced roads in India grew from 157 000 kms in 1950–51 to one million kilometres by 1990–91. But, registered motor vehicles grew from 0.3 million to over 21.3 million during the same period. It is not difficult to understand why the road system failed to cope with this level of traffic demand. It is projected that road traffic will account for 87 per cent of passenger and 65 per cent of goods traffic by the year 2000. It is also estimated that the total number of registered vehicles will increase to 54 million by 2001. The enormous investments needed, along with the organisational resources required, to transform India's crippling road transport system is currently beyond the reach of the government. Public sector allocation for road development as a portion of total expenditure has been declining over the various plans, from 6.7 per cent in the First Plan to 3 per cent in the Eighth Plan.

Poor investment in public transport led to the boom in two-wheelers in India which registered an annual growth rate of 20.7 per cent in the 1960s,

16 per cent in the 1970s and the 1980s, compared to an overall rate of growth of 7.6 per cent for cars and jeeps. Unlike the Chinese, the majority of Indians depend on fuel driven two-wheelers for their daily transport. The lack of adequate public transport and the high price of cars have contributed to the enormous growth of scooters, motor-cycles, mopeds and auto-riskshaws. The State Road Transport Undertakings operate a fleet of over 100 000 buses employing 830 000 employees, but their level of service is extremely poor and many of the buses are not roadworthy. These undertakings face severe financial constraints due to a combination of factors like having to operate on uneconomic routes without cost-based fare structures, gross overmanning, poor management and a resulting loss of incentive to improve the situation.

The amendment of the Motor Vehicle Act, which came into force from 14 November 1994, giving more powers to the state government in the matter of granting driving licences and permits for motor vehicles, has spurred the growth in private motor vehicles without matching growth in roads leading to further road congestion. The amended Act removed the ceilings on the number of stage-carriage permits that can be held by an individual or company. The growth in urban population and the matching need for transport has reached alarming proportions in various cities in India. Given the high density of population and the scarcity of land, it is going to be impossible to increase the road capacity substantially. It will not be possible to satisfy the growing demand for vehicles and roads in certain cities in India taking into account the constraints of land availability, the high cost of capital, along with the need to lower the existing rates of pollution. Thus the transport demands of India's highly congested cities have to be addressed separately from that of the nation as a whole.

In the past, roads have been financed from budgetary sources and constructed by the Public Works Department. As public resources are not available to meet the level of investment required, the National Highways Act has been amended to allow the levy of a fee on certain routes of the national highways, bridges and tunnels. This amendment is to enable private sector participation in the construction, maintenance and the operation of roads on a build-operate-transfer basis. The road sector was declared an industry to help market-borrowing and the issuances of bonds for raising capital. Customs duty on construction equipment has been reduced and clearance procedures streamlined. Monopolies and Restrictive Trade Practices Act provisions have also been relaxed to enable large-scale private investment. However, it will be difficult to fund the construction through toll finances alone.

Since the changes made to the National Highways Act in 1995, steps have been taken to finance projects via the private sector, both domestic and foreign. The Thane Bhiwandi bypass was awarded on a build-operate-transfer (BOT) basis. Global tenders were invited for five more national highways projects relating to the construction of bypasses and bridges on a BOT basis. Global tenders have been invited for feasibility studies for a proposed supernational highway connecting the major metropolitan cities and manufacturing towns with the major ports in India. Additional support for the development of the national highways is being sought via loan assistance from various international agencies like the World Bank, the Asian Development Bank and the Overseas Economic Cooperation of Japan.

The slow implementation of the first national highways project through the state governments as agents of the Ministry of Surface Transport forced the World Bank to reduce the quantum of foreign assistance by $96 million. It was therefore decided to make the National Highways Authority autonomous to speed up the pace of implementation of externally-aided projects. Despite India's resource crunch, it has to be noted that the country has consistently lost out on aid and assistance from multilateral agencies through inadequate policies that result in slow implementation. As there was no simple solution to the question of land acquisition, the policy framework for the development of roads remained fundamentally flawed. The private sector was not able to provide a solution to that conundrum. It was up to the government, albeit the Ministry of Surface Transport, to provide a way out of the impasse.

To meet the traffic expansion, the national highways network needs to be drastically improved. Higher transportation costs have proven costly to the Indian economy affecting its international competitiveness. A broad assessment of the needs of India's main roads over the next decade indicates that Rs 320 billion would be required between 1996–97 and 2000–01, 28 per cent of which will have to be spent on maintenance. India's expenditure on roads is about a third of the revenue raised through road taxes and related levies compared to developed countries where road-user taxes are entirely set aside for the development and maintenance of roads. In light of the massive funding requirements, The India Infrastructure Report recommends a Highway Development Fund as an assured extra-budgetary source of funding. The report also recommends a Highway Infrastructure Savings Scheme to provide assured funds for commercial roads; further, the resolution on the Central Road Fund approved by Parliament in 1988 be implemented. The comprehensive amendment of the National Highways Act encompassing issues of land acquisition, environmental clearance, simplification of procedures, introduction of toll-levies and equity participation in the highway sector should bring in greater private sector investments.

Civil Aviation

The partial liberalisation in civil aviation begun in 1990 with the cargo open-skies policy was to enable international airlines to operate cargo flights without any restrictions, thus allowing them to charge rates without having to refer the matter to the Directorate General of Civil Aviation. It is worth noting that liberalisation in the civil aviation cargo sector was introduced prior to the reforms of 1991 in response to the demands of exporters who needed timely availability of capacity, greater choice of rates and economies of scale that were achieved through a larger flow of trade. The Air-Taxi Operators Scheme, also launched in 1990 but given a secondary role to the main domestic carrier Indian Airlines, received a poor response due to the restrictive environment in which private operators were expected to run their business.

It was not until the repeal of the 1953 Air Corporation Act on 1 March 1994, ending the monopoly of both Indian Airlines and Air India, that real competition was introduced into the civil aviation industry. Seven private operators have been granted the status of scheduled airlines and 21 air-taxi operators the permit for charter or non-scheduled air transport services. Private investment in civil aviation now allows 40 per cent foreign equity in domestic airlines. Thus, domestic air services are currently operating in a reasonably competitive environment with private air services catering to just over 40 per cent of the domestic air transport market.

One of the consequences of liberalisation has been the rise in prices in most sectors of the economy which necessitated steep rises in domestic airfares. But these increases did not meet the spiralling costs of fuel and oil, airport landing and parking fees, interest charges, insurance costs, depreciation, spare parts, repairs and other related expenses which account for 87 per cent of total costs. Due to partial liberalisation, the cost structure faced by the industry remains high. The price of aviation turbine fuel, for example, accounting for 35 per cent of total costs, is about 2.5 times that of international prices. The government permitted the import of the fuel under the Special Import License scheme during 1994–95. But the imposition of a surcharge on the import of fuel against such a scheme made these imports uneconomical, thus annulling the benefit that would have accrued to Indian Airlines (IA) during 1995–96. IA has not been able to rationalise its fare structure, particularly on short-haul flights. Long-run marginal cost was used as the guiding principle for pricing services on short haul while marginal revenues were less than long-run marginal costs. The main trunk routes, on the other hand, were over-priced and extremely lucrative. Understandably, these routes came under severe competition from private airlines.

The deregulation in domestic services was started in April 1993. As a result, IA has been under severe strain as it has had to share the market on its more profitable routes and lost skilled personnel to the rival private operators who were able to attract key pilots and other personnel by offering higher compensation packages. This affected the ability of IA to deploy its existing aircraft capacity. Besides, IA has been plagued by irresponsible unionism, and unresponsive and impolite staff. Political interference resulted in the total subversion of professionalism within the company. The new environment in the domestic services sector has helped greatly in the quality of service provided to airline passengers. However, the financial performance of IA is not strong enough to enable the company to raise sufficient internal resources to fund its future expansion.

The profitability of Air India (AI) has come under pressure due to a combination of factors like poor customer service due to industrial unrests leading to cancellation of flights and disruption of flight schedules. Depreciation costs and interest charges have risen as the small number of carriers available for long-haul flights and the overall aging of the fleet has made it necessary to acquire newer aircraft. The increase in expenditure due to higher insurance, fuel oil, landing, leasing, rental and hire charges, wages and salaries of staff have all contributed to the high cost structure of the industry. These costs are not being fully offset via rises in fares or higher bookings. The company incurred a net loss of Rs 2.7 billion in 1995–96. While profits have declined with rising costs, the company's performance has improved in most of the physical parameters. But, Air India's overall load factor of 62 per cent remains low compared to international airlines. Its share of international traffic originating from India has declined from 42 per cent in 1981 to 20 per cent by 1994 as passengers switched to other carriers with superior service. Through aggressive marketing, AI improved its market share to 22 per cent in 1995.

The airport infrastructure demands a higher level of investment. Keeping in view the resource constraints of the government, domestic and foreign investors have been invited to participate in the development of new international airports and the expansion of infrastructural support at some domestic airports. It has also been decided to privatise the ground handling at Delhi and Mumbai to facilitate decongestion and improve aircraft turnaround time. India's domestic air transport industry is still in its infancy. The cost structure is too high for the industry to generate sufficient internal savings for expansion or to attract massive foreign investment until the issues relating to the high cost structure are properly addressed by the government.

Shipping and Ports

India's shipping capability has grown steadily since 1960–61 when the gross registered tonnage was 0.4 per cent of world capacity, but represented 1.5 per cent of world capacity in 1994–95. The 1960s and 1970s saw a 10 per cent growth rate in tonnage acquisition. The worldwide slump in shipping in the 1980s affected India and the vigorous growth rates of the previous decades were hard to sustain. The slowdown in acquisition since the 1980s resulted in raising the average age of the Indian merchant fleet. The addition of new vessels in the last few years brought down the average age of the Indian fleet to 14 years by 1994 against a global average of 17 years. The average age of the Indian cargo fleet of 411 vessels was 10 years compared with the international average of 16 years. However, Indian ports face alarming capacity shortages and low productivity levels due to low labour and equipment productivity.

India's fleet has largely evolved in direct response to the growth in imports. A major portion of the Indian fleet comprises of dry cargo bulk carriers, dry cargo liners and crude oil tankers and POL carriers. Imports of POL and fertilisers and exports of ore have resulted in this unusual composition. POL account for over 42 per cent of traffic in major ports. Indian bulk carriers have been limited to smaller size vessels, compared with international standards, due to the inability of the domestic ports to handle larger vessels. Containerisation which ushered in a technological revolution in the industry has yet to make any impact in India. In 1993–94, container traffic accounted for less than 7 per cent of total traffic. Indian ports are significantly costlier than other ports for handling containers and the losses due to delays and the use of second and third generation vessels are estimated at over $300 million per annum.

Most Indian shipping is currently owned and operated by the public sector. The Shipping Corporation of India (SCI) set up in 1961 with a mere 16 per cent of total tonnage, currently accounts for half of it. With a few other state level public sector units, the public sector owns 55 per cent of the total. The remaining ownership is distributed among private sector companies which is dominated by a handful of private companies like Great Eastern Shipping, Essar Shipping and a few smaller players like Chowgule Shipping, Garware Shipping, Varun Shipping. The industry has been blamed for its complacency because Indian shipping companies have never handled more than 42 per cent of India's international trade. The share of Indian ships in overseas cargo was about 29 per cent in 1994–95.

Spread over India's 5560 km long coastline there are just 11 major ports and 139 minor ones that are operable. Of the 11 major ports, the five ports of Bombay, Madras, Vishakapatnam, Kandla and Marmagoa account for over 90 per cent of total freight. During 1995–96, the total cargo handled at major ports rose to 215 million tonnes or 91 per cent of the total traffic handled by the port sector. Dry and liquid bulk constituted 80 per cent of the traffic volume with general cargo, including containerised cargo, accounting for the remaining traffic. The total capacity of India's major ports was estimated at 177 million tonnes at the end of March 1996. Most Indian ports are operating at over their capacity limits. Thus, for India to be able to maintain its export growth rate, development of port capacity will be vital. The India Infrastructure Report (IIR) recommends the development of two megaports, one each on the east and west coasts, as warehouses for the Indian subcontinent.

Long-term targets for Indian shares in bulk carrier and liner traffic are quite aggressive at 50 per cent and 40 per cent of the total traffic respectively. But to achieve these aims requires a substantially higher level of investment in the shipping and ports sector. In its effort to provide globally competitive multimodal transport facility for containerised cargo, the Container Corporation of India has been diversifying its operations with a view to rise to the growth in container traffic in the future. As the composition of port traffic has been changing over the last few years with the new emphasis on exports, the availability of item-wise capacities at major ports has not been possible. There is an increasing need to restructure the capacity of the existing ports to handle such volumes. While port productivity has improved in recent years, productivity levels still remain low due to the usual problems of over-manning, outdated equipment and various operational constraints. By international standards, the level of productivity in India's ports do not even stand scrutiny.

Overall port capacity was estimated to increase to 325 million tonnes by 2000–01 and 540 million by 2005–06, requiring investments of Rs 100 billion in the first stage and a further Rs 150 billion over 2005–06. Compared to actual expenditure of Rs 16 billion between 1992–96 and a total plan allocation of Rs 42 billion, the resources required have to be internally generated or come from private sources. The internal accruals of the ports were expected to amount to Rs 60 billion between 1996–97 and 2000–01 and Rs 75 billion from 2001–02 to 2005–06 leaving a deficit of Rs 40 billion and Rs 80 billion respectively to be raised from external sources. The SCI's gross internal resources were only Rs 5.5 billion in

1995–96 compared to Rs 3.9 billion in 1994–95. The projections for internal accruals made by the IIR appear to be optimistic.

The privatisation of ports has been initiated to attract private investment and modern technology. The port activities that are being opened up for private sector participation include the building and maintenance of container terminals along with cargo-handling facilities, the setting up of storage and warehouse facilities, operation and maintenance of port crafts and other equipment, dredging and pilotage services. The government has given clearance to the Jawaharlal Nehru Port to award the licence for the construction, management and maintenance of a two-berth container terminal for a period of 30 years on a build-operate-transfer basis to the P&O Ports, an Australian led consortium. Proposals for the privatisation at other ports are also under way. Under the present system, ports are governed by the Indian Ports Act 1908 and the Major Port Trusts Act 1963. Both these Acts have flexibility to allow privatisation of port activities. But greater delegation of financial and administrative powers to the port trust boards has to be introduced to encourage and sustain the participation of the private sector.

The Telecommunications Sector

India's telecommunication network represents the highest level of unfulfilled demand in the services sector. It offers among the lowest level of penetration of the population in developing countries. The National Telecom Policy (NTP) of May 1994 reassessed the Eighth Plan targets aiming to link all villages to the telecommunication network by 1997. This target had to be revised for completion in the Ninth Plan. Out of 603 906 villages in India, 35.8 per cent had access to public telephones by March 1996. The other major feature of the NTP was the proposal to make telephones and lines available on demand by 1997. This was to be achieved by the introduction of competition in basic telecom services. The NTP envisaged a private sector initiative to complement the Department of Telecommunication's (DoT's) efforts at resource mobilisation. The progress of the NTP stalled with the arrest of Sukh Ram, the ex-Minister of Telecommunication in the Congress Party, on charges of corruption in 1996.

India had a network of over 21 328 telephone exchanges with a capacity of 15.16 million lines and 12.61 million working connections in September 1996. The exchange network has been growing at the rate of 22 per cent per annum over the past few years. A switching capacity of 2.6 million lines was added during 1995–96 registering a 17 per cent growth over the previous year. A quarter of this increased capacity was in the four major cities of Delhi, Mumbai, Chennai and Calcutta. While the growth rate of providing new telephone connections has been increasing, the number of people waiting for new connections remains high. On 31 March 1996, there were 2.28 million people 'officially' waiting for telephone connections. However, Mahanagar Telephone Nigam Ltd (MTNL) was in a position to provide a telephone connection on demand to its customers by March 1997. This level of growth would never have materialised without greater competition being introduced to the sector.

Basic telecom services in India have been the monopoly of the government. Despite recent privatisations, the government's shareholding in MTNL, which handles the two most profitable telephone systems of Bombay and Delhi, and Videsh Sanchar Nigam Ltd (VSNL), which controls the international switching and transmission systems, remain at the 66 per cent level. Telephone services for the rest of the country are handled by DoT. Production facilities have also been the sole preserve of the public sector. The Indian Telephone Industries produced switching systems and telephone instruments and Hindustan Teleprinters made the telex and fax-machines. But the NTP of May 1994 aimed at transforming India into a major manufacturing base and an exporter of telecom equipment. Until 1991, the production of telecom equipment was reserved for the public sector, though private investment in the production of customer premises telephone equipment was allowed in 1984. In July 1991, the telecom equipment manufacturing industry was delicensed allowing the automatic approval of foreign equity up to 51 per cent in the sector. By 1995–96, exports of telecom equipment were at Rs 16.5 billion.

Value-added services were opened up to the private sector in 1992. These services include cellular mobile phones, radio-paging, electronic mail, voice mail, audio and video text services, video conferencing along with credit card authorisation services. One major initiative to introduce cellular phones was thwarted after the unsuccessful bidders took recourse to legal action as a means of invalidating the selection process. The decision to award radio-paging was similarly challenged. Most observers concede that the problems arose because the tenders were issued prior to the government framing adequate rules and procedures relating to the issue of licenses. The NTP statement of May 1994 provided clearer guidelines indicating the scope of the private sector in providing basic telecom services. In the value-added services sector, the government has permitted foreign equity participation of up to 51 per cent, but this limit is lower at 49 per cent for basic services like cellular mobile phone and radio-paging. Private sector investment is also welcome in the manufacture of telecom cables.

On the basis of licences issued in 1994 for the four metro cities of India – Delhi, Mumbai, Chennai and Calcutta – cellular mobile phone services have already started on a commercial basis in these cities. Government inexperience meant that it failed to adopt the highest-bid route. Thus, these four licences were given away very cheaply. It is expected that a cellular mobile telephone service will be operational all over the country as letters of intent have been issued to successful bidders to operate in 17 of the 20 circles for a period of 10 years. In January 1995, tenders were invited from the private sector companies registered in India for the award of licences for providing basic telecom services for 15 years in the various areas of the country. Letters of intent have been awarded to eight bidders in 12 telecom circles to provide basic telecom services. The DoT will continue to provide basic telephone services in all circles. Only one licence to a private operator is being given, in addition to the DoT, in each circle.

The original outlay for the telecommunications sector as outlined in the Eighth Plan was Rs 251.4 billion. With restricted budgetary support and limited options for market borrowing in 1991–92, additional resources were drawn up by rationalising the tariff structure, issuing subscriber bonds and supplementing market borrowings by equity issues of VSNL and MTNL. The revised Eighth Plan outlay was Rs 239.5 billion for DoT including MTNL. In the first four years of the Plan, 1992–96, total expenditure on developmental schemes was Rs 255.5 billion, over 80 per cent of which was financed internally and 19 per cent through market borrowings. There was a small amount of budgetary support. For the remaining year of the Plan it was estimated that investment would increase the total expenditure to Rs 355.3 billion, 79 per cent of which would come from internal resources.

India's installation, rental and local call charges of fixed lines are among the cheapest in Asia. Revenue per line to the government has therefore been among the lowest in Asia, marginally above that of China. As in the power sector, residential phone tariffs in India are subsidised by the business sector. It is inevitable that the private, fixed-line operators have targetted business customers so as to maximise revenue with minimal investment. Usage level in India is highly dispersed: 80 per cent of the revenue comes from 20 per cent of users, and 40 per cent of subscribers pay only their monthly rentals which include 100 free calls every two months. 60 per cent of international calls are also made from two cities in India, Mumbai and Delhi. The rate structures are revised infrequently; there was one made in March 1996. The previous one was in June 1993.

Though the demand for fixed lines remain high, poor fixed-line infrastructure is expected to provide impetus to the growth of mobile phones in

India. However, with airtime charges among the highest in Asia, substantial discounts need to be provided to encourage usage of cellular phones even though monthly rentals are low along with installation and deposit charges. Marketing price wars are set to put pressure on these rates. The high cost of hand-sets due to high import tariff along with the liquidity crunch in the financial markets has depressed the level of demand from the corporate sector. Airtime charges are also anticipated to fall as capital equipment prices, import duties and prices decline. Licence fee liabilities are the second largest item of cost for the private operators after access charges to DoT. External factors like funding costs, tariff regulation and import duties also influence the profitability of private cellular and fixed-line operators. Increased competition can only benefit the customer.

One of the future concerns for the industry is that there are many different levels of technology operational within the Indian telecommunications framework. Officials do not seem overly worried about system-compatibilty, having carried out extensive validation tests on the various systems in use. As the replacements costs of upgrading equipment and standardising them along international lines can be exorbitant, the current emphasis is on growth and on providing basic services to consumers. With increasing globalisation, India's telecom sector will need to fall into line with international standards. Even in the case of Japan, the telecommunication industry which had long depended on indigenous technology developed by NTT (Japan's former monopoly national telecom company) was often out of line with international standards. But in 1989 Japan agreed under intense pressure from the USA to adopt a US standard for analogue phones. Currently, Japanese cellular phone companies are considering adopting a US standard for digital phones as well as using radio frequencies more effectively amid rapidly expanding demand for cellular phones.

There is significant potential for growth in the sector. At current rates of growth India is expected to become the sixth largest network by 2001. But substantial investments will be required to ensure that India becomes a global player in the telecom sector. The government has realised the need to attract foreign companies to set up manufacturing bases in India. The establishment of the Telecom Regulatory Authority has been a welcome development. It has been estimated that an additional 19 million lines would be required over the next five years of which DoT and MTNL would provide 10.3 million lines; the rest are expected to come from the private sector. Total funds required by the sector for the provision of basic and cellular telecom services by 2006 was estimated by the India Infrastructure Report at Rs 1915 billion, 47 per cent of which is to come from the DoT's internal revenue generation. Between 1992–96, internal sources provided about Rs 206 billion for investment. Unless the government pursues an aggressive policy of greater privatisation and liberalisation, the level of funding required from the private sector or from the public sector itself will not be forthcoming.

INVESTMENT IN THE SOCIAL SECTORS

The fact that India lags behind other developing countries in its social sector development has been established by various World Bank reports. Scholarly studies by Dreze and Sen make a compelling case for swifter reforms in education. India's ranking in the United Nations Development Programme's Human Development Index (taking into account purchasing power parity, adjusted real per-capita GDP, life expectancy at birth, adult literacy rates and other social development criteria) reinforces the nation's low development status. An examination of the details of reforms desirable in the various social sectors is beyond the scope of this book. However, as the problem of the eradication of poverty is vital to the development of India, it is important to address the principles involved in achieving that. It is becoming increasingly important for governments around the world to enhance human development. The most effective way of assisting the poor is to help them to invest in themselves.

Table 5.4   Public expenditure on education and health

Country	Education		Higher education (as % of all levels)	Health	
	1960	*1990*	*1992*	*1960*	*1990*
	(% of GNP)			*(% of GNP)*	
India	2.3	3.5	15	0.5	1.3
China	1.8	2.3	19	1.3	2.1
Indonesia	2.5	0.9	na	0.3	0.7
Malaysia	2.9	6.9	16	1.1	1.3
Pakistan	1.1	3.4	18*	0.3	1.8
Philippines	2.3	2.9	15*	0.4	1.0
South Korea	2.0	3.6	7	0.2	2.7
Sri Lanka	3.8	2.7	14	2.0	1.8
Thailand	2.3	3.8	16	0.4	1.1

Note: * Data refers to a period other than specified.
Source: *Human Development Reports*, 1995 and 1996.

While India's poor showing in the world's league table for human development is cause for concern, what is worrying is that the level of public expenditure on social sectors in India compares favourably with that of other

Asian countries (see Table 5.4). This only confirms the suspicion that the impediment to India's development has not always been the lack of investment. Poor returns on the investments made are due to policy failures triggered by inadequate assessment systems and other factors such as poor project implementation, lack of training or incentives, inadequate monitoring, not to mention nepotism and corruption in the hiring of staff; in brief, an inefficient management system resulting in low productivity. The problems in India's social sector mirror those of the general economy where reasonably high rates of investment do not translate to levels of productivity seen in other economies.

The transfer of wealth to the poor can be facilitated by increasing the demand for their services. One of the functions of reform was to remove the bias against unskilled labour within the domestic market which could benefit from the availability of cheap labour by exploiting the global market. The East Asian countries were able to increase their real wages through exporting their cheap labour in the 1960s and 1970s. A rise in private investment in infrastructure with an increase in trade should have generated a higher demand for semi-skilled and unskilled labour in India. Instead, liberalisation increased the demand for skilled personnel in certain sectors of the economy leading to an escalation of salaries that became comparable to those in the West such as the investment banking sector. The success of the software industry in India is an example of the extent to which the country is benefiting from its export of cheap, skilled labour. As private sector investment in the development of infrastructure rises, demand for unskilled and semi-skilled labour should also increase. Policy bottlenecks have delayed such investment flows stalling the growth in employment generation.

Alleviation of poverty created due to unemployment and under-employment continues to be the long-term objective of economic and social development in India. As under-employment is the primary cause of poverty, the pace of poverty reduction was higher in the 1980s than in the 1970s as overall employment levels improved in the 1980s with the higher growth rate of the economy during that decade. Since poverty has been largely a rural phenomenon, there is a strong case for land reform. As that is deemed to be not viable politically, greater liberalisation in agriculture will improve the prospects of those employed in the sector. While economic reforms in India threaten workers in the public sector, the higher rate of growth in private investment should lead to greater job creation in the private sector. The public sector employs about 19.5 million people or less than 8 per cent of India's labour force. Thus, much of the productive capital of the country is concentrated on the few.

The average level of poverty in India tends to hide the high level of disparity among the states. The higher incidence of poverty in the more populous states like Uttar Pradesh also illustrates that population growth is the major factor in the higher level of poverty. These are also the states with the lowest literacy rates. The need for stepping up literacy programmes along with family welfare schemes is thus vital for reducing poverty. India has no option but to invest heavily in its social sector development. With better education and a flourishing private sector, the level of poverty in the country can be lowered substantially over the next 50 years. An improvement of two percentage points in GDP growth is enough to double incomes every 35 years. However, if the population is also expected to double over the same period, the government has to fast-forward its investment in the social sectors. Setting up adequate systems to monitor the investments made is as important as building schools for girls in remote villages where the teachers and inevitably the pupils turn up irregularly. This 'absenteeism' has frittered away precious resources over the years.

In view of the importance of tackling the issue of rising unemployment in the country, the National Development Committee appointed a committee in early 1991 to suggest the means of achieving near-full employment within a ten year period. The Eighth Plan targeted the generation of 8.5 million additional employment opportunities per annum during 1992–97. This target was sought to be achieved by emphasizing crop-wise and geographic diversification of agricultural growth, wasteland development, promotion of agro-based activities and rural non-farm activities including rural industries like the decentralised and small-scale sector of industry and the urban informal sector with the services sector. The expansion of rural infrastructure in housing, education and health services was also seen as part of revamping the special employment programmes. Thus, the thrust areas for job creation were the diversification of agriculture, irrigation, stimulation of rural non-agricultural employment, small-scale industries, large-scale programmes of construction, faster growth of services and the informal sector. But, slippages between policy and implementation meant that employment generation fell short of the target.

Reforms were meant to benefit the poor. Instead the partial implementation of reform has extracted a high social cost. Real per capita increases in expenditure were made on social sectors like elementary rural education, health and family planning, housing and urban development. The Eighth Plan outlay on social sectors and rural development was 180 per cent higher than in the Seventh Plan. The aim of reform was to accelerate the reduction of poverty but the successful pursuit of these social objectives by the government implies a sound fiscal base and reduction in public expenditure to release public resources for the social sectors. Budgetary support for activities which can be sustained by private sector funding are being cut but further scope for reduction in unproductive subsidies remains. The Eighth Plan's allocation for social services at 18.2 per cent of expenditure was the highest since that of the Third Plan. But, it does not alter the fact that decades of inadequate investment in the social sectors coupled with the inefficiencies inherent in past policies have resulted in a high level of poverty.

The aim to boost investment in human capital development by enhancing budget provisions for anti-poverty programmes and accelerating labour intensive growth is reflected in the sizeable increases in the central Plan allocations for social sectors and poverty alleviation programmes. The allocation for education as a percentage of total outlay has increased from 3.6 per cent in 1992–93 to 5 per cent in 1995–96. But, the significant shift lies in the rising trend in expenditure on elementary education which rose over 100 per cent over this period. One of the main criticisms aimed at India's educational funding is the heavy subsidisation of higher education at the cost of primary education. The other discernible change is the rise in the expenditure on rural development which included major programmes for poverty alleviation and employment generation. What is unclear is whether the government has established any mechanism for evaluating the success of these programmes initiated as a result of the higher expenditure, because higher expenditure by itself does not necessarily translate into productivity and growth.

Total outlays for the social services and rural development programmes rose annually with the major contribution coming from higher central allocations. Over 62 per cent of the expenditure in 1995–96 was from the centre. The centre initiated a programme addressing the critical issue of investing in the nation's most vital sector during the Eighth Plan (see Table 5.5), but the centre's strategy for developing rapid and sustained growth of productive employment opportunities and the alleviation of poverty was not fully reflected at the state level.

India's inadequate social and economic development with its high incidence of poverty and regional disparities warrants a higher level of public expenditure on the social sector. What is necessary is a system of monitoring the utilisation of these investments. India scores poorly in the provision of sanitation where 86 per cent of the population has no access to it. It was also estimated that 70 million children under the age of five were suffering from malnutrition, which explains the high infant mortality rate. Considering India's healthy foodgrain situation, the whole issue of malnutrition among children has more to do with the inefficiencies of India's public distribution system, the lack of proper health education among young mothers, and the social mores of family life in India. Thus, increasing investment in the education of women should yield significant returns in the long term. In one stroke, it will reduce population growth and infant mortality, improve the overall health of the nation and help in wiping out the divisions over caste in India. Besides, higher literacy is fundamental to India's democratic and secular institutions. Investment in social sectors is not only necessary to underpin growth but to keep Indian values and democracy alive.

Table 5.5   Eighth plan outlay for social sectors (Rs billion)

	Eighth Plan	1992–93 actual	1993–94 actual	1994–95 RE	1995–96 R E
Rural development	344.3	50.9	70.3	82.7	94.7
Social services	790.1	113.2	140.2	182.2	232.4
education	196.0	26.2	31.5	42.8	61.2
health	75.8	12.1	13.0	17.1	20.1
family welfare	65.0	10.1	13.1	14.3	15.1
housing	52.7	6.5	12.9	13.6	19.7
urban development	52.8	7.9	8.6	10.7	17.9
other	347.9	50.4	61.1	83.7	98.3
Total	4341.0	728.5	880.8	1062.0	1198.9
Central plan	2478.7	436.9	552.2	683.2	745.9
State plans	1799.9	279.2	315.0	358.3	430.0
UTs plans	62.5	12.4	13.6	20.6	23.0

Source: *Indian Economic Survey*, 1996–97.

AGRICULTURE

The importance of agriculture to the Indian economy cannot be overlooked as it provides employment to about 65 per cent of the population, represents 30 per cent of GDP and accounts for 20 per cent of India's exports. Under a centrally planned economy, agriculture received a high share of India's total expenditure. Large capital outlays on rural infrastructural development helped to expand irrigation facilities, improve productivity through the use of higher-yielding seeds and the increased use of fertilisers while achieving better disease control through the use of pesticides. Rural credit mechanisms were put in place to provide the farmer with access to cheaper capital and agricultural support prices were established by the government. India thus allocated considerable resources towards its 'green revolution' to alleviate food shortages and build up a comfortable buffer of food stock.

India devoted Rs 685 billion in 1994–95 or 8 per cent of its GDP to agriculture, but it has not translated into significantly higher productivity in the sector. Tax revenue from agriculture, as a percentage of government's total revenue, declined from 6.7 per cent in 1961–62 to 0.8 per cent by 1991–92 reducing the scope for the creation of any investible surpluses within the sector. While expenditure on agriculture, irrigation and allied services has risen exponentially since the 1960s, the rate of growth of gross capital formation in agriculture was low at 2.3 per cent per annum between 1970–91. The rate of growth of gross value-addition in the sector was also poor at 2.8 per cent per annum between 1969–91. Since 1990–91, gross domestic capital formation in agriculture has declined in real terms but the share of the private sector has risen from 75 per cent of gross capital formation in agriculture in 1990–91 to over 79 per cent in 1995–96. Improved trade policy and expectations of greater liberalisation in the sector has attracted a higher level of private investment. A large portion of public investment in agriculture has disappeared in current expenditures on subsidies instead of going into asset creation.

The growth of India's food production has outpaced its population growth but the per capita availability of foodgrains has risen more sporadically. In spite of the progress in agricultural production, the annual variations in output remain a cause for concern. Experts have attributed it to changing agro-climatic conditions in which the new technologies have been put into use. With the new seeds and nutrient technology, output has become more dependant on irrigation. But much of the irrigation potential developed remains sensitive to rainfall because more than half the irrigated area is served by minor sources. The per capita growth of agriculture and food products in India has lagged behind that of China's since the 1980s and yet the food content of China's imports has been higher. The compound annual growth rate of per capita food production in India between 1979–92 was 1.6 per cent compared to China's 2.9 per cent.

As India gets more industrialised and labour shifts from agriculture to industry, the current self-sufficiency in foodgrain production, thanks to nine good monsoons, may appear in hindsight as the golden decade of prosperity. While productivity gains have been made, the average yield of most major crops in India is low. India's liberalisation has touched most areas of manufacturing but it has not been applied to the agricultural sector where major productivity gains can be made. It is true that agriculture in most countries is considered to be something of a sacred cow and that no nation would like to surrender its sense of security in terms of food. But, it is only a matter of time before nations need to address the question of the sustainability of subsidies that generate inefficiencies in productivity in an environment of increasing constraints in the availability and allocation of financial resources.

The problem with any policy is that no single policy holds good forever. So, whatever economic policies India adopted in the 1950s had long outrun their usefulness and needed changing. It goes without saying that the policies being implemented today will need changing in a couple of decades. Policymakers need the flexibility to adapt to changes in the economic environment without waiting for a crisis to enforce it upon them. The turning point in India's determination to be self-sufficient in food came in 1965 when a severe drought led to a 19 per cent fall in foodgrain production which precipitated imports of 10.3 million tonnes of foodgrains representing 14 per cent of the total foodgrain availability. India's foodgrain position has always been influenced by the monsoon. India experienced three severe droughts since Independence. In four out of the 10 years in each of the decades of the 1960s, the 1970s and the 1980s, the country was under drought conditions that were categorised as 'moderate' to 'near severe'. India has now had nine uninterrupted 'normal' to 'good' monsoons since 1988 which has boosted foodgrain production and raised the level of the nation's buffer stock.

India's current level of self-sufficiency in foodgrain production was achieved through increases in cropped areas, the higher use of irrigation, fertilisers, high-yielding seeds and the availability of subsidised credit to farmers. The rise in productivity growth came in the 1980s and can be attributed to the rise in the yield of wheat. Forty-three per cent of the total geographical area was used for agricultural activity in 1990–91 compared to 36 per cent in 1950–51. As some parts of the net sown area were cropped more than once, the gross sown area was 28 per cent higher in 1990–91 compared to 11 per cent in 1950–51. Of the net sown area, less than 18 per cent was irrigated in 1950–51 compared to 33 per cent in 1990–91. The proportion of the gross area under major crops using high-yielding varieties of seeds also rose from 12 per cent in 1970–71 to 51 per cent by 1990–91.

However, the system of subsidies in agriculture has created an imbalance in the allocation of resources, encouraging concentration on elite cereals to the exclusion of pulses, oilseeds and other coarse cereals. In 1950–51, the production of cereals was 83.5 per cent of foodgrain production compared to 16.5 per cent for pulses. By 1994–95, this ratio had not improved but deteriorated to 93 per cent for cereals and only 7 per cent for pulses. Among cereals too, production is dominated by rice and wheat which together comprise 77 per cent of foodgrain production. Most of the irrigated land has been devoted to foodcrops, specifically rice and wheat. The area devoted to pulses has stagnated at 23 million hectares and production has hovered at 12–14 million tonnes. As a result of this stagnation in production over the last several years, pulses have declined from 11 per cent of the foodgrain basket in 1970–71 to 7 per cent in 1995–96. Per capita availability of pulses has declined substantially from about 70 grams in 1961 to 39 grams in 1996.

Despite government efforts to boost production by increasing both minimum support prices and retail prices, there has been a reluctance by farmers to increase their production of pulses. Larger price spreads for pulses translated to a lower share of the profit to the producer in the consumer price for pulses than it was for cereals. This is a good example of how production growth is a direct result of a profit motive; and, if the latter is withdrawn, the incentive to produce more is also reduced. The whole point about introducing market orientation to a centrally planned system is to inject that incentive. The market, as it has operated under a centrally directed economy, has favoured certain crops above others. The returns from introducing market orientation will also decline in time, and policy changes will then have to be made.

After decades of central planning and public investment in irrigation facilities, the total irrigated area as a percentage of the area under foodcrops rose from 24 per cent in 1970–71 to 38.7 per cent in 1993–94. Despite the preference for rice and wheat production, only 48 per cent of the area under rice production and 85 per cent of the area under wheat production were irrigated by 1993–94. While rice productivity lagged as a result of the inadequate irrigation coverage, it is worth noting that the major rice producing states in India have wide variations in irrigated areas devoted to rice. Thus, for example, states like Uttar Pradesh or West Bengal which are major rice producers have 58 per cent and 25 per cent respectively of their rice acreage irrigated while states like Tamil Nadu and Andhra Pradesh have over 93 per cent of their rice area under irrigation. The higher level of irrigated areas in the south has more to do with the cheaper supply of power in those states.

An efficient and irrigated cropping system alone can sustain the growing needs of India's population. While the creation of irrigation potential and its optimum utilisation remains the government's priority, the rate of success remains poor. The rate of utilisation of irrigation potential has improved but was still at 89 per cent in 1995–96. The irrigation potential created for major and medium irrigation systems was estimated to be 33

million hectares in 1995–96 and 58 million hectares under minor irrigation. The total area under irrigation has increased but the growth rate declined significantly in the 1980s compared to the 1970s reflecting the
decline in utilisation rates. As the costs of irrigation has risen sharply, government investment has declined. The system of subsidised tariffs for irrigation, which does not even cover the basic maintenance costs of the
irrigation networks, has ensured that the existing facilities are not fully
utilised and thus fresh capacity creation has declined. This has restrained
growth in agricultural productivity.

The increasing demand for fresh water has been causing acute pressure
on the development of water resources in India bringing into focus the user-
cost of water. There is a broad consensus that the country's irrigation rates
should cover the annual maintenance and operational expenses along with
some percentage of fixed costs. The Economic Survey of 1995–96 pointed
out that 'the water rates . . . need to be rationalised with due regard to the interests of small and marginal farmers', while 'the issue of sound financial
restructuring of irrigation projects must receive greater attention at the
policy making level in the States'. Public canals and tube-wells have been
the major sources of irrigation accounting for 65 per cent of the total irrigated land while other forms of wells account for a further 21 per cent. The
use of tanks in irrigation declined in the 1960s with the growth in publicly-
funded canals and the huge spurt in the growth of tube-wells. During
1971–91, the rate of growth of canals lagged behind that of tube-wells with
the net irrigated area growing at 2 per cent per annum.

The use of fertilisers has been encouraged to some extent by the government subsidy, but its use lags behind that of other developing countries like
China, Indonesia or Malaysia because the subsidy has been directed more
at the producer rather than the consumer. India's agronomists point out that
the use of fertilisers remains below recommended levels for many crops
and that enhancing its use could boost foodgrain production by as much as
20 per cent. While fertiliser subsidies have encouraged higher usage, with
annual fertiliser subsidies amounting to virtually the combined outlay of
central and state governments on agriculture, doubts have been cast on the
long-term advantages from such an expenditure not to mention its inequitable bias. The implicit subsidies on irrigation and power supply as a result
of non-recovery of basic economic costs from the users are estimated to
be even larger than the fertiliser subsidies and together they have been
potentially damaging to the rise of real investment in agriculture as they
have worked against the generation of investible surpluses. There has been
a growing realisation that subsidies need to be cut and the resources thus
freed be invested to improve the productivity of the agricultural sector.

Fragmentation of holdings has been another obstacle for farmers. The average size of operational holdings declined from 2.69 hectares in 1960–61 to 1.68 hectares in 1985–86. While it has affected all classes of farmers, it affected marginal farmers the most; they constitute over half the farmers in India. The least affected were the large farmers who comprise 2 per cent of all farmers indicating that India's land reform programme is heavily overdue. According to various studies, the minimum holding size required to earn an income above the poverty level is 1.7 hectares. That implies that 76 per cent of farmers are barely equipped to earn a subsistence income through farming. The inadequate targeting of subsidies has not helped subsistence farmers.

In order to encourage foodgrain production, India adopted the minimum support prices (MSP) policy for farmers. The government also used MSP as a strategy for controlling inflation and thus may find it difficult to contain inflation in the process of introducing market pricing. But in a world that has to restructure itself globally in order to survive, it is inevitable that domestic pricing will need to be aligned along global lines. The combination of subsidies and MSP created an inefficient system so that the value-added in agriculture remained low. This is reflected across the board from the growth in irrigated area to the yield per hectare in the major crops which is reflected in the gap in yields per hectare of major crops between the world's top producers and India's. It is clear that Indian yields have a lot of catching up to do as they are well below the world averages. Despite India's major achievements in the agricultural sector, restrictions on agricultural activity has inhibited the development of this key sector of the economy.

Various restrictions in terms of licensing requirements for agro-processing industries, restrictions on exports and barriers in internal trade and storage together with input price distortions have reduced incentives for producers and inhibited growth in agricultural productivity. According to an IMF study, 'labor productivity in India's farm sector has grown by an average of 1/2 of 1 per cent a year over the past two decades, compared with productivity growth in East Asian farming of over 2 per cent a year' (IMF, 1995, *India: Economic Reform and Growth*, p. 62) India's low productivity has contributed to the slow growth of farm wages and persistent poverty in rural areas. Indeed, broadening the reforms to cover agriculture which employs 65 per cent of India's population should help to spread more equitably the benefits of reform and improve income distribution.

India remains among the largest producers of rice, wheat, millet, groundnuts, rapeseed, sugar, soyabean, jute, cotton, tobacco and tea among other food products. But its ranking in terms of yield per hectare globally is significantly low in all the major crops. India has undoubtedly achieved a lot in terms of its ability to produce foodgrains since the 1950s, however in the next phase of India's growth the emphasis has to be on better utilisation of existing resources to maximise production. Despite greater success in food production and a lower rate of growth in population, economic prosperity leads to higher consumption leaving less for exports. The story of Indian tea is well-known; increased domestic demand and stagnant production ultimately dislodged India as the world's major tea exporter. In 1980, India exported 0.22 million tonnes of tea and was the world's largest exporter with almost a quarter of the global market. By 1992, Indian tea exports had fallen to 0.16 million tonnes representing 14 per cent of the world market. Unless action is taken to improve India's productivity in tea, it may not be long before India ends up having to import tea. This could happen in some areas of foodgrain production as production to consumption ratios fall.

The timely supply of cheap credit to farmers is also vital to boosting their productivity. Thus, providing access to institutional credit for small and marginal farmers to enable them to adopt modern technology has been the major objective of India's agricultural credit policy. Though there has been a rise in the availability of credit to farmers, there has also been the problem of debts which has been inhibiting credit expansion to the farmers and has cast doubts on the economic viability of the commercial lending institutions. The recovery rate in 1995 was at 59.9 per cent having gone up from 54 per cent in 1992. In October 1994, the Reserve Bank of India deregulated the interest rate structure for cooperatives for lending as well as for raising deposits, and this is expected to improve the viability of these cooperatives. But agricultural loans waived in 1990, during the brief reign of the Janata Dal, aggravated the problem of recovery and inhibited credit expansion and threatened the economic viability of lending institutions.

The liberalisation of the agricultural sector has greater potential for dynamic, labour-intensive growth that would spread the benefits of economic reform more rapidly to a larger section of India's society. Thus, the political priority should be to relax the controls on agriculture in the way the industrial sector was deregulated in 1991. This would involve the same process of elimination of licensing requirements for wholesale trade and storage in agriculture. The public sector procurement programme and the minimum support pricing mechanism will need to be phased out gradually and the import and export of agricultural items should be allowed. Most of the restrictions on agricultural exports have already been removed. The items on the restricted list have also been reduced considerably and only a few items remain which require licensing or quantitative ceiling. Rice and wheat are now major Indian exports. Fruits, vegetables and flowers are also emerging as products with tremendous export potential. The new policy provides greater flexibility to growers in the export market. However, trade in agricultural commodities continue to be subject to quantitative restrictions.

There exists an argument in favour of foreign participation to bring in funding and technology, but the process of liberalisation in agriculture can be made initially at the domestic level to encourage the participation of the domestic private sector. The system of price incentives should reflect market conditions. The distortions in pricing are gradually being corrected while the subsidies are being reduced in real terms. Since 1991, the minimum support price mechanism has been used to smooth out the pricing distortions of the past, thereby gradually reducing the gap between domestic and international prices.

The regional imbalances in India's food production can be potentially destabilising for the country unless the various states are united through exchange of goods and services. Uttar Pradesh can de declared as India's granary with 20 per cent of production, followed by Punjab at 11 per cent, Madhya Pradesh 10 per cent, and Bihar and West Bengal each at 7 per cent in 1994–95. These five states together produced over half of India's foodgrains. Andhra Pradesh, Haryana, Maharashtra and Rajasthan produced a further 6 per cent each. Thus, almost 80 per cent of India's foodgrains came from nine states. These states can be further broken down into a few districts which have produced the nation's supply of food. It is not difficult to understand why India needs an excellent national food distribution system covering its 25 States and 7 Union Territories. The highly concentrated growth could have an adverse impact on food security as productivity increases begin to plateau in the existing high-growth areas.

The emergence of regionalism in Indian politics is a guide to the fact that the centre's influence has been waning. There is also the problem that extending the growth of foodgrain production to larger areas will be prohibitively expensive and thus beyond the scope of any government. Since the Seventh Plan period, the government has been targeting the eastern and north-eastern region, traditionally the low-productivity areas, for rice production. They are also among the poorest regions in the country. Considering that the eastern region accounted for 66 per cent of gross area under rice, the concentration was justified. With new cultivation techniques for the rain-fed lowlands, which account for 40 per cent of the regions' cropped area, improved seed varieties and superior fertiliser application, researchers are confident of increasing the productivity growth in the eastern region. Unless governments recognise the need to enable the private sector to invest, the chances are that India could become a nation divided within itself between the producers and the non-producers of foodgrains.

India is among the world's largest producers of fruits and vegetables. But restrictions in licensing requirements for agro-processing industries means that less than 5 per cent of the nation's production gets processed. Spoilage was estimated to be as high as 25 per cent. The easing of restriction in agro-processing industries has helped on both counts. Efforts are being made to boost the productivity of horticultural crops by the increased use of drip irrigation. Restrictions relating to acreage under drip irrigation was removed in 1995–96 and assistance is being provided for the entire holding to be devoted to growing horticultural crops. India loses approximately $1 billion annually through post-harvest losses of fruits and vegetables due to poor infrastructure and the lack of organised marketing of such produce.

There is great scope for private investment in the processing and food preservation sector. But the food processing industry's potential can only be unlocked by restructuring the industry which has been dominated by small-scale units. In February 1997, the Finance Minister dereserved rice and dal milling, poultry feed, vinegar, synthetic syrups, biscuits and ice-cream. There were still 822 items that were reserved for the small-scale sector. Since the mid-1980s, partial liberalisation in the food processing sector attracted the participation of large-scale industry, and most of the major global players now have a presence in India awaiting further reforms.

CONCLUSION

The United Front government's Common Minimum Programme (CMP) highlighted the inadequacies in infrastructural development for sustaining a higher level of economic growth. The reforms initiated in 1991 addressed these constraints by ending the monopoly of the public sector in the provision of the nation's infrastructure. In order to sustain greater private sector participation, a transparent policy framework needs to be established in all sectors involving changes in existing laws with regard to employment, taxation, land and competition. The progress in introducing the regulatory and administrative framework required to accommodate the private sector has been slow. It is vital that public spending in the various sectors is maintained during the period of transition.

The non-agricultural reforms which were launched in the 1980s and accelerated in the 1990s created a favourable environment for the agricultural sector, but major policy issues threaten the growth of agriculture. The public spending on agriculture has not been supportive of equitable or sustainable growth in the sector and trade restrictions continue to affect agricultural profitabilty, both external as much as domestic trade. The rural financial credit system is unable to help the small marginal farmers. Reforms in agriculture will be vital to poverty reduction in India. Public sector investments in rural infrastructure and human capital tend to encourage private investment. Investment in technological advancement and development of human capital can reverse the decline in productivity growth. The global environment is benign for agricultural liberalisation in India, and it is hoped that the nation's planners will take advantage of it.

An examination of public sector expenditure on infrastructural development, social sectors or on agriculture reveals that there is scope to improve returns on investments. Reforms include the introduction of private sector investment, switching public expenditure towards more targeted and growth-enhancing programmes, initiating market pricing of both inputs and outputs, and greater liberalisation of trade. Domestic markets in India need to operate more freely to support an effective open trade policy. India faces a favourable external environment and needs to utilise this opportunity to progress precipitously with its economic reforms which were initiated in the midst of a global crisis. Unfortunately, over the past few years, the pace of reform has slowed. Lack of progress in fiscal adjustment is also linked to India's remaining structural weaknesses which together are limiting improvements in productivity growth.

6 Investing in India

Efficient market theory has far-reaching implications for the future of the market as it is premised on the fact that the creation of wealth is based on the optimal allocation of capital which is most likely to be achieved through the market. If the market can be relied upon to mirror economic signals, then it can also transmit useful signals to both suppliers and users of capital; the former in building up their investment portfolios and the latter in establishing the criteria for the disposal of funds. As market orientation is being introduced to the Indian economy, it would be appropriate to indicate that it refers to international pricing indicators. The assumption is that, by doing so, India can open itself to the global market and exploit its competitive advantage through trade.

Like the economy, the Indian stockmarket is riddled with inefficiencies. It is thus critical to establish a reliable market pricing mechanism. Lack of confidence in the pricing efficiency of the market tends to draw the attention of both investors and users of capital to methods of exploiting these inefficiencies and away from the positive messages implicit in the market. But as pricing inefficiencies appear in most markets, active portfolio management can compensate for market inefficiencies and failures. Emerging markets (EMs) do not display the level of pricing efficiency to be found in the securities markets of industrial countries. These inefficiencies thus become a reason for fund flows seeking higher returns. While these funds may not be considered large by developed-country standards, they represent substantial percentages of the market capitalisation of emerging countries. The enhanced level of risk associated with EMs implies that investors end up with exploiting market volatility. While this phenomena distorts efficient market theory, there is a large body of evidence to support the fact that EMs are simply not efficient.

This is clearly a hindrance to the recipient country which has to deal with volatile fund flows, but investors have a responsibility to manage the volatility of such market flows on behalf of their clients. One of the challenges of a successful investment strategy in EMs is to neutralise the speculative aspect of such investments. Thus, if one learns to manage the risk in EMs, the reward is invariably more than optimal. Many successful investors in more mature markets have been able to ignore market timing in favour of the fundamental valuation of the companies they invest in. But in EMs investors cannot afford to ignore timing because extreme market volatility can lead to significant overpricing as well as underpricing. The illiquid nature of EMs means that any sizeable inflow of funds inflates financial assets swiftly.

One of the major attractions of investing in India is that the country has all the classic characteristics that feature in any investor's criteria for investment. The country offers a functioning democracy and has built up some kind of a consensus on reform. It boasts of an independent judiciary and a credible legal system. It has a large pool of skilled and cheap labour not to mention some of the most able administrators in the developing world. India has an established local equity culture supported by a high savings rate. It has an acceptable level of disclosure at the corporate level. It has established stockmarkets with over 7000 listed companies and 21 stock exchanges, and a developing banking and financial infrastructure along side a growing middle class. All this is supported by governments pledged to implement reforms, to deliver higher levels of economic growth than it has achieved in the past.

India has built an entire political and social infrastructure that is not in place in various other Asian countries, but the major problem with India is an inefficient management with inadequate policies. To what extent this is attributable to the low level of educational development is beyond the scope of this book. But what deters investors is that India's vast potential may remain more of a promise than a reality unless policy changes are implemented with some urgency. The advantage of investing in India today lies in the belief that the country, under new management as distinct from new governments, will succeed in achieving a higher level of efficiency and productivity growth than it has done in the past. Various studies on net factor productivity in India's private sector reveals that it compares favourably with that of East Asia. Increased competition with excess capacity, a weak trend in output prices and lower protection from imports will combine to put pressure on the manufacturing sector's profit margins. But it will be compensated by increased demand, lower incremental costs of capital, raw materials, physical infrastructure and distribution costs. All these attributes of growth can be acquired selectively in the Indian market without paying fancy prices in other established Asian markets.

As global EM investment strategies mature from an analysis of international flow of funds in financial markets to investing in industries and companies on a global basis, they will increasingly reflect foreign direct investment (FDI) flows. Currently, FDI flows into India remain small compared to portfolio investments. However, if Global Depository Receipt flows can be classified as a form of FDI, then FDI has overtaken portfolio flows into India. As the infrastructure develops and India is able to absorb a higher level of FDI, such flows will boost economic growth. India has a diverse industrial base in one of the largest developing consumer markets in the world, and it will not be long before FDI begins to find its way. The relationship between the stockmarket and the economy tends to be a contrapuntal one. The potential portfolio investor is well-advised to remember that financial markets can flourish in an environment of relatively weak investment activity as funds get transfered from the economy to the stockmarket and vice versa.

Studies also indicate that it has been difficult for EMs to compete with the US market. Since 1988, the US equity market performed better than most markets within Europe, Australia and the Far East (EAFE) as a group in 72 out of 96 rolling 12-month periods. In these 72 periods, when the US delivered better returns than EAFE markets, EMs outperformed the US market in only 23 periods. Thus, there is only a 32 per cent chance of EMs outperforming the US market when it is doing better than EAFE markets. But when EAFE outperforms the US, then EMs tend to outperform EAFE. In 18 out of those 24 periods when EAFE did better than the US, or a 75 per cent possibility, the performance of EMs was better than EAFE. In conclusion, it can be said that when the outlook for the US market is favourable, money stays at home. But when the US market looks lacklustre, US investors understandably invest overseas. And due to the illiquid nature of EMs they tend to outperform EAFE when this flow of funds takes place. When global allocations to EMs rise, fund flows into India automatically go up.

The Morgan Stanley Capital International (MSCI) Emerging Markets Free Index allocation for India was 9 per cent at the end of December 1994, but 5.7 per cent at the end of December 1995 due to the introduction of South Africa into the index. This allocation for India is likely to decline further with the introduction of newer EMs. But actual allocations to India within the EMs index reflect the short-term views of asset allocators with regard to the performance of the Indian stockmarket. An analysis of the average for India within a selection of EM funds revealed that the allocation was at 6–7 per cent of global EM portfolios during January as well as in December 1996. Fund managers maintained an overweight position in India through 1996 despite the political uncertainty. India's macroeconomic fundamentals in 1996 compared well with those of other Asian economies as well, and so did market valuation.

The Indian market compares favourably with other EMs due to its higher level of industrialisation and potential for service sector growth. While the

Indian economy is fairly evenly distributed between agriculture, industry and services, the private sector's representation of the overall economy is no more than 10 per cent. Inadequate land reform laws mean that land ownership is denied to the private corporate sector. In the services sector, the government dominates the financial and infrastructural sectors. Even the industrial sector is dominated by the public sector. As the private sector's access to the economy increases, so will the securitisation of the public sector. These developments will reflect in the market capitalisation which has been dominated by the private industrial sector compared to other sectors of the economy. India's market capitalisation of about $150 billion thus reflects a fraction of its economy. With increasing privatisation and the enhanced role for the private sector in India's economy, the structural changes will begin to reflect in its market capitalisation.

The Indian economy grew at an average rate of 4 per cent during 1951–81 and at 5.6 per cent during 1981–91. Growth between 1991–2001 is expected to average 6.5 per cent. If India succeeds in the structural reform of its economy, whereby capital to output ratios reflect better utilisation of capital than in the past, there will be a rise in capital investment in the economy. Even a slow and steady improvement in capital to output ratios could yield growth rates of 8–10 per cent in the economy. As GDP per capita improves, so will consumer expenditure and savings. All these developments will be enacted on the stage of the capital market which, with greater maturity, will begin to provide investors with greater protection and returns.

As the demand and supply of stocks generally tend to influence the price level in any market, it is prudent to accumulate stocks when the market is out of favour. Liquidity is the life-blood of markets. If there is high supply of stock in the form of public or rights issues, and as pricing in EMs tends to be inefficient, there is every possibility that intermittently there will be a mismatch between demand and supply leading to rapid and unexpected market adjustments. In India, the potential supply of stocks to the market over the next decade will be sizeable. But, so is the amount of global pension funds that have little exposure to Indian investments. The basic implication of markets, their open and efficient nature, implies that demand and supply is matched in the price. Thus, the very concept of markets, where market forces determine price levels, implies that some lose out in the process. The market does not reward all investors. In more mature markets the risk is lower and weaker investors are better protected. In all markets, however, investors are ultimately risk-takers. Fund managers are thus rewarded or penalised for their ability to gauge risk.

There is no mechanism within a market system for the demand and supply of stocks to be managed in such a way that both investors and corporates benefit equitably. In highly sophisticated markets such results can be aspired to, but in markets that are in the early stages of their evolution it is practically beyond the scope of the market to deliver such protection. In fact, such an idea runs contrary to the 'market' concept itself. But unless market blindspots are catered to in developing democracies, the social implications of the introduction of market reforms can be fatal to the reform process. Thus the regulatory authorities have a crucial role in ensuring investor protection, adequate compliance and timely disclosure by corporates. Unfortunately, due to the lack of resources including expertise and experience, the regulatory authorities find the task extremely challenging. Treading the thin line between establishing free market conditions while ensuring a high level of investor protection through regulation is perhaps the most difficult challenge for India's market regulators. But the success of the market depends on the successful monitoring of the market.

The US Congress recently introduced legislation authorising the SEC to collect a fee of 1/300th of one per cent of the aggregate dollar amount of sales of certain securities transacted by or through a member of the National Association of Securities Dealers, Inc. The new fees are similar to the transaction fees that have been levied on exchange transactions since 1934, and are being collected to recover costs to the government of the supervision and regulation of securities markets and professionals and the related costs of activities including enforcement, policy and rulemaking, administration, legal services and international regulation. India could impose such a separate fee to implement an efficient and better regulated market. Once the benefits of such a tax are clearly demonstrated, most investors will pay for it. However, due to the existing inefficiencies in the system the cost of transaction is inordinately high in India. Asking investors to pay even more than they already do may not be the right approach. But introducing legislation that will bring about greater competition in providing such services will lower transaction costs which would enable the Securities and Exchange Board of India to introduce fees for covering other costs like legislation and regulation. It was the lack of an appropriate legal framework that prevented the government, the law courts or any other regulatory authority from successfully bringing about any indictment against the participants in India's stockmarket scam of 1991–92.

The demand and supply of stock is reflected in the valuation of the market. There are various ways of determining value, and one of the simplest is the price to earnings ratio (P/E). This ratio for Indian companies was low until 1991 when the introduction of reforms and capital market liberalisation led to a surge in demand for stocks, resulting in the securities scam of 1992. Subsequently, with the opening up of the stockmarket to FIIs, similar levels of over-valuation were reflected in the P/E for the market. Taking into account the low turnover ratio of stocks and the small free-float of shares, the P/E of the market went up from 10× in 1990 to over 50× in 1992. Market capitalisation to GDP ratios also soared. In highly illiquid markets, value distortions can occur rapidly; the necessary adjustment of valuation can be painful for those investors who entered the market at the higher levels of valuation. A significantly undervalued market can equally turn swiftly under the weight of funds from being an attractive investment to one to be avoided, all within a short period of time.

Under the demand – supply scenario anticipated for India, there is the very real prospect of only a modest rise in the stockmarket index as any rise in demand will be met with a higher supply of stock. Thus, one could have a rise in market capitalisation through the privatisation programme alone without any appreciable rise in the level of the market index. Most investors have been spoilt with highly speculative returns on their investments. Even investors in corporate debt securities in India have been rewarded with unusually high returns. These unrealistic expectations from EMs have put pressure on market operators as investing starts to resemble gambling. There is thus a need for discipline when operating under such conditions. Investors must learn to prune their expectations when investing in EMs.

INDUSTRIAL POLICY DEVELOPMENT

India's central planning for development assigned industry a crucial role in employment generation, capital accumulation and economic growth. However, once the initial thrust of industrial investment for import-substitution was satisfied, the strategy of centrally-determined policymaking with an inwardly-oriented trade and investment programme yielded inferior rates of return on investment, resulting in higher capital to output ratios. Thus, the rapid growth of value addition in the early 1960s was followed by a prolonged phase of stagnation which lasted until the 1980s. While there was disillusionment regarding the resource generation aspect of the public sector, its role as the driving force behind India's development continued to be paramount and additional budgetary resources were directed at the public sector. The harsh reality was that policy failures were rewarded with lower productivity growth, depreciating currencies, declining global market shares and falls in employment and wage levels.

Despite the substantial investments made in the public sector, its lower levels of productivity meant that the public sector's share in GDP rose from

8 per cent in 1960 to 25 per cent by 1990–91. The share of the government in the paid-up capital of companies went up from 3 per cent in 1950 to a staggering 73 per cent by 1990–91. By 1989–90, the public sector owned just over half of the productive capital in the industrial sector but accounted for only a quarter of the gross value of its output, compared to the private sector which owned 41 per cent of the productive capital but contributed 65 per cent of the gross value of output. In 1994, India had more than 1000 PEs of which 800 were owned by the states. The SEBs and state transport boards still account for a large share of the state enterprises' assets and production.

The New Economic Policy of 1991 aimed at stimulating greater private sector participation in the economy with a view to injecting greater efficiency into the public sector through competition, improving the management of PEs by increasing their autonomy, and giving them the mandate to become profit centres and not remain mere high-cost centres. The introversion in policymaking was responsible for the low productivity increases in the inefficient PEs which constrained growth. Successful planning and development involve not only high levels of investment but efficiency with which resources are put to use. In India, investment grew faster than output; investment increased by a compound annual rate of 4.4 per cent a year between 1960–61 and 1993–94 compared to a 4 per cent growth rate for GDP. As productivity growth is the central basis of economic dynamism, India's industrial sector was not generating acceptable returns on investment.

India's PEs continue to dominate industries such as coal mining and energy, steel and fertilisers. The number of areas reserved for the public sector has been reduced from 18 in 1991 to six – defence products, atomic energy, radioactive minerals, mineral oils, coal and lignite and railway transport. The PEs have tended to be more capital-intensive, or the more capital-intensive industries were kept under the control of the public sector as it was perceived that the private sector did not have the resources to invest in such capital-intensive industries. The government's initial import-substitution policy favoured investment in heavy industries for economic development. These enterprises in due course became bureaucratic and inefficient under government control and lost their initial commercial outlook. Gross profit over capital employed was 11 per cent in the central PEs in 1993–94 compared with 20 per cent for the private sector. After taxes, net profits of PEs amounted to less than 3 per cent of capital employed, which was insufficient even to cover depreciation costs; and the annual financing needs of the central PEs exceeded 5 per cent of GDP, or about a quarter of domestic savings, between 1991–94. The performance of the state enterprises has been worse.

That India generated reasonably high rates of both investment and savings within a comparatively stable macroeconomic environment cannot be denied, yet the low returns in the public sector held back growth. Government policy encouraged industry to invest in physical capital, new technologies and skills in the early 1980s through the partial easing of licensing controls and a modest liberalisation of the financial markets. The strong depreciation of the rupee during the 1980s boosted exports. The private sector responded positively to these changes which was reflected in their improved profitability, but the same cannot be said of the PEs. The partial deregulation and increased market orientation of the 1980s led to an improving trend in output and productivity growth in the industrial sector. It also resulted in rising inflation and a rapid deterioration of the country's external accounts as aid flows were not adequate to cover the current account deficit which was increasingly being financed by external government borrowing on commercial terms. The fiscal deterioration stemmed from rising current expenditures, especially for interest payments and subsidies.

Despite the many shortcomings of India's centralised planning, there was one respect in which it had a definite impact on the progress of industrialisation and that had to do with building up a significantly diversified industrial base. In 1956, consumer goods accounted for half the weight in the industrial production index and capital goods less than 5 per cent. By 1970, consumer goods were less than a third with basic goods representing a third of the index and capital goods 15 per cent. This trend was also reflected in terms of value added in total manufacturing (see Table 6.1).

Table 6.1   India's diversified industrial base (weights of use-based sectors in the index of industrial production)

Items	1956	1960	1970	1980	1990
Capital goods	4.7	11.8	15.2	15.0	16.4
Basic goods	22.3	25.1	32.3	33.2	39.4
Intermediate goods	24.6	25.9	20.9	21.3	20.5
Consumer goods	48.4	37.2	31.5	30.5	23.6
of which non-durables	NA	31.6	28.1	26.6	21.0
durables	NA	5.7	3.4	3.8	2.6

Source: *Annual Survey of Industries*, various issues.

India's development strategy constituted mainly in building a large, publicly owned, heavy industry sector while leaving the production of consumer goods and agriculture to private enterprise. Employment growth was to be achieved through growth in the consumer goods sector or through the development of the small-scale sector and rural industrialisation, all of which were expected to be labour intensive. Thus, the majority of the labour force is employed in the informal sector as employment in the formal or organised sector of the economy dominated by the public sector has been constrained by legislation. The proportion of employment in the organised sector has remained unchanged at 8 per cent of total employment. Therefore, employment generation in the industrial sector has been extremely poor. The performance of the small-scale sector in terms of generating employment has been uneven and the policy of industrial dispersal only modestly successful resulting in inter-state inequalities in the 1970s. However, some reduction in disparity was achieved through higher economic growth in the 1980s leading to an improvement in employment during the decade. But growth across India's states varied considerably during the 1980s.

With the reforms of 1991, along with the intention of the United Front government to accede more power to the states, the future success of India's 25 states will depend on fiscal prudence at the state level and the incentives for investment offered by the states rather than on decision-making at the centre. Already one notices the predominance of certain states in attracting more investments than others. While information on the distribution of investments in the states is available infrequently, it is evident that new investment since 1991 has gone into states like Gujarat, Maharashtra, Tamil Nadu and Uttar Pradesh. FDI has also been confined mostly to these states, with the addition of Delhi, Orissa and West Bengal. Maharashtra and Gujarat have lighter and more dynamic industries which have benefited from the reforms, while states like Orissa and Bihar, endowed with natural resources, are skewed towards heavy, public-sector-type industries which have taken longer to adjust to the new environment. India's southern states fared worse than the richer northern states of Maharashtra, Gujarat, Haryana and Punjab due to inadequate state government policies.

Many of India's 25 states are thus starting off with a comparative disadvantage. While competition within them for private resources is desirable, it could also widen the existing gap between the more successful states and those that are less able to attract private investment. The role of the centre is in enabling the weaker states to implement market oriented policies, improve infrastructure and provide an environment conducive to private investment. As the states increasingly need to compete for funds, it is important for the centre to ensure that the strategy for social sector development is on a national basis.

The link between macroeconomic and structural conditions and growth cannot be over-emphasised. Macroeconomic instability is associated with lower growth as it affects both investment and productivity. India's macroeconomic policies were conducive to rapid output growth, capital accumulation and productivity gains in the 1980s. But, the negative impact of a weak fiscal policy along with distortions in the trade and exchange rate regime stunted its growth potential. A healthy export policy enforces discipline on the producers and introduces an awareness of global pricing and quality consciousness. Thus, trade and changes in the terms of trade have a high impact on productivity growth.

The point that is worth reiterating is that the rate of growth, being related to the rapid accumulation of assets and productivity, tends to increase with improvements in total factor productivity. While growth can be broken down into its component factors such as capital and labour, output growth cannot always be explained by changes in these factors, as has been evident in India where reasonably high levels of investment do not translate to commensurate returns on investment. That element of growth which cannot be explained by the factors of production usually reflects the more efficient use of resources or the adoption of newer production technologies; in other words, improvements in total factor profitability (TFP). According to a study made by the IMF, the East Asian countries grew significantly faster than India not only because of faster growth of their capital stocks, but also on account of higher TFP growth. The results for the period after 1980 show that India's productivity improved markedly in the 1980s overtaking that of East Asia. This increase in TFP also contributed to rising output in the 1980s in the Indian economy (see Table 6.2).

A detailed study of the growth of TFP in the organised manufacturing sector in India between 1960 and 1989 by Isher Judge Ahluwalia (1985, 1991) revealed that after a long period of stagnation during 1960–80, TFP growth improved significantly in the 1980s. Her research indicated poor performance by intermediate goods and consumer non-durables in TFP growth. Capital goods and consumer durables fared better. The better performance of consumer durables and capital goods was in line with the performance in other developing economies, but the poor performance in the intermediate goods sector was not shared by the other developers. According to Ahluwalia, the rapid growth in value-added in the early 1960s was due to the high rates of growth of factor inputs and poor productivity growth, but the resurgence of growth in the 1980s was marked by a moderate growth of investment, a decline in employment and strong productivity growth.

Some of Ahluwalia's conclusions are revealing; for example, industries established for the sole purpose of import substitution (capital goods, for example) experienced lower TFP growth along with heavy industries with high capital-to-labour ratios. Encouraging investments in industries without taking into consideration market conditions or analysing the market-based reasons for growth created inefficient enterprises. It also accelerated the rise in capital – labour ratios. Under the stringent control of the government and its inflexible labour laws, the bias towards capital intensity rose within a highly-protected regime.

Table 6.2   Total factor productivity and growth

Country grouping	GDP	TFP
Period 1960–88		
East Asia*	7.4	1.9
South Asia**	3.6	0.6
of which India	3.1	0.3
Africa	3.4	0.3
Latin America	3.8	0.4
OECD	3.7	1.2
Period 1980–88		
East Asia*	6.2	1.6
South Asia**	4.5	1.3
of which India	4.8	2.3
Africa	2.1	−0.5
Latin America	1.2	−1.4
OECD	2.4	0.6

Notes: * Includes only the high-performing East Asian economics, Hong Kong, Indonesia, the Republic of Korea, Malaysia, Singapore, Taiwan Province of China and Thailand; ** includes Bangladesh, India, Nepal, Pakistan and Sri Lanka.
Source: *India: Economic Reform and Growth*, IMF Occasional Paper 134, December 1995, p. 10.

Studies made by others, including Joshi and Little (1994, 1996), also confirmed that the rates of return on public investment, especially in manufacturing, were very low between 1960 and 1987 at 0.1–2.1 per cent. Between 1976–77 and 1986–87, real rates of return on investment in public sector manufacturing improved to 3.1–5.2 per cent. This they attributed partly to the allocation procedures for public investment in sectors where India had little comparative advantage. But, rates of return on private manufacturing at 16.7–22.6 per cent in 1976–87 were closer to that encountered in industrial countries. Greater aggregate demand accounted for higher growth rates but increased public infrastructure investment contributed to reducing bottlenecks in the supply of power, transport and communications – in short, costs to industry were lowered as a result of the reforms started in late 1970s.

Changes in the allocation procedures for investment were ushered in through the process of liberalisation in 1991 leading to rising profit-to-capital-employed ratios in the public sector. While the level of diversification in India's industrial base could not have been achieved without the role played by the public sector, most sectors of the economy have now been opened up to the private sector. Industries still requiring licensing approval account for less than 15 per cent of the value-added in the manufacturing sector. The number of industries reserved for the public sector has been reduced to six and private sector participation in some of these sectors is also permitted on a case-by-case basis. Private sector participation is encouraged in the development of infrastructure like power, telecommunications, roadways, shipping and ports, airports and civil aviation. However, a host of obstacles remain as the process of obtaining various permits and licenses at the state level still deters FDI.

The government had a policy of reserving production of some 822 items, including most non-durable consumer products, for the small-scale sector which received various subsidies in the form of loans, purchase and price preferences and protection via quantitative restrictions on imports. Thus, the ability to exploit economies of scale inhibited investment, innovation and production efficiency. The manufacture of ready-made garments, for example, which was the preserve of the small-scale sector, was opened up for the participation of large-scale industrial undertakings subject to an export obligation of 50 per cent of production. Since 1991, the authorities have made an effort to correct the multitude of distortions inherent in the economy by introducing market orientation in the management of resources and reducing state intervention in determining such decisions to expand the economy's productive capacity.

India's structural reforms concentrated on the industrial sector and aimed at eliminating constraints to private investment. The response of the private sector to economic liberalisation has been positive. Private capital inflows have risen substantially since 1992–93 as the costs to industry have been lowered. One of the major developments in establishing this trend has been the reduction of import tariffs and its contribution to industry's cost structure. The rationalisation of excise duties for lowering costs and prices by relieving tax on the inputs has also helped in mitigating the cascading effect on the cost-effectiveness of the final product. In the capital goods sector, for example, where India does not have a competitive advantage, imports accounted for 66 per cent of value-added in 1989–90. In the non-electrical machinery sector, the ratio of imports to value-added was a staggering 90 per cent. Though capital goods imports fell sharply in the initial period of adjustment after the economic crisis, the ratio of imports to value-added was still over 60 per cent in 1993–94. As India's capital goods sector continues to add to capacity and invests heavily in technological upgradation, value addition has recovered to levels manifest prior to the crisis of 1991.

With the elimination of import licensing requirements for intermediate and capital goods, the share of value-added that was subject to quantitative restrictions (QRs) in the manufacturing sector declined from 90 per cent in 1990–91 to an estimated 51 per cent in 1994–95. The lowering of tariffs impacted directly on productivity growth. Imports of consumer goods remain severely restricted and QRs on agricultural imports were also prevalent covering 93 per cent of value-added in 1994–95. It is difficult to quantify the degree of effective protection from foreign competition to Indian industry since the licensing system was used extensively and tariffs were used to supplement protection at various stages of production. India's tariffs were among the highest in the world and, after six years of reform, remain high by international standards.

The structural adjustment programme of 1991–92 had a depressive effect on the industrial sector as it affected the availability of raw materials, spare parts and components along with the cost of finance. It also affected total domestic demand. Industrial growth picked up strongly between 1994–96, particularly in the capital goods sector which had suffered the most during the recession of 1991–93 (see Table 6.3). The growth of consumer durables was particularly strong in 1995–96. This sector is most likely to perform in the years ahead in view of the major investments that have been made possible by India's liberalisation. As the production of basic goods is determined more by investment trends in previous years, it was little affected by the fluctuations in short-term demand. There has not been significant new investment in the sector as the framework for private sector investment in areas such as power and hydrocarbons was not available in the beginning and progress has been slow in establishing it.

Although the production of consumer non-durables recovered in 1994–95, lack of adequate data in this sector may have been the cause of the low recorded growth. India's index of industrial production, covering 352 items, does not cover the small-scale sector which is more dynamic and is the fastest growing sector of the Indian economy especially in the export-oriented segments-like garments, leather, gems and jewellery. The present index has not been rebased since 1980–81 and does not reflect the changes in India's industrial structure. Many of the fastest growing sectors such as electronics, computers and automobiles are understated. The other problem is that the index is understandably based on information from the registered sector while half of India's manufacturing output is in the

Table 6.3 Index of industrial production (% change)

Years inform 1993–94 etc	Weight**	1981–82 till 1990–91	1990–91	1991–92	1992–93	1993–94	1994–95	1995–96	1996*
Overall index	(100)	7.8	8.2	0.6	2.3	6.0	9.4	11.7	9.8
Capital goods	(16.4)	11.5	17.4	−12.8	−0.1	−4.1	24.8	17.8	16.6
Consumer goods	(23.6)	6.7	10.4	−1.8	1.8	4.0	8.7	12.5	8.2
durables	(2.6)	13.0	14.8	−12.5	−0.7	16.1	10.2	37.1	9.8
non-durables	(21.0)	5.7	9.4	1.2	2.4	1.3	8.4	6.4	7.7
Basic goods	(39.4)	7.5	3.8	6.2	2.6	9.4	5.5	8.7	6.7
Intermediate goods	(20.5)	6.2	6.1	−0.7	5.4	11.7	3.7	10.2	10.8

Notes: * April to October 1996; ** weight in the index.
Source: Indian Economic Survey, 1996–97.

small-scale sectors about which there is little comprehensive information. Currently the index of industrial production comprises the manufacturing sector (77.1 per cent), mining and quarrying (11.5 per cent) and electricity (11.4 per cent). It is increasingly being acknowledged that an independent industrial reporting system should be set up and that reporting be made compulsory for items covered in the index.

With the recovery in industrial production, there was evidence of a resurgence in private investment in 1994–95. Increased credit availability and a growing business confidence led to this investment recovery. The cost and availability of credit to the private sector has a significant impact on capital formation. Industrial entrepreneurs' memorandums and letters of intent filed since the initiation of reforms up to December 1996 has been buoyant and overall investment intention totalled Rs 5437 billion with an estimated employment generation of about five million. The number of FDI approvals between August 1991 and October 1996 amounted to Rs 249.7 billion with actual inflows totalling Rs 63 billion. More than 80 per cent of FDI flows are in high-priority sectors such as power generation, oil refinery, electrical equipment manufacturing, chemicals and the export-related sectors. The level of FDI in India is admittedly small, compared to China. Improved infrastructural facilities are required to accelerate FDI emphasising the importance of enhancing investment in infrastructure.

International capital movements tend to intensify the impact of domestic policy by richly rewarding it when it is sound and punishing it when it is not so. Faster capital flows are making domestic policy far more important for workers around the world because sound macroeconomic and structural policies are crucial to attracting and keeping capital and thus achieving the productivity necessary to create competitive jobs at rising wages. But when policies fail, portfolio investments and savings leave the scene and labour suffers the consequences of such withdrawal. The delays experienced in FDI inflows into India is not only bad for local labour and the prospect of jobs, but continued frustration by investors may lead them to take their investments elsewhere. The inferior quality of India's infrastructure is thus one of the major obstacles to India being able to attract any significant level of FDI investment in the medium term.

A combination of political uncertainty, delays in implementing reforms, and the high cost of capital and infrastructural constraints led to a decline in business confidence as reflected in the lower approvals for FDI in 1996 as well as in proposed investment plans. The cost and availability of capital is as decisive a factor in attracting private investment as is the availability of physical infrastructure. Reforms in the financial sector improved the prospect of the availability of cheaper capital to the corporate sector. But, greater fiscal adjustment is required to reduce real interest rates in India. The pressure on real interest rates that emerged after August 1995, due to the limited progress in fiscal correction, threatened to crowd out private investment. The fiscal pressures emphasise the need to bolster state finances as the risk of fiscal adjustment at the centre being derailed by the profligacy of the states remains all too real. Investment flows are summarised in Table 6.4.

Table 6.4   Investment flows since 1991

| Year | Industrial investment intention | | Foreign direct investment | |
| | Through IEMs and LOIs+ | | Approvals and investment flows | |
	proposed investment (Rs bn)	proposed employment ('000)	Amount** (Rs bn)	Actual inflow (Rs bn)
1991*	783.8	803	5.3	3.5
1992	1298.6	1020	38.9	6.7
1993	768.2	803	88.6	17.8
1994	1067.1	959	89.6	29.8
1995	1397.7	1205	308.2	63.7
1996	1032.1	877	249.7	63.1
Total	6347.6	5669	780.3**	184.6

Notes: + Industrial Entrepreneurs Memorandum (IEMs) and Letters of Intent (LOIs); * August to December; ** excludes the approvals of GDRs.
Source: *Indian Economic Survey*, 1996–97.

The inconclusive nature of the outcome of India's general election in 1996 has made the task of the central government more difficult in implementing expenditure reforms or in addressing key issues relating to the financial situation of the states. The overall fiscal deficit needs to be reduced to relieve pressure on domestic savings which continues to be usurped by the public sector as the flow of funds from the banking sector to the government remains significant. Little has been done since 1991 to address the distortions in the PEs, the labour markets or the agricultural sector. Reforms in all these sectors are necessary to sustain the momentum of industrial growth in the country. As the macroeconomic policy of a country has a significant impact on investment and industrial output, the challenge for industry and management lies in their ability to influence the formulation of policy at the centre.

The government's role will remain crucial not just in the formulation of policies but also in encouraging private investment by releasing resources in the financial system. Private sector investment is influenced by the cost and availability of credit as much as by regulatory access to key areas of industry and the presence of price uncertainty. The real lending rate plays a key role in determining private investment as much as the availability of both financial and physical resources. The private sector's investment response to the economic crisis bears testimony to that. Sharp tightening of credit conditions after the crisis of 1991 brought about a decline in private capital formation. Private investment would have declined even further were it not for the reduction in the PSBR which ameliorated the 'crowding out' effect due to the competition between private and public sectors for physical as much as financial resources.

As credit conditions eased and the lowering of banks' cash and statutory liquidity requirements released resources, the private sector's access to credit was increased. However, with the liberalisation in the financial markets and the chance for firms to raise equity capital at attractive rates, corporate borrowing switched from debt to equity. Many Indian firms were successful in securing foreign financing to restructure their balance sheets by reducing their exposure to the high-cost domestic debt. Hence the decline in domestic commercial bank borrowing in 1993–94. Corporate foreign debt also declined significantly from around 10 per cent of total financing to negative figures. The momentum of investment by the private sector was affected by the lagged effects of the initial contraction in demand and the unutilised industrial capacity which was influenced by social and political tensions in 1993–94. It was not until 1994–95 that the recovery in private capital formation was reflected in the growth of exports and the rapid expansion of output in the capital goods sector. The high real interest rate environment in 1996–97 once again affected production, investment and growth.

Two-thirds of India's gross domestic capital formation was undertaken by the private sector long before the reforms of 1991. As the private sector is poised to play a larger role in the nation's development, private capital accumulation will be the main impetus to future growth. The private sector's share in investment has been significantly higher than that of the public sector in all areas of economic activity where private investment was permitted. It only declined in those areas where investment returns declined significantly due to interventionist government policies that crippled private enterprise as was the case in agriculture. Since 1991, steps have been taken to dismantle the system of controls to make the investment climate more open to private enterprise. There is reason to believe that various sectors of industry will continue to be able to build on their competitive advantage within a freer investment regime and will be able to establish successfully not just a domestic franchise but gradually an international one.

Productivity growth in India's manufacturing sector has been evident even within the constraints of an economic system that was not particularly conducive to growth. One of the reasons for the improvement in value addition in the 1980s was the partial liberalisation of the economy that made imports easier for the manufacturing sector. It encouraged a higher level of capital formation which had declined significantly in the 1970s. With a huge domestic market, relatively high trade barriers and serious infrastructural constraints to FDI, Indian industrialists have been cushioned in an increasingly globally competitive environment. FDI shied away from India due to the high-cost structure for industry. It thus prevented a higher level of long-term capital flow into the country and with it the technological upgrading of industry.

It is important, therefore, that economic policies are acted upon swiftly for the benefits of reform to filter through to the whole economy. Concerted efforts have been made to lower industrial costs so that the Indian entrepreneur can compete on a level playing field in the global market. The key costs to industry are capital, raw materials, energy, distribution, labour, management and technology. In most of these areas, except for labour and distribution, India lacks any significant global competitive advantage. The real cost of capital in India is high due to a combination of loose fiscal policy and tight monetary policy. Persistent power shortages add to the existing problem of high energy costs to industry. Poor investment in infrastructure is compounded with poor financial management, operational inefficiencies and inadequate maintenance. Lower import tariffs have reduced the cost of raw materials but more needs to be done in bringing down the rates further. The role of management remains crucial in improving total factor productivity assuming that macroeconomic policies will be geared towards supporting investment and growth.

India's natural advantages in labour and distribution cannot be disputed but labour comprises a small component of overall costs in most industrial enterprises. It is true that in the more labour-intensive industries, countries like India and China are most likely to make the greatest gains in the global market. But, having an advantage in that segment is not going to impact on productivity growth unless the training of labour is matched to technological advancement. In fact, an inflexible labour force is a punitive cost even though it may be cheap. A skilled and disciplined labour force is essential to a country's long-term success even though in the short term unskilled labour has its uses in various sectors of the economy, mainly in the infrastructural sector. However, as seen in various East Asian countries, the productivity of the labour force has a lot to do with the level of technological advancement. Enhancing labour mobility and equipping workers for change is the key to a good labour policy. Retraining of labour can help groups of workers but is unlikely to provide a long-term solution to the re-structuring of labour in a global marketplace.

Labour policy reforms in India have been slow to crystallize as changes have been linked with introducing changes in the management of the public sector. Industrial 'sickness' in India refers to both public and private enter-prises that chronically make losses but continue to operate while the 'exit policy' refers to regulation that blocks the liquidation of such loss-making enterprises. The losses of such enterprises remain a significant drain on pub-lic resources. The losses of the SEBs, for example, in 1990–91 represented 0.8 per cent of GDP and the losses of the PEs amounted to 0.4 per cent of GDP the same year. The deficit of the central PEs constituted 3 per cent of GDP in 1994–95, a level unchanged from 1990–91. Decades of weak banking super-vision encouraged the continued lending of credit to over-leveraged, under-capitalised and often loss-making concerns through interest capitalisation. Substandard management compounded the problem of inefficiencies in op-erational terms and legal obstacles to restructuring ensured that industrial sickness was also associated with surplus labour.

The Industrial Disputes Act of India requires firms with more than a 100 workers to obtain prior approval of the state government to retrench labour. As a result only a small portion of India's labour force, a mere 3 per cent, is employed in the private organised sector and a further 7 per cent in the public sector. The majority of India's labour force is thus employed in the unorganised sector. Under existing property laws, the Urban Land Ceiling and Regulation Act, ensures that firms are unable to sell their urban and holdings or to liquidate their assets without state approval. A workable 'exit policy' for unviable units will require a complete change in current labour and land regulations to enhance the flexibility of management for corporate restructuring.

Those countries that have achieved the highest gains for their workers are those that decided early on in the cycle of growth to take advantage of international opportunities and to rely more on market forces rather than on the state for their resource allocation. Such benefits may be harder to reap in a fiercely competitive global marketplace. Many developing countries today, including India, are approaching industrial development based on a strategy of exports with the hope of creating the dynamics for economic growth. The success of such a strategy will depend on government policies, institutions and infrastructure along with the skills and knowledge base that can provide the necessary support for trade and manufacturing. Change in global technology has forced the market concept on most pro-ducers of goods and services.

Competitive pricing is a necessary condition for success but so is awareness of consumer preferences, quality, timeliness and the delivery of
goods; in short, marketing and distribution skills. The main consequence
of liberalisation is that the ability to keep up with international patterns of
technological change has become more important to the survival of industrial firms than it was in protected economies. This makes it difficult for
latecomers to follow successfully the path of export orientation as access to
'high technology' has become an important factor in determining competitiveness. Product life-cycles are becoming shorter as the pace of global
technological change quickens and production techniques restructure the
international division of labour and replace raw materials by man-made
substitutes. In a global market, with the evolution of a new concept of industrial competitiveness, developing countries have to be able to respond
to these challenges continually.

Industrial technology is being distributed faster than in the past, thanks
to superior global communications. The time required to implement
changes is also shrinking with developments in technology. Thus, it took
the UK well over half a century from the time of its industrial revolution to
double its per capita income. But, in Japan the process involved around 34
years from 1885. For Korea, it was possible to achieve that in just 11 years
from 1966 and in the case of China that was done in less than 10 years.
Developing countries are beginning to realise that their traditional advantages with respect to natural resources and cheap labour are no longer the
key ingredients for achieving international competitiveness. Comparative
advantage is being forged with equipping oneself with technological capability and innovation with the ability to exploit new technologies in the
production process. The introduction of modern technologies has a negative effect on employment unless human resource development is kept
abreast of industrialisation. The challenge for a country like India is that it
needs to develop faster than the rest if only to keep pace with global technological trends.

INVEST IN COMPANIES, NOT IN THE STOCKMARKET

A 'contrarian' investment strategy may not be a prerequisite for investing
in developed markets but is essential in EMs. The key to successful investing in any market lies in identifying companies, with good management
and strong earnings' growth potential over the medium term, which are
currently trading at a discount to their future worth. The whole concept of
active portfolio management implies the possibility of exploiting market

inefficiencies. In EMs, substantial pricing inefficiencies occur. Thus, a correct analysis of the sensitivity of the earnings potential of a firm leads to significant returns.

One of the basic principles of equity investment emanates from the notion that the investor shares in the future prospect of the company. If a share is purchased at a 'reasonable' market valuation, the expectation is there that future earnings growth will accrue to the investor along with the annual payout in dividend earnings. This is usually reflected in the market value of the company. Hence, the relevance of assessing the earnings per share (EPS) growth prospect of a firm and researching its past EPS history or its dividend payout policy in determining annual cash returns. That may not always be rewarding in India. Thus, the price performance of Reliance Industries Ltd has consistently lagged in EPS growth over the past several years. The shareholder would not have benefited from Reliance's explosive growth in market capitalisation if the shares had been bought in the open market during a period when they were 'over valued'. Timing one's entry and exit, in short trading, would have been critical to making reasonable returns on investment in this company. Reliance Industries is India's leading private sector company in the textiles and petrochemicals sectors and has been hugely successful in garnering funds from both domestic and overseas investors. The bulk of the company's foreign debt is long term. Reliance's historical growth was achieved through a process of backward integration from textiles and fibres to fibre intermediates and feedstock and eventually to oil refining and exploration. This growth was financed through funds raised via equity and debt issues. However, if an investor had left the investment in Reliance untouched over the past five years, price appreciation would not have matched EPS growth.

Most Asian companies do not pay out a high dividend as earnings get ploughed back into investment. In India, dividends are calculated as a percentage of the face value of the stock. Thus, if the face value of a stock is Rs 100, then a 40 per cent dividend payout means Rs 40 per share which, as a percentage of the market value of the company, can be less than 3 per cent. Investing in India is aimed at capital growth rather than on dividend returns. As companies in developing economies tend to be capital intensive, fund-raising via equity issues often results in the periodic dilution of EPS estimates leading to rapid distortions in value projections. The management of companies try to deliver steady EPS growth, but the market itself is influenced by short-term fund flows resulting in extreme volatility. When investing in EMs, potential earnings dilutions must be factored into an investment decision. It is often the case that equity issues tend to flood the market at higher valuations than at lower valuations. No self-respecting management would agree to issue its shares at a low valuation. And, investors find that buying companies at high valuations dilute their returns. Thus management and investors have opposing priorities as both aim to maximise returns.

As one of the problems of dealing in EMs is illiquidity, most investors end up buying what they can get in the market when liquidity rises in their fund accounts instead of what they want to buy at a price they consider appropriate. The Global Depository Receipt (GDR) issue of State Bank of India is a case in point. Unless, an investor had established a holding in SBI over a period of time when the shares were trading at about Rs 160, it would have been sensible to subscribe to the GDR issue which garnered over $400 million from FIIs. The issue was made at a 'fair' value and, with the GDR issue, it reached its FII-ownership limit of 24 per cent. FIIs then faced the option of avoiding the stock altogether or buying the stock at a premium to the domestic price. The evolution of premium or discount in the foreign pricing of firms can be traced to the lack of any arbitraging opportunity between the two markets. It happened in the Korean and Thai markets as the foreign ownership limit was reached in companies. When investors were optimistic about the prospects of Korea in the late 1980s, premiums on Korean stocks ranged from 100–400 per cent. Currently, Korean GDRs trade at domestic market values or at discounts; such is the perception of investors of the Korean economy.

If one were to turn to companies in India that generate a higher level of cash and do not need to dilute their capital base, like Hindustan Lever (HLL) in the consumer products sector, one realises that the market tends to value such companies highly. HLL's price-to-earnings ratio (P/E) has fluctuated between a low of 30× earnings to over 65× earnings since 1991, depending on the overall valuation of the market. A limited free-float of shares also tends to aggravate the problem of valuation. Companies like HLL have a devoted shareholder base who have held on to the stock for decades. Any 'value' investor averse to chronically high P/E's would have missed out on the growth of HLL which has to be counted among India's few well-managed companies. The point is that despite its high P/E, the share price performance of the company kept pace with its EPS growth while Reliance Industries' low P/E did not translate to its share price performance reflecting its EPS growth.

Thus, one needs to look at other valuation measures like price-to-sales ratio (PSR), price-to-operating-profit-per-share ratio or the return on capital invested (ROCE). One way of determining a companies' ability to put its capital to good use is to examine its ROCE. The majority of Indian firms earn less than 20 per cent on capital employed. If adjusted for inflation at 10 per cent, then real rates of return fail to keep pace with the real cost of capital which has generally been high but, more recently, has been higher at 15–18 per cent. Increasing the equity base through share issues or borrowing at a high real interest rate implies that adequate rates of return on capital is unsustainable. Herein lies the basic problem of investing in India. If the rationale for investing is reaping higher returns on capital, then the returns in India are not competitive. An analysis of 99 companies monitored by ING Barings showed that on 29 January 1997 there were 20 companies with ROCE over 30 per cent. They were Hindalco (aluminium); ITC (agro-based products); Bajaj Auto and Tempo, Hero Honda, Mahindra and Mahindra, Punjab Tractors, TELCO, TVS Suzuki (automobiles and ancilliaries); Madras Cement and Raasi Cement (cement); Marico (consumer products); Infosys, NIIT, Satyam Computers (information technology); IPCL (petrochemicals); BPCL and HPCL (refinery/oil); and MTNL and VSNL (telecommunications). It is worth noting that five of the 20 companies operate in the public sector. Also, past measures of ROCE can be unreliable in an increasingly liberal business environment.

High real interest rates translate to a low P/E for the stockmarket. If the real cost of capital is zero, then an EPS growth rate of 15 per cent would justify a P/E of 15–20. But where the real cost of capital is 10 per cent, then an EPS growth of 25–30 per cent would be required to warrant a P/E of 15. In high-cost economies there is little scope for upward revaluations of the market. Companies have to work harder to service their debt and deliver the required returns on capital as capital is becoming increasingly mobile. India may not provide mobility to its investors but the rest of the world does not operate under such constraints. Genuine investors may keep faith in India for a while. Unless the government recognises that fact and addresses the problem of its fiscal deficit, the only option available is to trade the market when the opportunity presents itself. But taking into account the size of the market along with the dealing, settlement and liquidity constraints; even that has not been worth the effort.

After the reforms, Indian companies' profit figures benefited from changes in tax and depreciation laws as well as in their ability to raise funds at market valuations not to mention the reduction in various duties such as excise and imports. Profits of firms improved without any structural adjustments being made in industrial practices. The prospect of an improvement in corporate India's economic value added (EVA) was swiftly reflected in stock prices. EVA is usually measured by adjusting a firm's profit figure for non-cash accounting items and subtracting the notional cost of capital including equity. India's corporate law and reporting procedures still lag international standards. Thus, evaluating a firm's EVA can be misleading and any investment decision based solely on such analysis might not deliver the desired returns. India thus remains a quantitatively-oriented investor's nightmare but a stock selector's paradise.

One of the results of India's past restrictive industrial policies was the creation of conglomerates like Grasim Industries which produce products as diverse as viscose staple fibre, cement and sponge iron. Understanding the financial performance of such companies can be problematic as there is no regulatory requirement to give a detailed account of sales and costs for the various businesses separately in the annual accounts. Besides, companies owned by the same family group produce the same products in different holding companies. It is only a matter of time before corporate India has to restructure itself along product lines. While the break-up value of these companies is expected to be more than that of the whole, investing in Indian companies on their net asset value, book value or breakup value can turn out to be a frustrating experience as restructuring cannot be implemented without radical changes in company, labour and land laws. It might be useful to work out the replacement cost of the underlying assets of the firm but it will be futile to conclude that one had assessed accurately the cost of land, licences and franchises. A bird in hand can be worth four in the Indian bush.

Concepts like market value added (MVA) or realised economic value are not the sort of tools used or recognised by corporate managers in India. It does not necessarily reflect on the ability of the managers. Companies in India made the owner-families rich but in creating shareholder wealth, the corporate structure has not been very successful. On the contrary, the restrictive corporate laws encouraged the siphoning of wealth out of the firms into privately-held vehicles. MVA reflects a company's market value minus all invested capital including retained earnings. Until 1992, Indian companies could not freely raise equity capital in the stockmarket. Thus, notions like 'realised economic value' which is a firm's cash flow minus the cost of capital, or its 'value creation quotient' which represents the ratio of market value to capital invested can be quite meaningless when investing in India. There are firms in India whose market value is lower than the amount of money the same firm raised via a GDR issue. The domestic market is indicating to the overseas investors that they made a big mistake in valuing those companies.

Most companies are financed with a combination of debt and equity. The firm's prospects are thus divided between various claimants. The risk and return is distributed in such a way that debt holders bear less risk and expect lower returns than equity holders. The enterprise value (EV) of a company is calculated as its equity market capitalisation plus debt minus cash plus any minority interest. The ratio of EV to operating profit measures the total investment in the firm to its return. The combination of high debt-to-equity ratios of Indian companies with the high cost of debt automatically depresses the equity market value. Taking into account the poor reporting requirements at the corporate level, investing on the basis of sophisticated measures like enterprise value to operating profit, market value added, economic value added, realised economic value or Tobin's Q ratio may not yield superior returns partly because the data available is not clean. It is profitable to know the quality of management, market shares of products, location and distribution franchises. While recognising the limitations of data, analysis can be useful in indicating broad trends in value addition rather than reflecting accurate value. Also, applying such measures of value to one's investments can influence the thinking of firms in India. When corporate managers in India start to evaluate their own companies on the basis of such valuations, it might encourage them to understand more about the quality of returns they are able to offer to global investors.

Even though there are over 7000 companies listed in India, when one screens stocks on the basis of good management, earnings potential, tradeability and other such criteria, the list does not comprise more than 100 companies. Finding companies with good management offering products or services in one sector and providing an acceptable level of transparency in their accounting procedures is not an impossible task in India. Companies like ACC, Gujarat Ambuja Cement, Madras Cement or Raasi Cement (cement); Bajaj Auto, Mahindra & Mahindra, TELCO or TVS Suzuki (automobiles); BSES or Tata Power (power); BPCL, HPCL or OIC (oil); Hindalco or Indal (aluminium); MTNL or VSNL (telecommunication); HDFC, ICICI, SBI or IDBI (finance); Crompton Greaves or Kirloskar Cummins (engineering); Ranbaxy Laboratories (pharmaceuticals); Hindustan Lever or Nestle (consumer goods); Infosys, Satyam Computers (software/IT); Essel Packaging (packaging) all fall into that 'desirable' category. Many of these shares are even available in Global Depository Receipts.

However, one could have easily lost a fortune in any of these 'highly recommended' companies depending on the timing of one's investment. In mid-1993 for example, shortly after FIIs started to invest directly in the Indian stockmarket, the price of VSNL was around Rs 300. Privatisation was not on the agenda and it was difficult to get a decent line of stock in the company. Most of it was owned by the government and the local financial institutions. The initial GDR issue was priced for FIIs at Rs 1400–1600 in mid-1994. It does not take a genius to conclude when to have bought and sold VSNL. The price of VSNL shares had fallen to Rs 700 by January

1995 when it was again in the 'buy' territory, but nobody was recommending the stock as a 'buy'.

The Indian stockmarket does not lend itself to active trading due to the lack of liquidity and the onerous settlement procedures. But, the volatility of the market forces genuine investors to turn into traders. Until such time that the stockmarket matures, it will continue to attract speculators. For a market to evolve from a 'flavour of the month' investment to a long-term investment requires a concerted effort by the government in tackling macroeconomic policy decisions and continuing with reforms. Markets are far from perfect but it is unproductive for governments to interfere with the market mechanism.

CONCLUSION

In conclusion, investing in Indian companies is no different to investing in companies in any other country. It would be to the immense advantage of any investor to have some understanding of the company one invests in. Understanding its products or services and the costs involved in producing them is the best investment advice one can get on any company. It may even be a good idea to avoid investing in a company if one does not fully comprehend what it produces or has no conception of the costs incurred in its production. It may be difficult sometimes to check out the company's production facilities and meet management on site. But it is vital to gauge the company's attitude towards costs and in motivating its workforce. Contrary to popular opinion, investing in India involves investing in a relatively high-cost structure for industry. Only labour is cheap. So, whether management have the ability to keep costs low needs to be examined carefully. The deepening of reforms will contribute further to the lowering of costs to industry. However, it is ultimately up to the management to maintain their global competitive edge.

Many Indian companies are family-owned and have professional management in place only at the second-tier level rather than at top-tier management level. But public sector companies and MNCs have had professional management in place for a long time. It is not clear if they are better equipped for the survival of their firms as experience has shown that in both these cases, ownership lies not with the managements but with the government or was shared with a foreign partner leading to a sclerosis of management and paralysis in decisionmaking. With the onset of liberalisation and competition, Indian companies increasingly recognise the importance of professional management in the success of their long-term survival strategies. This is not to imply that family-owned companies are not well-managed. On the contrary, the vested interest of the family can ensure that returns on capital employed are maximised.

As the world gets increasingly global and production shifts towards lower cost centres, firms that can offer a globally competitive product stand to benefit. In India, labour costs will rise faster than production costs in terms of energy and raw material costs. The cost of capital, which is high in India, could be reduced if the government puts its mind to dealing with its unsustainable fiscal deficits. While an independent central bank would help, the problem of high fiscal deficits needs to be tackled by the government. The combined deficit of the centre and the states has declined from 12 per cent of GDP in 1990–91 to 9–10 per cent currently. In a more open environment, companies have been able to raise cheaper capital abroad. Besides, foreign companies directly investing in India will find it most difficult to replicate the distribution franchises already in existence, built over the years by companies as diverse as Reliance Industries to Oil India Ltd. It is difficult to evaluate the worth of these distribution franchises and customer loyalty bonuses.

The investor can benefit from spotting companies that have their survival strategies in place; Indian companies cannot be expected to deliver miracles. Studies show that India's private corporate sector has the ability to rise to the challenge, but whether management strategies will lead to success or failure largely depends on other related factors like the cost of production and the ability to influence the pricing of their products. It is therefore significant for industrialists to work with the government to implement policy changes on an all-party basis. In an increasingly global marketplace, corporates in developing economies depend heavily on their governments to provide a stable macroeconomic framework for their success or failure. It is the goal of the investor to identify correctly the major variables in the Indian economy and gauge the sensitivity of the value of companies to changes in expectations regarding those decisive factors. Having identified those companies as potential investments, it is simply a matter of being patient and waiting for the right time to invest aggressively. T.S. Eliot once said that 'the great writer does not write about experiences he's had but experiences he's going to have'. Similarly, a top fund-manager displays the imagination, the power of anticipation and the ability to be ahead of others in the choice of investments.

Bibliography

Ahluwalia, I.J. (1985) *Industrial Growth in India: Stagnation since the Mid-Sixties* (New Delhi: Oxford University Press).
— (1991)*Productivity and Growth in Indian Manufacturing* (New Delhi: Oxford University Press).
Asian Development Bank (1994, 1995) *Asian Development Outlook.*
Bhagwati, Jagdish (1993) *India in Transition: Freeing the Economy* (Oxford: Oxford University Press).
Bhalla, A.S. and A.K.N. Reddy (1994) *The Technological Transformation of Rural India* (New Delhi: Oxford University Press).
Bhattacherje, S.B. (1995) *Encyclopaedia of Indian Events and Dates* (New Delhi: Sterling Publishers).
British Petroleum (1996) *BP Statistical Review of World Energy.*
Cassen, Robert and Vijay Joshi (eds) (1995) *India – The Future of Economic Reform* (New Delhi: Oxford University Press).
Centre for Monitoring the Indian Economy (1994) *Basic Statistics Relating to the Indian Economy*, August.
— *Economic Indicators*, various issues.
Chakravarty, Sukhamoy (1985) *Development Planning – The Indian Experience* (New Delhi: Oxford University Press).
Claessens, Stijn and Sudarshan Gooptu (eds) (1993) *Portfolio Investment in Developing Countries* (World Bank: World Bank Discussion Paper 228).
Confederation of Indian Industry (1995) *Handbook of Statistics.*
— (1996) *International Conference on Insurance: Vision 2000*, August.
Dreze, Jean and Amartya Sen (1995) *India, Economic Development and Social Opportunity* (New Delhi: Oxford University Press).
Eswaran, Mukesh and Ashok Kotwal (1994) *Why Poverty Persists in India* (New Delhi: Oxford University Press).
Galal, Ahmed and Mary Shirley (1994) *Does Privatisation Deliver?* (World Bank: Washington DC).
GATT (1993) *Trade Policy Review: India.*
Government of India: *An Economic and Functional Classificiation of the Central Government Budget* (New Delhi: Ministry of Finance), various years.
— *Annual Financial Statement of the Central Government* (New Delhi: Ministry of Finance), various years.
— *Annual Survey of Industries* (New Delhi: Ministry of Industry), various years.
— *Budget at a Glance* (New Delhi: Ministry of Finance), various years.
— (1993) *Economic Reforms – Two Years After and the Task Ahead* (New Delhi: Ministry of Finance).
— *Economic Survey* (New Delhi: Ministry of Finance), various years.
— *Expenditure Budget* (New Delhi: Ministry of Finance), various years.
— (1995) *Export and Import Policy* (New Delhi: Ministry of Commerce).
— (1992) *Final Report of the Tax Reforms Committee* (New Delhi: Ministry of Finance).

249

Government of India (1995) *Hydrocarbon Perspectives: 2010* (New Delhi: Ministry of Petroleum and Natural Gas).

— *Indian Petroleum and Natural Gas Statistics* (New Delhi: Ministry of Petroleum and Natural Gas), various years.

— *Indian Public Finance Statistics* (New Delhi: Ministry of Finance), various years.

— (1996) *India Infrastructure Report* (New Delhi: Ministry of Finance).

— *National Accounts Statistics* (New Delhi: Central Statistical Organisation), various years.

— (1994–95) *Public Enterprises Survey, Volumes 1–3* (New Delhi: Ministry of Industry).

— (1996) *Receipts Budget 1996–97* (New Delhi: Ministry of Finance), July.

— (1993) *Public Sector Commercial Banks and Financial Sector Reform: Rebuilding for a Better Future* (New Delhi: Ministry of Finance).

— (1991) *Report of the Committee on the Financial System* (New Delhi: Ministry of Finance).

— (1993) *Report of the Committee on Industrial Sickness and Corporate Restructuring* (New Delhi: Ministry of Finance).

— (1994) *Report of the Committee on Reforms in the Insurance Sector* (New Delhi: Ministry of Finance).

— (1994) *Report of the Tenth Finance Commission* (New Delhi: Ministry of Finance), December.

International Finance Corporation (1993) *India: Capital Markets Review* (Washington DC: IFC).

— (1993) *Trends in Private Investment in Developing Countries: Statistics for 1970–94* (Washington DC: IFC Discussion Paper 28).

International Monetary Fund (1995) *India: Economic Reform and Growth* (Washington DC: IMF).

Ishiguro, Masayasu and Takamasa Akiyama (1995) *Energy Demand in Five Major Asian Developing Countries: Structure and Prospects* (World Bank: World Bank Discussion Paper 227).

Jalan, Bimal (1996) *India's Economic Policy – Preparing for the Twenty-First Century* (New Delhi: Viking).

Joshi, Vijay and I.M.D. Little (1994) *India: Macroeconomic and Political Economy, 1964–1991* (Washington DC and New Delhi: World Bank and Oxford University Press).

— (1996) *India's Economic Reforms: 1991–2001* (New Delhi: Oxford University Press).

Kathuria, Sanjay (1996) *Competing through Technology and Manufacturing* (New Delhi: Oxford University Press).

Kessides, Christine (1993) *The Contribution of Infrastructure to Economic Development* (World Bank: World Bank Discussion Paper 213).

Kurien, C.T. (1994) *Global Capitalism and the Indian Economy* (New Delhi: Orient Longman).

Little, I.M.D., D. Mazumdar and J.M. Page (1987) *Small Manufacturing Enterprises: A Comparative Analysis of India and Other Economies* (World Bank and Oxford University Press).

Mohan, Rakesh (1996) *Public Sector Reform and Issues in Privatization*, OECD Development Centre Conference Volume.

— (1996) *The India Infrastructure Report* (New Delhi: Ministry of Finance).

Muir, Russell and Joseph P. Saba (1995) *Improving State Enterprise Performance: The Role of Internal and External Incentives* (Washington DC: World Bank).

Nayyar, Deepak (1996) *Economic Liberalization in India* (Calcutta: Orient Longman).

— (ed). (1994) *Industrial Growth and Stagnation: The Debate in India* (Bombay: Oxford University Press).

Piramal, G. and M. Herdeck (1985) *India's Industrialists, Vol 1* (Washington DC: Three Continents Press).

Ramesh, S. and Arun Gupta (1995) *Venture Capital and the Indian Financial Sector* (New Delhi: Oxford University Press).

Rao, C.H. Hanumantha (1994) *Agriculture Growth, Rural Poverty and Environmental Degradation in India* (New Delhi: Oxford University Press).

Reserve Bank of India: *Annual Report*, various years.

— *Finance of State Governments*, various years.

— *Report on Currency and Finance*, various years.

— *Reserve Bank of India Bulletin*, various issues.

Sader, Frank (1995) *Privatizing Public Enterprises and Foreign Investment in Developing Countries, 1988–93* (Washington DC: World Bank).

Securities and Exchange Board of India: *Annual Report*, various years.

— (1994) *Indian Securities Markets: Agenda for Development and Reform* (Bombay: RBI).

Sen, Amartya (1992) *Inequality Reexamined* (Oxford: Oxford University Press).

Shaw, Timothy M. (1995) *Economic Restructuring in East Asia and India* (London: Macmillan).

Srivastava, Vivek (1996) *Liberalization, Productivity and Competition* (New Delhi: Oxford University Press).

United Nations Industrial Development Organisation (1995, 1996) *Industrial Development Global Report* (Oxford: Oxford University Press).

United Nations Development Programme (1995, 1996) *Human Development Report* (New York: Oxford University Press).

World Bank (1993) *The East Asian Miracle: Economic Growth and Public Policy* (Oxford: Oxford University Press).

— (1995) *Economic Developments in India: Achievements and Challenges* (Washington DC: World Bank).

— (1996) *Global Economic Prospects and the Developing Countries* (Washington DC: World Bank).

— (1996) *India: Country Economic Memorandum – Five Years of Stabilization and Reform* (Washington DC: World Bank).

— (1995) *World Development Report: Workers in an Integrating World* (Oxford: Oxford University Press).

— (1996) *World Development Report: From Plan to Market* (Oxford: Oxford University Press).

Index